D1521069

The Metaphysics and Ethics of Relativism

# The **METAPHYSICS**
# and **ETHICS**
# of **RELATIVISM**

Carol Rovane

HARVARD UNIVERSITY PRESS
*Cambridge, Massachusetts*
*London, England*
*2013*

*Library of Congress Cataloging-in-Publication Data*
Rovane, Carol A. (Carol Anne), 1955–
The metaphysics and ethics of relativism / Carol Rovane.
pages  cm
Includes bibliographical references and index.
ISBN 978-0-674-72571-3 (alk. paper)
1. Relativity.  2. Ethics.  I. Title.
BD221.R68 2013
149—dc23          2013007373

*For Akeel,*
*my own true love*

# Contents

Introduction      I

**PART ONE**
## How to Formulate the Doctrine of Relativism

1. The Prevailing Consensus View: Disagreement,
   Relative Truth, and Antirealism      15

2. Relativism as Multimundialism      71

**PART TWO**
## Evaluating the Doctrine of Relativism

3. Relativism concerning Natural Facts      125

4. Relativism concerning Moral Values      195

References      273
Acknowledgments      279
Index      281

The Metaphysics and Ethics of Relativism

# Introduction

When philosophers argue against a metaphysical doctrine, they do not usually rest with the charge of mere falsity. They tend to register the much more radical charge of incoherence. In the case of relativism they have tended to go further yet, to say that the doctrine cannot so much as be formulated in a satisfactory way. As a result, contemporary defenders of relativism are well advised to concern themselves primarily not with establishing its truth but with clarifying its content. In setting out to write this book, I have administered this eminently sound advice to myself, seeking such a clarification, and asking: What would we be establishing the truth *of,* if we were able to establish the truth of relativism, and what sorts of considerations would we look for in seeking to establish its truth?

As I attempt to answer these questions, I will be guided by four desiderata that I think any satisfactory formulation of the doctrine should meet: (1) It should capture a central and important *intuition* about its content; (2) it should attribute to the relativist a distinctive *metaphysical commitment* that is at once controversial and yet nevertheless worth taking seriously; (3) it should contain the resources to allow the relativist to *avoid the charge of incoherence* that is so often levied against her; and (4) it should show how we could meaningfully *live* in accord with the doctrine. In this book I develop and defend a particular formulation that satisfies these desiderata, and then I evaluate various arguments for and against relativism in two domains—the domain of natural facts that are appropriate objects of scientific investigation and the domain of moral values.

I will devote the remainder of these introductory remarks to three tasks: motivating the four desiderata; introducing three intuitive conceptions of relativism that seem to me to merit particular attention; and saying just a bit about the direction of my arguments to come.

The first and third desiderata require little defense. It is obvious that a satisfactory formulation of the doctrine of relativism must capture a central and important intuition about its content, and that it must portray the doctrine in a coherent way. The motivation for the second desideratum is perhaps less obvious. There is a significant variety of philosophical stances and themes that we associate with the word "relativism," and not all of them are metaphysical, and indeed some of them are avowedly *anti*metaphysical. So why is it desirable to formulate the doctrine as a metaphysical one? And if that is what we desire, why does it not speak against the fourth desideratum, that our formulation show how we could meaningfully *live* relativism, since so little metaphysics has practical import?

Only a pragmatist would lay it down as a general desideratum that *all* metaphysical doctrines be formulated in such a way that they emerge as having practical import. Although I do have pragmatist leanings, it is certainly not my aim to formulate the doctrine of relativism in a way that only a pragmatist would find satisfactory. My aim is to formulate what has been at issue in recent debates about relativism, where by "recent" I mean both the current debates and also the main twentieth-century debates from which the current ones descend. The following intellectual movements and projects in the last century were all regarded as having potentially relativistic implications: one conspicuous understanding of logical positivism, certain strands in cultural anthropology, certain developments in the philosophy of science, and some forms of pragmatism. Although it was not always clear exactly what the "threat"—or perhaps I should say, more neutrally, the "prospect"—of relativism is, it was generally taken for granted it would have real consequences for the conduct of inquiry and interpersonal relations. While the current debates have taken a somewhat more technical turn than their twentieth-century precursors, focusing mainly on certain issues in formal semantics, they too generally conceive the doctrine of relativism as holding practical significance. It is this recent tradition of thought about relativism in the last hundred or so years to which I want to do justice in my formulation—in which the issue of relativism has seemed to be worth arguing about in part because it is not just an academic exercise, but might bear on life.

Thus, I am not making any claim of greater generality than I need to. I am not demanding that all of metaphysics have practical import, but only a certain metaphysical conception of relativism that has come down to us from the major debates of the twentieth century. The question remains, however: Why should we conceive the issue being debated as a metaphysical one at all, especially since by the end of the last century some self-described "relativists" claimed to be *against* metaphysics, or at least to have *dispensed* with it?

It will be useful to distinguish two different antimetaphysical stances that are commonly thought of as relativist.

One involves a generalized hostility to all forms of, or claims to, "objectivity"—as we find when the relativist is portrayed as claiming that *there is nothing more to truth than mere opinion.* Young college students are prone to take up this position at least for the sake of argument, and it may be that some postmodernists are prepared to take it up more seriously. But regardless of whether we should or should not take this position seriously, it is not the one that I aim to formulate in this book. I aim to formulate a doctrine of relativism that does not already go by another name, and it seems to me that this one should really be called "nihilism."

Richard Rorty had a more nuanced antimetaphysical stance, the point of which was not to renounce all notions of objectivity, but to renounce a particular philosophical project, which first raises and then attempts to solve an alleged problem about the "mind-world relation"—the problem being to explain how the mind is able to "represent" things "outside" it. This problem came to the fore in the modern period and was successively addressed by Descartes, Leibniz, Locke, Berkeley, Hume, and Kant, and it continues to have a grip on the philosophical imagination. But we might well join Rorty in eschewing the problem without necessarily being against metaphysics in the broad sense I have in mind when I wish to portray the doctrine of relativism as carrying a distinctive metaphysical commitment. As I will be using the term "metaphysics," it refers to any inquiry into the most general aspects of what there is, or how things are, or the nature of the things that are.

I should clarify that on my broad understanding of what falls within metaphysics, the important contrast is not the one that Kant emphasized, between metaphysics and science—where metaphysics employs a traditional philosophical methodology of a priori argumentation from first principles while science employs methods of induction and confirmation. On my understanding, when science addresses the most general aspects of nature it is every bit as "metaphysical" as a priori philosophizing. The contrast that matters for my purposes is between metaphysics and epistemology—the topic of a metaphysical inquiry is, as I have said, the most general aspects of what there is, or how things are, or the nature of things, whereas epistemology is concerned with what we can or cannot *know* about these things, or, indeed, about anything at all.

Accordingly, when I say that I aim to capture a metaphysical doctrine of relativism, I am saying that I aim to capture something that goes beyond what might be called "epistemic relativism." Epistemic relativists hold that justification is always relative to a standard of justification, and moreover, that there is more than one such standard, and there is no neutral basis on which to comparatively evaluate those standards or to settle disagreements about them. These difficulties that arise under the heading of epistemic relativism are really skeptical difficulties, and they have held a prominent place in the longer history of philosophical debate about relativism extending back to the ancient Greeks. But as I have said, I do not aspire to formulate a doctrine of relativism that already goes by another name. Just as I do not attempt to formulate a doctrine that might as well be called "nihilism," I also do not attempt to formulate a doctrine that might just as well be called "skepticism." It seems clear to me that something *else* has been at issue in the more recent debates about relativism, which is not a skeptical issue, but a metaphysical one. It is in order to ensure that my formulation of relativism captures what this issue is that I have imposed my second desideratum.

Let me expound this metaphysical dimension of the doctrine of relativism in a preliminary way, by briefly surveying three intuitive conceptions of its content—all of which I will be exploring in much greater depth in Chapters 1 and 2.

There is one intuitive conception that predominates in the current debates, according to which relativism arises with a certain kind of disagreement that is said to be *irresoluble*. Call this the *Disagreement Intuition*. It is natural to suppose that what makes a disagreement irresoluble is the fact that the parties involved cannot figure out which of them is mistaken and which of them (if either) is right. On this supposition, the Disagreement Intuition tracks an epistemic and not a metaphysical doctrine of relativism. But most current advocates of the Disagreement Intuition have a different understanding what would render a disagreement irresoluble, which is that neither party is mistaken, or to put it positively, *both parties are right*. This is not a claim about what the parties to a disagreement can or cannot *know* about their situation, but a claim about *what is the case* in their situation, and so on my broad construal of metaphysics it counts as a metaphysical claim.

In the very recent literature, some philosophers who work in formal semantics have invoked a second intuitive conception of the doctrine's content, according to which the relativist holds that truth is relative to context. Call this the *Relative Truth Intuition*. Although the Relative Truth Intuition is almost irresistibly suggested by the very name of the doctrine of relativism, its current advocates do not see it as standing on its own; for them, its primary interest lies in whether it can help us to elaborate the Disagreement Intuition in a coherent way. I do not think it can. But regardless of whether I am right, what I want to underscore now is that if we portray *truth* as relative, and not merely justification as I described above in connection with epistemic relativism, the resulting relativism would indeed be a metaphysical doctrine. (It bears mentioning that not every advocate of the Disagreement Intuition sees the Relative Truth Intuition as required, or even helpful.)

If these two intuitions about the doctrine's content are in themselves metaphysical intuitions, they also incorporate a further background assumption about the doctrine's metaphysical significance, which is that *relativism and realism are mutually opposed doctrines.* Advocates of the Disagreement Intuition are quite explicit that relativism-inducing disagreements can arise only in domains where antirealism holds on the following grounds: they take it that there is no more to truth in domains where antirealism holds than what suitably well-informed subjects judge to be true, and they take it to follow that if such suitably well-informed subjects were to disagree, then there would be no metaphysical basis on which to say that either of them was mistaken, and so their disagreement would be relativism-inducing; whereas, they think there would be such a basis in domains where realism holds, for then there would be more to the truth than what the disagreeing parties judge to be true. When the Disagreement Intuition is supported by the Relative Truth Intuition, the truth of the parties' claims is portrayed as relative to the different standards of justification by virtue of which their claims count as true (when they are suitably well informed); this preserves the assumption that relativism arises only in domains where antirealism holds, because it is assumed that where realism holds, truth is not relative in this way.

It is striking that neither of the intuitive conceptions that are now so central figured much at all in the main twentieth-century debates about relativism. They were guided by a third intuitive conception of relativism, which I will call the *Alternatives Intuition.* It is fair to say that the meaning of the word "alternative" has never been satisfactorily elucidated—though it was closely associated with another word whose meaning was also never made entirely clear, namely, "incommensurable." Yet however obscure the idea of an alternative may be, there is no denying that it figured centrally in the main twentieth-century debates. That is why, when Davidson set out to refute relativism in his 1974 address to the American Philosophical Association, he took aim at *the very idea* of a conceptual scheme. He thought that by undermining that idea he could also undermine what he took to be the relativist's central commitment, which is that there are *alternative* conceptual schemes.

Although the twentieth-century debates were guided by a different intuitive conception of relativism than the current debates are, they nevertheless shared the same background metaphysical assumption that relativism and realism are mutually opposed doctrines. For them, an important source of the assumption—and indeed their whole argumentative strategy in favor of relativism—was to be found in Kant. He argued (in the very philosophical spirit that Rorty had counseled against) that we cannot make sense of the possibility of knowledge within a realist metaphysics that portrays the objects of knowledge as radically mind-independent, because it follows from such a realism— which he called "transcendental realism"—that we could not come to know objects without transcending the conditions of our own subjectivity—something he claimed to be impossible. As he put it, we can coherently aspire to know things, not as they are in themselves, but only as they appear to us through the forms of our sensibility and understanding. Many contemporary realists retain the aspiration that Kant rejected, though they are somewhat divided about where it leads. Scientific realists have an optimistic vision, on which the history of science has brought us progressively closer to an objective form of knowledge that successfully corrects for the distortions imposed by our own subjectivity, so as to get at how things really are; whereas skeptics argue that we can never transcend the conditions of our subjectivity so as to verify that what we think corresponds to how things really are. These views share a realist assumption but draw different epistemological conclusions. Kant came to his own positive view with a pathbreaking move—a "Copernican revolution" that would cease to define knowledge in terms of objects but would instead define objects in terms of knowledge. The result was "transcendental idealism," the doctrine that defines the world as the knowable world and, accordingly, as subjectively conditioned. Although Kant did not present his Copernican move as a first step on the path to relativism, that is how it appeared to many twentieth-century philosophers. This trajectory is utterly familiar to both philosophers and intellectual historians, but it is worth traversing it in its bare rudiments so as to situate the arguments and claims of the chapters to come.

In the various movements and projects of the twentieth century that I described above as holding potentially relativistic implications, arguments for relativism generally followed a roughly Kantian pattern: First it was claimed that if the world is to be known at all, it must meet the conditions in which subjects are able to know it; then it was argued that there is more than one kind of knowing subject, each of which imposes different subjective conditions that the world would have to meet in order to be knowable; from all this, it was concluded that there are as many worlds as there are kinds of subjects, and subjective conditions through which a world might be known. So, for example, Carnap held that if the world is to confer truth on our claims, it must provide empirical confirmation of them; but he argued that such empirical confirmation is possible only in the context of a particular linguistic framework that supplies a vocabulary and a logic in which to frame empirical claims; and, according to him, it lies within our power to devise many such linguistic frameworks, each generating its own particular form of empirical objectivity. Goodman agreed with Carnap that we can devise many different languages, and claimed that in doing so we literally construct different worlds. Whorf and other anthropologists who flirted with relativism made a similar claim, suggesting that inhabitants of different cultures who speak different languages are thereby put in touch with different forms of reality. Kuhn described scientists who work within different scientific paradigms as inhabiting different worlds. Although Rorty stood somewhat apart, because he eschewed metaphysical debates for and against realism, even he argued for a plurality of different "conversational practices" that condition our thought. What I want to underscore is that, *overall*, the common pattern was to argue that there is a plurality of different subjective conditions on which reality might be said to depend, and that there is no objective basis on which to say that any one set of subjective conditions is more or less valid than another. In contrast, realists contend that their conception of reality as mind-independent provides a standard by the light of which it would in principle be intelligible to evaluate whole systems of logic, thought, and language as more or less apt for capturing the facts *as they are*. On the realists' view, that is the form of objectivity to which we should aspire, namely, knowledge of the facts as they are in themselves, conceived as independent of our particular forms of subjectivity; and in their view, to embrace this aspiration is to oppose relativism.

One surprising conclusion that will emerge in the longer course of my arguments in this book is that the longstanding assumption that relativism and realism are mutually opposed doctrines does not stand up to critical scrutiny.

Another, perhaps less surprising, conclusion is that the two intuitive conceptions of relativism that govern the current debates—the Disagreement Intuition and the Relative Truth Intuition—also do not stand up to critical scrutiny. I say this is a less surprising conclusion only because some others—mainly opponents of relativism—have already argued for it. But their arguments are substantially different from mine. The reason is that their underlying aim in making their arguments is also different from mine. Their aim is a wholly negative one, which is to show that there is a difficulty in formulating or making sense of the doctrine of relativism at all, whereas my aim is not entirely negative. When I argue against the Disagreement Intuition and the Relative Truth Intuition, I shall be drawing lessons about how else we might intuitively conceive the content of the doctrine of relativism, so that we can ultimately arrive at a satisfactory formulation of it.

This will be the work of Chapter 1, whose negative arguments against the two intuitions that now predominate will lead us back to the Alternatives Intuition that informed the twentieth-century debates, and a new way of developing and making sense of it.

In Chapter 2 I will go on to elaborate three related ways of conceiving what alternativeness amounts to: logical, metaphysical, and practical.

*Logically* speaking, alternatives are *truths that cannot be embraced together;* or equivalently, alternatives are *truths that are not universal,* in the sense of being truths for everyone. It will be my claim that when this is so, logical relations do not hold among all truth-value-bearers, but instead some of them fail to stand in any logical relations at all. That is why they cannot be embraced together when true.

Here is what follows from this, *metaphysically* speaking: If there are alternatives, then there is not *one* world but rather *many* worlds. My nomenclature for this distinction will be to call the one-world thesis "Unimundialism" and the opposed, many-worlds thesis, which I am attributing to the relativist, "Multimundialism."

If there are alternatives, then *practically* speaking what follows is this: there are boundaries *within* which logical relations hold among all truth-value bearers, but *across* which logical relations cannot reach. When this is so, both our inquiries and certain forms of interpersonal engagement must be confined within such boundaries, and we must view what lies outside of them with a profound *epistemic indifference*. We shall have to acknowledge that the truth-value bearers that are outside of the boundaries within which we operate are not candidates for belief by us; and we shall have to acknowledge as well that we have nothing to teach, and nothing to learn from, other people who reside outside of those boundaries—that is the practical implication of their inhabiting a different world.

The language of many worlds is familiar from much writing about relativism in the twentieth century, most prominently in Goodman and Kuhn. It is also prominent in contemporary physics—I have in mind the "many worlds" interpretation of quantum mechanics, as well as the recent postulation of "multiverses"—but there it speaks to issues somewhat different from the ones relating to relativism as I am formulating it in this book. When I initially encountered the language of many worlds in Goodman and Kuhn, it struck me as mere metaphor. But if the arguments that I present here for taking the Alternatives Intuition as our basis for formulating relativism are convincing, then that language can be taken literally. This ensures that the resulting formulation satisfies the second desideratum I have laid down—though, of course, I will be at pains to show that it satisfies all four desiderata. First, it captures a central intuition about relativism, which is that relativists are committed to the existence of alternatives. Second, as I have just explained, the metaphysical significance of alternativeness—Multimundialism—qualifies as a distinctive and controversial metaphysical commitment. Third, the idea of an alternative can indeed be elaborated in a coherent way. Fourth, Multimundialism provides for a distinctive normative stance through which to live relativism.

After having developed and consolidated my proposed formulation of relativism in Part One of the book, I will turn in Part Two to the task of assessing what grounds there are to affirm or deny the doctrine so formulated—not in general, but in two specific domains.

Chapter 3 takes up relativism in the domain of natural facts as the sciences study them, and brings to bear considerations from philosophy of language, philosophy of science, and philosophy of mind on the question whether there is room for alternativeness in nature. Throughout the chapter, I shall be exploring the significance of holism—its implicit role in Davidson's general argumentative strategy against relativism, as well as its explicit role in Kuhn's and Feyerabend's arguments for incommensurability in science. I will also be exploring the significance of scientific realism, which is normally assumed to rule out relativism. The emerging lessons will be curiously at odds. On the one hand, considerations from holism entail that there is no occasion for adopting the Multimundial stance in science—that is, there is no prospect of *living* relativism in the context of scientific inquiry; and yet, we will see that the realism that governs the scientific outlook deprives us of grounds on which to affirm that nature is definitely *one*, but on the contrary supplies us with grounds for allowing that it may be *many*.

Chapter 4 addresses relativism in the domain of morals, by considering in some depth two different accounts of the foundations of morals that are widely regarded as having relativistic implications. One is the explicitly conventionalist account of "morals by agreement" that was pioneered by Hobbes and that served as the main premise for one prominent (Gilbert Harman's) defense of moral relativism; the other is the vision of morals that underlay the relativism of the early anthropologists as well as that of Bernard Williams, on which morals are unintended products of their historical and cultural situatedness. If the general Davidsonian strategy against relativism could successfully be carried over to the domain of morals, then neither of these accounts could offer any support for relativism. But I will argue that the Davidsonian strategy does not carry over, and so there is a real question that remains: Might there be some conditions that warrant our adopting the Multimundial stance toward others with respect to moral matters? In the course of the discussion, it will turn out that the neo-Hobbesian account does *not* give us such a warrant, in spite of its explicit conventionalism, whereas the cultural-historical account that Williams favored *might* do so. These considerations will help to confirm a point that I want to steadfastly stress throughout: there is no particular opposition between realism and relativism; that is, no particular dependence of relativism on antirealism. This point allows, for instance, that we might side with McDowell and hold that morals can be objective even though they are a product of historically situated social and cultural conditions, while still leaving room for relativism in the sense that my book will have argued in earlier chapters to be a coherent metaphysical possibility.

# PART ONE

# How to Formulate the Doctrine of Relativism

# 1

## The Prevailing Consensus View:
## Disagreement, Relative Truth, and Antirealism

In my introductory remarks, I said that there are four desiderata that any satisfactory formulation of the doctrine of relativism should meet. It should (1) capture a central and important *intuition* about its content, (2) attribute to the relativist a distinctive *metaphysical commitment* that is controversial and yet nevertheless worth taking seriously, (3) ensure that the doctrine is *coherent,* and (4) show how we could meaningfully *live* in accord with the doctrine. A good method to set up, therefore, would be to start with (1) by looking at the chief intuitions we have about the content of the doctrine of relativism and assess them by the lights of the other desiderata, that is, by considering how well they meet the other three desiderata. That is the broad dialectic with which I will proceed in this first part of the book.

Among contemporary philosophers who seek to formulate the doctrine of relativism, there is a broad consensus that *the* most central intuition about its content that we should aim to capture is the *Disagreement Intuition.* On this intuitive conception, relativism would arise with a certain kind of disagreement that is said to be, first of all, "irresoluble," but also, second, irresoluble for the specific reason that both parties are right.[1] Let us call disagreements of this sort "relativism-inducing disagreements." The most commonly cited examples of such relativism-inducing disagreements in the recent literature are so-called "disputes of inclination" in which the parties disagree about such matters as whether snails or fish sticks are delicious, but the more interesting and pressing possibilities would arise in the domains of morals and politics, and it is widely agreed that there, too, relativism would arise, if at all, with irresoluble disagreements in which both parties are right.

In spite of the impressive consensus surrounding the Disagreement Intuition, there is much to be said against it, and indeed much has been said against it—one main charge being that it is logically incoherent because it lands the relativist in a position of having to allow exceptions to the law of noncontradiction. Recent attempts to rescue the Disagreement Intuition from this charge of logical incoherence have resorted to a *second* intuition about the content of the doctrine of relativism, namely, the *Relative Truth Intuition,* according to which the relativist holds that truth is relative to context. Although this latter intuition does hold a central place in popular conceptions of relativism, in the more strictly philosophical literature the view tends to be that it cannot stand on its own independently of the Disagreement Intuition, and that its interest lies mainly in the support that it might give to the project of elaborating that intuition in a coherent way—that is, in such a way as to satisfy the third of the four desiderata I have set.

The current consensus in favor of the Disagreement Intuition is strong enough that when objections are offered against it, they are not just taken as objections against a particular intuitive conception of the doctrine of relativism, but rather as objections against the broader project of trying to formulate the doctrine at all, and the question is not so much as raised as to whether there might be yet another, *third,* intuition from which we might proceed in that broader project. I shall

---

1. Contemporary philosophers who take the Disagreement Intuition as their starting point include Crispin Wright (2001, 2006, 2007), Max Kolbel (2002), Francois Recanati (2007), and John MacFarlane (2005, 2007, 2008).

be arguing that the consensus is wrong on this score. There is indeed another, quite different, intuition available from which to proceed, one that figured prominently in the twentieth-century debates about relativism but that has been left to the side in the recent debates. According to this third intuition, relativism arises with what were then generally referred to as "alternative conceptual schemes"—so I will call this the *Alternatives Intuition*. It is quite understandable that this third intuition has been set aside, because it was never, in my opinion, elaborated in a sufficiently clear or compelling way. Nonetheless, the main burden of my arguments in this chapter is that we ought to return to it.

I will begin, not by directly launching an argument in favor of taking the Alternatives Intuition as our starting point for formulating the doctrine of relativism, but rather by undertaking a critical examination of the Disagreement Intuition. As a path of argument, this more oblique approach is better for a number of reasons: first, given the consensus surrounding the Disagreement Intuition, we should not turn our backs on it without first considering its merits; second, insofar as there is more than one intuition about what relativism involves, we ought to compare their respective merits rather than fasten our attention exclusively on just one of them; finally, there is much to be learned by thinking through the difficulties that confront the Disagreement Intuition—in doing so, we shall learn much about what drives and supports the Alternatives Intuition.

Here, then, is a preliminary statement of the detailed plan of argument for the rest of this chapter.

Since the first desideratum I mentioned asks us to begin with intuitions, I will begin in Section 1 with an initial exploration of the Disagreement Intuition. Given the prevailing consensus, it obviously meets the first desideratum, of capturing a central intuition about the doctrine of relativism. Prima facie, there is no difficulty about its meeting the second as well—of attributing to the relativist a distinctive *metaphysical* commitment. It does so by construing relativism-inducing disagreements as being *irresoluble* for a very nonstandard reason, which is that both parties to the disagreement are right. This is to be contrasted with another familiar account of how irresoluble disagreements might give rise to relativism, on which the doctrine does not emerge as carrying a distinctive metaphysical commitment but amounts to mere "epis-temic" relativism. The latter doctrine does not claim that both parties to a disagreement really can be right, but only that in some cases there is no way for the parties to determine which of them is wrong and which of them is right. In many philosophical contexts—especially when the disagreements in question are political disagreements—it has seemed to many that this epistemic version may be all that is meant by "relativism." But my project in this book is to formulate and evaluate a metaphysical doctrine, and so my interest in the Disagree-ment Intuition lies in the fact that, when it claims that both parties to a disagreement can actually be right, it seems to introduce an idea of metaphysical and not merely epistemic significance—in other words, insofar as relativism-inducing disagreements are to be characterized as *irresoluble,* they are to be characterized as *metaphysically* irresoluble. In Section 1, I will set this idea of a metaphysically irresoluble disagree-ment against a philosophical background of more general and long-standing ideas about the nature of disagreement, and about the pos-sibility that disagreements could ever be irresoluble in any sense at all, metaphysical or epistemic. We will learn that, in general, disagreements have a *distinctive normative significance* that is entirely missing in the situations that are alleged to be metaphysically irresoluble disagree-ments, and this puts into doubt whether we should regard them as disagreements at all. Merely to raise this doubt will not automatically suffice by itself to undermine the Disagreement Intuition, because its advocates might respond by simply admitting that relativism-inducing disagreements do not hold the very same normative significance that other disagreements do. But then the question arises, What is their distinctive normative significance? Eventually we will find that the answer to this question will lead us away from the Disagreement Intu-ition and back to the Alternatives Intuition that had been so central in discussions of relativism in the last century.

In Section 2, I will temporarily shift my focus away from the norma-tive issues that I raise in Section 1, in order to explore how the Dis-agreement Intuition might nevertheless be elaborated in a coherent way, thereby meeting the third desideratum I have laid down. Because it alleges that both parties to relativism-inducing disagreements can

be right, it seems to saddle the relativist with allowing outright violations of the law of noncontradiction. As I have said, the Relative Truth
Intuition is standardly brought to bear in order to rescue the Disagreement Intuition from the threat of logical incoherence that appears to arise when we allow that both parties to a disagreement can
be right—the thought being that there would not be any outright contradiction if the truth of the parties' respective claims could be portrayed as relative to different contexts.

It is often objected that even if we can succeed in rescuing the Disagreement Intuition from logical incoherence in this way, we shall
nonetheless end up failing in the larger project of arriving at a satisfactory formulation of the doctrine of relativism, because once the appearance of outright contradiction is removed in the situations that
are generally characterized as relativism-inducing disagreements, so
too is the appearance that they involve a genuine disagreement. Contemporary relativists take it for granted that the *only* intuitive conception of relativism that is worth trying to elaborate is the one suggested
by the Disagreement Intuition, and so they have responded to this
objection by trying to refine their accounts of relative truth accordingly, so as to do what the objection says cannot be done—which is to
retain the appearance of a disagreement while removing any outright
contradiction. But in Section 3 I shall offer a very different strategy of
response. With the help of an illustrative example, I will bring out that
there are further reasons we should not expect to be able to retain the
appearance of a genuine disagreement in the situations that are so often characterized as relativism-inducing disagreements. In addition to
the fact that it is hard to retain the appearance of a genuine disagreement without supposing that the parties involved really are contradicting each other, there are, in any case, strong grounds for interpreting their claims in such a way that there is not even a surface appearance
of contradiction between them. This interpretive point is very much in
line with the difficulty I raise in Section 1, that the situations that
are supposed to give rise to relativism-inducing disagreements lack
the distinctive normative significance of a disagreement. Yet the example will bring out that there is nevertheless a *distinctive normative response* that such situations call for. It is distinctive in the following

sense: although it is not the normative response that *disagreements* call for, it is also not the normative response that *agreements* call for either. Once we come to appreciate this fact about the situations that are alleged to be relativism-inducing disagreements—namely, that from a strictly normative point of view they are not properly characterized either as disagreements or as agreements—we can begin to see what supports the Alternatives Intuition. But it will take all of Chapter 2 to unpack that intuition, and to show that it can be elaborated in a satisfactory way, so as to yield a formulation of the doctrine of relativism that meets all four of the desiderata that I have imposed.

I will close this chapter by introducing the relevance of the fourth desideratum. This will be done via a discussion of a recent and influential attempt to rescue the Disagreement Intuition via the Relative Truth Intuition. Here again, the aim is the usual one of trying to absolve the relativist of the charge of logical incoherence, while preserving an appearance of genuine disagreement in the situations that are generally taken to give rise to relativism disagreements. But again, I will argue, the particular normative response that is called for in these situations is quite different from the normative response that disagreements generally call for. The conclusion that will emerge is that although we may be able to find logically coherent ways to portray these situations as disagreements, such portrayals do not help us to make sense of how it is possible to *live* in accord with the doctrine of relativism. Meeting that fourth desideratum will require making adequate normative sense of a situation that is neither disagreement nor agreement, and, as I have said, it is this task that will lead us back to the Alternatives Intuition.

## 1. A Prima Facie Difficulty for the Very Idea of a Relativism-Inducing Disagreement

Prior to contemporary debates about relativism, disagreement had been the implicit subject of a range of philosophical doctrines and positions ranging from Kant and Mill down to the positivists, and in those debates, the idea that some disagreements might be irresoluble met with varying degrees of hostility. I want to begin this section by considering why the idea was met with such hostility—not necessarily with a view to undermining the very idea of a relativism-inducing disagreement, but in order to get clear on what might be at stake in ever allowing or disallowing that some disagreements might be irresoluble. Once we get clear on this, we will be better able to see what, in general, the normative point in registering a disagreement really is. This in turn will afford a deeper understanding of the special character that relativism-inducing disagreements are supposed to have, and why they might be regarded as holding metaphysical and not merely epistemic significance—and hence, why starting with the Disagreement Intuition seems to promise a formulation of the doctrine of relativism that satisfies the second desideratum that I have set. However, we will also see that this special character of relativism-inducing disagreements ensures that they lack the usual normative significance of a disagreement—that is, the usual normative point of registering a disagreement is entirely missing in them. I will argue that this poses a prima facie difficulty for the Disagreement Intuition, one whose gravity will become more apparent as the chapter proceeds.

The idea of a relativism-inducing disagreement is to be contrasted with the idea of what I shall call an "ordinary" disagreement. In the former, it is supposed that the parties are both right, whereas in the latter it is taken for granted on all sides that the parties cannot both be right—at least one of them is mistaken. It is natural for us to approach such ordinary disagreements as occasions on which to figure out which party is mistaken and which (if either) is right, and when the parties do this to their mutual satisfaction, they thereby *resolve* their disagreements.

Some philosophers follow John Stuart Mill in placing a high epistemological value on promoting ordinary disagreements, because they view the process of resolving them as a good way to identify and correct errors, thereby advancing the overall state our knowledge. It is a little unclear to me whether this view entails that we are rationally required to always respond to our disagreements with others by trying to resolve them. But I do think it is clear that if anyone were to hold this, they would be going too far, because it is easy to imagine circumstances in which it would be rational to forego such an effort at

resolution. All we need to do is imagine that we have much more confidence in our own judgments than the judgments of certain others
with whom we disagree, and yet also have reason to refrain from trying to persuade them that they are mistaken—perhaps because we
think they should be free to make their own mistakes, or that their
mistakes are harmless, or that the chances of actually convincing
them are too low to be worth the bother of trying. The important
point is that even if we do not go so far as to place a supremely high
value on always trying to resolve ordinary disagreements, we must
still acknowledge that they always present the parties involved with
something *to be* resolved, in the sense that they cannot both be right,
and that so long as their disagreement is left *un*resolved, at least one
of them will remain mistaken.

If ordinary disagreements present the parties involved with something *to be* resolved, it does not necessarily follow that such disagreements always *can* be resolved. Yet, I have noted that the suggestion that
some of them might actually be irresoluble has been viewed with hostility by some philosophers. Reviewing the grounds of their hostility
will enable us to identify some conditions that would have to be met in
order to take the suggestion seriously.

The radical empiricist wing of logical positivism deliberately aimed
to rule out the possibility of irresoluble disagreements by embracing
an "empirical criterion of cognitive significance" according to which
the meaning of any truth-value-bearer is exhausted by its empirical
confirmation conditions, from which it follows that any issue over
which we can meaningfully disagree can in principle be resolved by
empirical means.[2] They did acknowledge that some traditional metaphysical issues that have generated controversy among philosophers
appear not to be resoluble in this way. But they argued that if it really
is the case that these controversies cannot be resolved, then the issues
allegedly at stake in them do not satisfy the empirical conditions for
meaningfulness, and on this ground they dismissed such "issues" as
mere pseudo issues that do not present us with anything to meaningfully disagree about. In taking this attitude, they were self-consciously

---

2. A. J. Ayer (1936) provides a useful summary of their position.

following through on a line of thought that Kant had initiated in the Antinomies of Pure Reason, where he aimed to dissuade philosophers from persisting in metaphysical disagreements that cannot be resolved by empirical means. But there is a difference between Kant and the positivists. Unlike the positivists, Kant did allow that we *can* meaningfully *frame* issues for ourselves that cannot be resolved by empirical means. What he did not allow is that it is rational to take a stand on such issues once we recognize that there is no empirical basis on which they could be resolved. The significance of this Kantian point for my purposes here, concerning the nature of ordinary disagreements, is as follows: If we cannot rationally take a stand on certain issues, then we cannot rationally disagree about them either, because it is only when the parties involved actually *hold* contrary beliefs or make contrary claims that they can be said to disagree. Other philosophers who are less committed to empiricism than Kant was—some pragmatists, for instance—take a similar view of why irresoluble disagreements should not arise. In their view, if we ever came to believe that a given disagreement of ours cannot be resolved by any means, empirical or otherwise, then the only rational response on our part would be to suspend belief on the matter in dispute, and in that case we would no longer be faced with an irresoluble disagreement *per se,* even though we would be faced with an irresoluble *issue.*

Having reviewed these positions from which the possibility that ordinary disagreements might be irresoluble is not in view at all, we can now clarify what is required in order to make room for it. We need to conceive a philosophical perspective from which it would be rational to retain our beliefs even in the face of our disagreements with others, and even in the face of believing that we shall never find any rational basis on which to resolve them. I find I can conceive at least one philosophical position that might afford this perspective: the position combines a *radically internalist account of rationality* with *a highly self-confident epistemic attitude that severely restricts the scope for reasonable doubt.*[3]

---

3. Isaac Levi (1990) takes this to be the (correct) epistemological position of pragmatism.

This self-confident brand of internalism allows, or really directs, inquirers to assess truth by their own best lights, which is to say, by the lights of what they already take to be true, or what decision theorists would call their "priors." When we follow this directive, we ought not to regard the mere fact that we disagree with someone as a ground on which to doubt our own belief about the matter in dispute, in the way that Mill recommended, nor even to reconsider it in any way, but should rather presume that the other party's belief is false because it contradicts one that we take to be true. This does not mean that this form of self-confident internalism does not ever allow that inquirers might have reason to take their disagreements with others as occasions on which to reconsider their own beliefs. They would have such reasons if they happened to regard the others with whom they disagree as being in at least as good an epistemic position as they with respect to the matters in dispute. But the point is that there is no guarantee that they do or should regard others in this way, and when they do not, they can in principle find themselves embroiled in irresoluble disagreements with them.

So, given this form of self-confident internalism, such irresoluble disagreements could arise if the following conditions all held: Two inquirers find themselves in a disagreement; neither of them regards the mere fact of their disagreement as providing her with an internal reason to open her mind about the matter over which they disagree, because each regards the other as being in a worse epistemic position than she to judge that matter—to be more specific, each of them has an internal reason to close her mind to the other's attempts to persuade her that she is mistaken, because she believes that the other's attempts would proceed from false beliefs; both believe that there is no prospect that further inquiry will provide them with new information on the basis of which they will ever be able to resolve their disagreement, because they foresee that their contradictory beliefs will lead them to attach different significance to any such new information.[4] In

---

4. This may seem to be the situation that Kuhn (1962) had in mind when he described certain scientific theories (or theoretical paradigms) as "incommensurable." But although we shall see (in Chapter 3) that there is good reason to view the form of incommensurability for which he argued as

these conditions, the parties involved might reasonably regard their disagreement as irresoluble and nevertheless persist in disagreeing, contrary to the recommendations of Kant, Mill, and many others.

Actually, the point cannot quite rest just there—that is, this is still not a complete list of conditions for the disagreement between them to be genuinely irresoluble. One has also to rule out the roughly and broadly Hegelian view that *future history might always bring to light a way to resolve the disagreement that is not yet foreseeable, or perhaps even conceivable.* In other words, the parties to the disagreement might think: There is no current resolution that is visible on the horizon, but future history might introduce some considerations, hitherto not visible, that bring about grounds for resolution, and so a resolution is in principle still possible. What would rule this possibility out? I think something like the following doubt: How can one ever know that such a Hegelian attitude is correct? If one is not in a position to know this, then one must grant the *possibility* that a given disagreement with others might be truly irresoluble, not only in the sense that it appears to be irresoluble now, but in the sense that it will remain irresoluble in the full course of time. In short, the denial of the Hegelian attitude just mentioned puts down a final, *diachronic* condition for the irresolubility of ordinary disagreement.

Now, I have just said that such an irresoluble disagreement is an ordinary disagreement, which implies that it does not induce relativism. That, however, is not a view held by all philosophers. For some, the conditions I have just described are exactly the conditions that establish relativism—it is what relativism intuitively involves—it is nothing else than the relativism-inducing disagreement we are after. The parties to a disagreement are consigned to allow that their disagree-

---

involving disagreement, that is not how he himself portrayed it. On his account, incommensurable theories do not share meanings, and if they do not share meanings, then they cannot logically conflict, and if they cannot logically conflict then those who hold them cannot disagree. The most familiar cases of disagreement that actually meet the conditions I just spelled out are certain religious disagreements, especially disagreements between Christian theists and their atheistic opponents.

ment is in principle irresoluble owing to the internal character of reasons and the existence of a multiplicity of viewpoints that are not internally constrained to respond to the same reasons in the same way. But if this qualifies as a variety of relativism, it is *not* the variety into which I am inquiring in this book, and it is also *not* the variety that advocates of the Disagreement Intuition have in mind when they describe relativism-inducing disagreements as "irresoluble." Why not? Because it fails to meet the crucial second desideratum, that requires the disagreement to be metaphysical.

I have emphasized that the disagreement I just described above would be an *ordinary* disagreement in which it is assumed by both parties that they cannot both be right. This means that the problem presented by the irresolubility of their disagreement would be purely epistemic. Each party would believe that she is right and that the other is mistaken, and so each would take the irresolubility of their disagreement to indicate that the other is incorrigibly mistaken. As a result, each would regard the other as subject to some form of epistemic limitation that prevents her from learning the truth about the matter over which they disagree, and although they would disagree about which of them is subject to such an epistemic limitation, they would agree that at least one of them is, and moreover, they would agree that the presence of such an epistemic limitation is precisely what makes their disagreement irresoluble.[5] So it should now be clear why I have said that if ordinary disagreements should prove to be irresoluble, this will only give rise to mere *epistemic* relativism.

---

5. The phrase "epistemic limitation" tends to conjure up a picture of diminished or impaired cognitive capacities. But the irresolubility of an ordinary disagreement would more typically be due to false beliefs. It might seem strange to refer to false beliefs as epistemic limitations, but it should seem less strange if we bear in mind that we are trying to envisage a case where false beliefs figure as the measure of all other candidates for true belief and, so, cannot be corrected by any further argument or new information. *That* is what is limiting about it—not merely that it is false, but the role it plays in the subject's epistemic life.

The prospect of epistemic relativism is disturbing, and philosophically interesting in its own right. But epistemic relativism is not the doctrine that I seek to formulate, nor is it the doctrine that philosophers have in mind when they take the Disagreement Intuition seriously. When they say that some disagreements are relativism-inducing because they are irresoluble, this is supposed to be a form of irresolubility that is *not* due to any form of epistemic limitation. That is, it is not due to the fact that the parties do not know, and cannot know, which of them is right. *The supposition is rather, as I have said, that both parties actually are right.* This is a *metaphysical* condition that is supposed to make their disagreement *metaphysically irresoluble*—and therefore relativism-inducing in the requisite metaphysical sense.

Before closing this exposition of how exactly relativism-inducing disagreements are supposed to be different from ordinary disagreements, I should say just a word about a still weaker version of the Disagreement Intuition that has figured prominently in the recent literature, which characterizes relativism-inducing disagreements in negative terms. Rather than say positively that *both parties are right,* this version says that *neither party is mistaken.*[6] But there does not seem to be a compelling reason to avoid the positive version. We can see this by briefly reflecting on the stock examples of relativism-inducing disagreements that I mentioned above, of so-called disputes of inclination. If I affirm that snails are delicious and you deny that they are, why should I see this as a relativism-inducing disagreement rather than as an ordinary disagreement in which you are mistaken if I am right (and vice versa)? The stock answer is that the truth concerning gustatory matters is a matter of how things taste to the parties who make gustatory judgments. But if that answer is right, then I must allow that you are not merely not mistaken in your judgment about snails but positively right. We will see in Section 3 that the same holds in situations where moral disagreements appear to be relativism-inducing—there too, the parties have good reason to regard each other as positively right, and not merely as not mistaken.

---

6. See Wright 2001, 2006, 2007.

The foregoing, initial sketch of what is claimed by relativism-inducing disagreements makes evident that the prevailing consensus view of relativism can reasonably expect to meet the first two of the four desiderata that I have set for any satisfactory formulation of the doctrine of relativism. The first is met because the very existence of the consensus suffices to show that the Disagreement Intuition is a central one, and the second is met because the intuition does seem to attribute to the relativist a distinctive and controversial metaphysical commitment, in the form of a commitment to the possibility of metaphysically irresoluble disagreements in which both parties are right, the second desideratum is also satisfied.

It is not immediately obvious, however, that the consensus view can satisfy the third desideratum, of coherence, for the apparently familiar and straightforward reason that if the relativist is committed to allowing that both parties to a disagreement are right, she would appear to be committed to allowing exceptions to the law of noncontradiction.[7]

It is in order to avoid this particular and rather familiar threat of incoherence, which is a threat of *logical* incoherence, that contemporary relativists have proposed to fortify the Disagreement Intuition by bringing tools from formal semantics to bear, in order to portray truth as relative to context. It is in order to ground these tools in intuitive considerations, that these Semantic Relativists invoke the second intuition about the content of the doctrine of relativism that I have mentioned, namely, the *Relative Truth Intuition*.[8]

Of all intuitive conceptions of the doctrine of relativism, this one is most strongly suggested by the very name "relativism." Perhaps that is why it tends to figure prominently in popular discourse about relativism, where it is typically associated with a *universally* formulated doctrine according to which *all* truth is relative. This popular theoretical

7. This is one of the problems that Wright has in view when he proposes the weaker version of the Disagreement Intuition according to which neither party is mistaken.

8. The central work along these lines is Kolbel 2002. Another related proposal that has attracted much interest in the last several years can be found in MacFarlane 2005, 2007, 2008.

understanding of the intuition is often said to be quickly refutable by a logical or perhaps quasi-logical difficulty of its own: if relativists hold that *all* truth is relative, then it would seem that any statement of their doctrine would have to constitute an exception to itself, and it would seem to follow that the doctrine is self-refuting.[9] Whether this refutation is too quick or not, contemporary philosophers who are interested in formulating the doctrine of relativism, including the most recent Semantic Relativists, do not conceive relativism as a universal doctrine about *all* truth, so they are not, in any case vulnerable to such refutations. They conceive it rather as a domain-specific doctrine, which means the issue of relativism can be raised separately and piecemeal in connection with specific domains, such as those studied by science, mathematics, logic, ethics, politics, aesthetics, and so on. Although they sometimes do acknowledge the quasi-logical difficulty that is routinely raised for the universally formulated doctrine, they

---

9. I have never been sanguine that the problem of *stating* a universal doctrine of relativism, according to which all truth is relative, is a devastating objection. We are accustomed to find limits on what we can coherently express, especially in connection with the concepts of truth and universality—as we find in the semantic paradoxes that are associated with a universal truth predicate, and also the problem of the universal set. We do not generally infer from the presence of these paradoxes that the concepts in question—truth and sets—do not generally work in the way that we suppose. Rather, we look for ways to employ them without falling into paradox, and in tandem, we look for ways to do without expressing what we cannot coherently express. So it seems to me that, if we really did have good reasons for taking seriously the idea that truth is in general relative, then we ought not to give up on the idea just because there is a problem about stating it—any more than Russell was prepared to give up on his general conception of sets because of the difficulty posed by the universal set, or indeed, any more than any of us would be prepared to give up on our general conception of truth because of the semantic paradoxes. However, I am only reporting a philosophical instinct here about how defenders of a universal doctrine of relative truth might proceed—it lies beyond my formal expertise and, for that matter, my interests, to assess whether it is on the right track. See Wright 2008 for some interesting reflections on the problem of conceiving and portraying all truth as relative.

generally do so only in order to set it aside as irrelevant to their project. Their interest in the Relative Truth Intuition lies in whether it provides a way to rescue the Disagreement Intuition from logical incoherence when it is employed in order to make sense of a domain-specific doctrine of relativism.

Prima facie, it would seem that this invoking of a second intuition by Semantic Relativists offers a promising strategy by which to fortify and rescue the Disagreement Intuition from its logical difficulty. If advocates of that intuition aspire to allow that truth-value-bearers of the form $P$ and $not\text{-}P$ can both be true, it does seem to be a plausible strategy to avoid outright contradiction by portraying the truth of $P$ and $not\text{-}P$ as relative to different contexts—provided, of course, that suitable contextual parameters are available. The trouble with this, however, is that it is really just a formal solution to a formal problem, and its availability does not guarantee that the Disagreement Intuition affords a formulation of the doctrine of relativism that is fully coherent in all respects, or that it provides for the possibility of living relativism—in other words, it does not really ensure that the resulting account of relativism would satisfy the third and fourth desiderata that I have set.

What stands in the way is a fundamental difficulty confronting the very idea of a relativism-inducing disagreement that no amount of formal maneuvering can get around. The difficulty is this. *The situations that are construed as relativism-inducing disagreements lack the distinctive normative significance of a disagreement, which arises only in situations of ordinary disagreements in which the parties cannot both be right; and so we should doubt whether the situations that are construed as relativism-inducing are properly thought of as disagreements at all.*

This needs patient elaboration.

The reasons that underlie and prompt this difficulty are implicit in what I said above about the nature of ordinary disagreements. I will lay them out now with a somewhat coy-seeming warning to the reader that because the Disagreement Intuition is so entrenched, its advocates are unlikely to be persuaded by the *initial* statement of these reasons that I am about to offer, and so it will take the remainder of the chapter to fully bring out their significance—first by appealing to an example, and then later by offering a supporting philosophical discussion of what is really going on in the example when it intuitively seems to illustrate a relativism-inducing disagreement. In fact, since so many philosophers take the Disagreement Intuition to be the only available intuition from which to proceed in formulating the doctrine of relativism, it may also take the arguments of Chapter 2—in which I will show how the doctrine can be formulated without recourse to the intuition—before it is fully dislodged.

*Every* disagreement, no matter what kind—whether it is an ordinary one or an allegedly relativism-inducing one—registers some contradiction. The parties involved must make contradictory claims or hold contradictory beliefs. In the case of ordinary disagreements, there is a clear normative point in doing this, which is partly logical, and partly epistemological in something like the sense that concerned Mill.[10] The point is to register the normative force of the law of noncontradiction, according to which the truth-value-bearers at issue (the claims being made, the beliefs being expressed) cannot both be true, along with the epistemological implication that the parties cannot both believe only truths unless one of them changes her mind. This is why ordinary disagreements present the parties involved with something *to be resolved* in the sense I explained above, where resolving their disagreement would involve their coming to agree on the matter about which they had just disagreed. But if there is nothing to be resolved in this sense, then there is nothing *in dispute* between the parties, nothing that they disagree *about;* and because there is nothing that they disagree about, it is gratuitous and pointless—actually, that is too weak, it is downright misleading—to say that they disagree in any sense.

---

10. As I explained above, not every account of rationality would place such a high epistemological value on promoting and resolving disagreements as Mill did. Self-confident internalists might actually think that they would be in danger of *epistemic loss* if they suspended belief every time they could not resolve their disagreements with others. However, they would still attach epistemological significance to disagreements, because disagreements always indicate that *someone* is mistaken, if not always themselves; and in cases where they hold others in high epistemic regard they would find it rational to respond to disagreements in exactly the way Mill recommends.

The situations that, according to the Disagreement Intuition, count as relativism-inducing disagreements do not share this feature of ordinary disagreements, because they are stipulated to be disagreements in which both parties are right. That is why they are characterized as a special kind of disagreement, which I have described as "metaphysically irresoluble," in order to mark the difference between the special sense in which they are supposed to be irresoluble and the sense in which some ordinary disagreements might be irresoluble. But to call such disagreements "metaphysically irresoluble" does nothing to mitigate against the fact that they lack the usual normative significance of a disagreement—a significance that normally arises precisely because the parties cannot both be right owing to the law of noncontradiction.

It has sometimes been suggested that relativism-inducing disagreements have a distinctive normative significance all their own. It is said, for example, that the parties to such disagreements are consigned to *agree to disagree,* and that if they should ever try to resolve their disagreement, then they will find themselves *talking past* one another. But these aspects are present in *all* cases where parties find themselves faced with disagreements that they take to be irresoluble, including the cases of ordinary disagreement where the parties agree that they cannot both be right. The ordinary cases are cases of mere epistemic relativism, in which each party recognizes that whatever reasons count as reasons for her to cleave to her own view of the matter under dispute do not count as reasons for the other to go over to it. This internalism about reasons, along with a self-confident epistemic attitude, is what makes their disagreement irresoluble—and it is why they end up *talking past* one another when they try to resolve their disagreement, and why they are therefore consigned to *agree to disagree.* But none of this hangs on the idea, central to the Disagreement Intuition as it is normally understood, that both parties to a relativism-inducing disagreement are actually right.

What I am now suggesting is a correction of how I, myself, have set things up. Just as it was misleading to call the situations to which the Disagreement Intuition calls our attention "disagreements" to begin with, it was also misleading to say that they qualify as a special kind of "irresoluble" disagreement; and it was equally misleading on my part to add the qualification that they are "metaphysically" irresoluble. My aim in doing so was to elucidate the Disagreement Intuition as sympathetically as I could. But the correction is forced by the realization that these situations do not present the parties involved with anything *to be* resolved because they are both right, and I now want to clarify, further, that if there is not anything *to be* resolved in such alleged disagreements, then there is not anything that would be left *un*resolved by failing to resolve them, and so the ideas of resolubility versus irresolubility cannot intelligibly apply in such cases. This point is of a piece with the point that there is nothing in dispute in such cases, and that they therefore do not qualify as disagreements, not even as disagreements of a special kind—because, to repeat, when there is nothing to be resolved, there is nothing in dispute between the parties and nothing they disagree about.

For this reason, I think we should reject the very idea of a relativism-inducing disagreement. But contemporary relativists who take the Disagreement Intuition seriously would not draw this conclusion, even in the wake of all that I have just said. They would simply conclude that if there are such things as relativism-inducing disagreements, then they will lack the usual normative significance of a disagreement—precisely because, as I have just emphasized, they do not present the parties involved with anything to be resolved. They might add, however, that there are still reasons to regard these situations as disagreements, because regarding them to be such should not require that there be something to be resolved, as I have claimed, but rather it should only require, as they have all along maintained, that the two parties hold contradictory beliefs or assert contradictory claims, a requirement that they claim is met in these relativism-inducing disagreements.

In Section 2, I will consider in some detail why contemporary relativists think this—I will consider, that is, under what metaphysical conditions they think it is appropriate to portray parties as disagreeing even though they are both right and there is therefore nothing to be resolved between them. I will also present a fuller account of the basic strategy by which Semantic Relativists propose to make sense of such relativism-inducing disagreements without violating the law of noncontradiction, thereby trying to ensure that the Disagreement Intuition might satisfy the third desideratum as well as the first two—so that it emerges not only as a central intuition about the content of the doctrine of relativism that attributes to the relativist a distinctive metaphysical commitment, but also renders her position fully coherent. In Section 3 I will follow up with a critical look at their proposal with the help of an illustrative example.

## 2. How Relativism-Inducing Disagreements Are Generally Conceived

One conspicuous feature of the prevailing view that relies on the Disagreement Intuition is that it takes for granted that if relativism-inducing disagreements are possible at all, they would arise in domains where a strong form of antirealism holds. By "strong" antirealism I mean this: the truth in domains where strong antirealism holds is what our best-informed judgments would deem to be true.[11] Thus, the consensus view is that if two ideally informed subjects were to make contradictory judgments in a domain where strong antirealism holds, they would disagree and nevertheless both be right; and because they would both be right, their disagreement would be irresoluble in the sense that is required by a Disagreement Intuition that satisfies the second desideratum—it would be irresoluble for metaphysical rather than merely epistemic reasons.

I have mentioned that relativism-inducing disagreements are sometimes characterized negatively, as disagreements in which neither party is mistaken.[12] This negative characterization would go together

---

11. A weaker form of antirealism might assert that reality is in certain respects mind-dependent without going so far as to equate truth with what our best-informed judgments deem to be true. Establishing that this weaker form of antirealism provides for relativism-inducing disagreements would require a different line of argument than the one I offer above from strong antirealism.

12. As I have said, Crispin Wright (2001, 2006, 2007) is the main proponent of this negative characterization. He also gives an especially clear account of how we might see the connection between relativism and antirealism by drawing on his important earlier work on antirealism (Wright 1992).

with a negative formulation of antirealism as well. Rather than directly equate truth with what ideally informed subjects would judge to be true, the negative formulation specifies that there is *no more* to the truth than what such ideally informed subjects would judge to be true, and then goes on to point out that if such ideally informed subjects were to make contradictory judgments, there would not be any *further facts* in the light of which either of them was mistaken. But just as I shall concentrate my attention on a strong version of what relativism-inducing disagreements involve that positively affirms that the parties are both *right,* correlatively I shall concentrate my attention on the strong version of antirealism that positively *equates* truth with what ideally informed subjects would judge to be true.

Strong antirealism with respect to the domain of natural facts that are appropriate objects of scientific investigation is not a philosophical doctrine that has widespread allegiance among philosophers today. With respect to such facts, most contemporary philosophers are scientific realists—that is, they deny that *we* are the measure of *things* and, as a result, we cannot equate the truth about such matters with what fully informed scientific investigators would judge to be true. But many scientific realists are open-minded about the possibility that when it comes to the *value* of things, we *are* their measure, because in their view to have value is to satisfy certain normative standards, such as standards of conduct or taste, and they find it plausible that the truth concerning such matters of value consists in what ideally informed subjects would judge to be true on the basis of those standards. However, strong antirealism about values does not automatically afford room for the possibility of relativism-inducing disagreements in which both parties are right, because that depends upon whether there is a guarantee that ideally informed parties would agree in their evaluative judgments. Philosophers who are open-minded about the possibility of relativism-inducing disagreements concerning matters of value see no such guarantee, but allow that different subjects might legitimately apply different normative standards in such a way as to arrive at opposed evaluative conclusions even in the cases where they are ideally informed.

These different normative standards provide contextual parameters within which truth might naturally be portrayed as relative, and that is precisely how Semantic Relativists propose to rescue the Disagreement Intuition from violating the law of noncontradiction. In their view, subjects who arrive at contradictory evaluative judgments by applying different normative standards should be conceived as being in different contexts, and their judgments (and corresponding claims and beliefs) should not be conceived as absolutely true and false, but should be conceived as true and false *relative* to those contexts.

Although I have been focusing on domains of value, because it is there that the prevailing consensus sees scope for relativism-inducing disagreements, the Semantic Relativists' strategy for avoiding outright contradiction is a completely general one that could in principle be employed in any domains where there are suitable contextual parameters to which truth might be portrayed as relative. It is also a variable strategy, in the sense that there are different ways in which truth might be portrayed as relative to context. As I shall be discussing in Section 4, it has been suggested that truth may be relative to what are called "contexts of use" or to what are called "contexts of assessment." But for the moment I want to bracket this complication and simply note that, in all cases, the relativity of truth to context can be formally represented through what Quine called "semantic ascent," which allows us to refer to or mention the truth-value-bearers whose truth-values are at issue, and then specify the conditions in which they are true in a way that makes explicit the role of contextual parameters in determining their truth-values.

But there is a vital qualification that must be made. Semantic Relativists see an important disanalogy between the cases of relative truth that they link with relativism and other cases of relative truth that everyone must acknowledge even if they reject relativism—namely, cases involving indexical pronouns such as "I," "now," "here," "this," and so forth.

The sort of contextualization generated in these cases of indexicality is utterly familiar, so I will describe them only very briefly. Such sentences are not true or false *tout court*, but rather true or false depending upon the context in which they are used. The reason is that the reference of indexical pronouns varies across contexts—the referent of "I" is determined by who is using it, the reference of "now" by when it is used, the reference of "here" by where it is used, and so on. As a result, two different people can make true claims using indexical sentences that might appear to be contradictory if we were to judge them solely by their surface grammatical appearance—as when I say truly, "I am a woman," and my husband says truly, "I am not a woman." But as anyone who understands indexical pronouns knows, my husband and I would not be making contradictory claims because we would not be affirming and denying the same proposition, and this is due to the way in which the referent of "I" varies with contexts of use and, more specifically, with who is using it—in the case at hand, I would be saying of myself that I am a woman, while my husband would be saying of himself that he is not a woman. The point of portraying the truth of indexical sentences as relative to contexts of use is to make all of this explicit—that their truth-values vary with contexts of use due to the way in which the propositions they express vary with contexts of use, where this in turn is due to the way in which the reference of indexical pronouns varies with contexts of use. In making all of this explicit, we thereby make clear why the appearance of contradiction among true sentences containing indexical pronouns is *mere* appearance—though of course this hardly needs clarifying, since no one who understands the way indexical pronouns work would ever be taken in by this appearance.

When Semantic Relativists aim to formulate the doctrine of relativism by combining the Disagreement Intuition with the Relative Truth Intuition, they do not similarly aim to remove the appearance of contradiction among truths, for it is crucial to their project that they *preserve* the appearance as veridical—otherwise they would fail to preserve the appearance of disagreement that they think is intuitively required by relativism. They hold that mere *Indexical Relativism* is not an appropriate model for what they regard as *True Relativism,* and in their view, True Relativism can arise only insofar as the parties to an apparent disagreement affirm and deny the very same proposition—even though both are right.[13]

## 3. Further Considerations Against the Disagreement Intuition

Armed with this general account of how Semantic Relativists preserve the Disagreement Intuition, I turn now to the critical phase of my discussion with the help of an illustrative example. Through that example I will be able to bring out that relativism involves a distinctive normative stance that is not well captured in terms of the idea of a relativism-inducing disagreement, but requires a different idea, one that has been explicitly invoked in discussions of relativism and is almost always implicitly invoked—namely, the idea of an *alternative*. Before trying to elucidate that idea, however, which will be the task of Chapter 2, I will close this chapter with a discussion of so-called "Assessment Relativism," which is a refinement of the more basic strategy by which Semantic Relativists portray truth as relative context. The point of the refinement is to better capture the distinctive normative stance of the relativist without giving up the Disagreement Intuition.

Before presenting my illustrative example, some caveats about the misuse of examples in discussions of relativism. There are two characteristic forms that such misuse of examples tends to take: in one, a philosopher shows that it is possible to interpret a given example in accord with a particular view, and then takes this as decisive evidence for the view; in the other, a philosopher shows that it is not necessary to interpret a given example in accord with a particular view, and then takes this as decisive evidence against the view. The common expectation underlying both of these forms of argument is that an example could in principle carry the burden of proof in discussions of relativism. But this expectation is completely misplaced, for the simple reason that it is always possible to interpret any given example in a variety of ways. Advocates of different intuitive conceptions of relativism can

---

13. "True Relativism" is a phrase from Wright 2006; it aims to capture roughly the same idea that is now often associated with the phrase "nonindexical contextualism"—see MacFarlane 2009.

always interpret the same example so as to accord with their respective intuitions, and what is more, opponents of relativism can always interpret it so that it does not illustrate relativism at all.

If examples cannot bear the burden of proof in arguments about relativism, it might be wondered what legitimate philosophical use they could possibly have. The answer is that they can be used to *illustrate* different positions—both relativist and nonrelativist—and thereby clarify the contents of those positions, as well as the philosophical issues at stake in debates about them.

It is obviously important not to confuse such illustrative and exploratory uses of an example, which are entirely appropriate, with an inappropriate justificatory use. But it is more difficult to avoid this confusion than one might think, owing to a related methodological point that we shall need to bear in mind as we proceed. We need to distinguish two questions: (1) How ought we to formulate the doctrine of relativism? (2) What grounds are there for embracing or rejecting the doctrine? It should be obvious that the first question is prior, because it is impossible to properly evaluate an unformulated doctrine. Moreover, if it was not obvious from the start, it should have become evident by now that answering this prior question is not an entirely straightforward matter, because there are serious challenges to the very coherence of the doctrine of relativism. It should also be obvious that a satisfactory answer to this prior question will not automatically supply us with an answer to the second—in other words, to establish that there is a coherent formulation of the doctrine of relativism will not suffice to establish the truth of the doctrine, or even its plausibility.

The distinction between these two tasks—of formulation and evaluation—seems to disappear in connection with a priori propositions that are conceptually true or false. Once such propositions are properly formulated, due reflection on the concepts involved should suffice to tell us whether they are true or false—a case in point would be the proposition that God is either actual or impossible, the truth of which Duns Scotus claimed to follow from the concept of God as a necessary being. However, it is not clear why we should presume from the start that the doctrine of relativism is conceptually true or false in this way, especially insofar as we are construing it not as a universal doctrine but as a domain-specific doctrine. We will see in Chapter 2 that the presumption is certainly false in relation to the specific formulation of the doctrine that I offer there. (This is related to my point in the Introduction, that the topic of relativism invites a method of philosophical investigation that departs from the traditional paradigm of a priori argumentation from first principles.)

All the same, once we have an example before us, we shall find it difficult to keep the two tasks apart, because whenever we find that a given example provides intuitive support for a particular *formulation* of the doctrine of relativism, we also find it natural to view the example as providing intuitive support for the *doctrine itself so formulated*. So even if a philosopher makes clear that she is using an example merely in order to illustrate what relativists intuitively have in mind by one or another formulation of their doctrine, the temptation will be to presume that she must implicitly be arguing for relativism in the course of her appeal to example. But that would be to presume that she is misusing the example in the way I am warning against. Of course, sometimes the presumption is correct—sometimes philosophers do misuse examples in just this way. But they ought not to and we ought not to, because, to repeat, examples concerning relativism are always susceptible to a variety of interpretations, and for this reason they cannot carry the burden of proof in philosophical debate.

The right attitude toward any example that might be offered in connection with the topic of relativism is to view it as setting us several related tasks: We need to consider the various ways in which the example might be interpreted so as to illustrate various positions that might reasonably be classified as relativist; then we need to assess the relative merits of formulating the doctrine of relativism as equivalent to one or another of those positions; finally, after we have settled on a given formulation, we can go on to consider what reasons there are to affirm or deny the doctrine of relativism so formulated. Note that we cannot carry out any of these three tasks just by staring at the example itself; we shall need to do some philosophy.

The example.

Let us suppose that I am a middle-aged woman of middle-class origin who grew up in a family of modest means in a small town in middle America, and that at the age of eighteen I was awarded a scholarship to go to a distinguished university at a significant distance from my hometown. Although my parents would have preferred that I remain near home and get married and have children, I took the scholarship and attended university, and ultimately I went on to earn an MBA. In spite of the recent troubles on Wall Street, I am already enjoying an unusually early retirement after making a fortune in investment banking. I remain single even though my parents continue to wish that I had married and had children. I visit them and my siblings on major holidays each year, but otherwise I rarely see them. They are all less well off than I, but neither they nor I see this as a reason I should contribute to their finances. We all believe that individuals should take responsibility for their own affairs as soon as they reach the age of eighteen—or at the latest twenty-two, and then only if they pursue a bachelor's degree immediately after high school and their parents are in a position to support them without too much sacrifice. We also all agree that I deserve my greater wealth, partly because I worked for it, and partly because my ability to gain it for myself showed that my efforts (and perhaps even I myself) have a kind of merit that other, less successful people fail to have. Shortly after retiring, I decide that I would like to see India, and during my travels there I meet a woman named Anjali who lives in a rural village in the Punjab. We tell each other about ourselves as best we can through an interpreter. She tells me that her parents arranged her marriage when she was a very young girl, and that she was married in her early teens. Since then her life has been organized around family responsibilities. In her position as wife she has taken her assigned place in her husband's family, and her primary tasks are bearing and raising children, and cooking and cleaning house, and attending to various needs of the wider family. It becomes clear to me that she believes that she was morally obliged to defer to her parents' wishes about marrying and to undertake all of the duties to others that followed upon her marriage. When I tell her that I have gone against my parents' wishes that I should marry and have children, it becomes clear to her that I believe that I was not morally obliged to defer to their wishes, and that as far as I was concerned, my only duty was to pursue my own personal goals and projects as I saw fit.

If we want to interpret this example in accord with the Disagreement Intuition, we shall need to keep firmly in view the difference between the sorts of situations that are alleged to be relativism-inducing disagreements and ordinary disagreements. So let me start by offering a *non*relativist interpretation of the example, on which it illustrates an ordinary disagreement.

For the purposes of this nonrelativist interpretation, let us suppose that Anjali and I initially react to each other's life choices with strong moral disapproval. I think it is quite wrong that she lives entirely for and through others in the ways that she does, without striving in any way to live up to certain moral ideals associated with American individualism that I regard as paramount, such as the ideals of self-determination and self-fulfillment. In her turn, she thinks I am quite wrong to have gone against my parents' wishes that I marry and have children, and to have abandoned my family in the process. From her perspective, my life—one of living primarily by and for myself—looks devoid of moral virtue, which she sees as largely stemming from having a place in a familial and social network of the sort that Indian tradition affords. When she and I are in this frame of mind, we take ourselves to have an ordinary disagreement, in which we cannot both be right, and what is *to be* resolved—what we disagree *about*—is whether deference to parents is morally obligatory. In addition, because our opposed attitudes toward deference to parents follow from our more general moral commitments—to the values of American individualism and Indian tradition, respectively—we are bound to view ourselves as being in disagreement about these more general moral issues as well, and there too we presume that we cannot both be right. In all of these disagreements, we implicitly take it for granted that there are facts of some sort in the light of which we cannot both be right, and that is why there is something to be resolved between us. (This nonrelativist interpretation of the example does not require that Anjali and I have any very clear ideas about what the relevant facts might be. All that is required is that we conceive them as something over and above our respective moral standards, to which those standards would have to answer in order to yield true moral claims. In the limiting case, we might simply take it to be a brute fact that one set of standards is right and that the other set is wrong. But it is more likely that we would believe that there are other facts in the light of which this is so. If we were philosophers, we might look to one of the major moral theories for help in identifying such facts. Thus, if we were eudaimonists, we might expect to find them in an adequate account of human flourishing; if we were hedonistic utilitarians, we might try to discover them by estimating and comparing how living by the principles of American individualism and Indian tradition would affect aggregate happiness; if we were contractualists, we might try to figure out what implicit agreements hold between parents and their adult offspring; and so on.)

If we want to consider how a *relativist* might interpret my example as illustrating the Disagreement Intuition, we will need to embellish it slightly, in order to incorporate the sort of antirealist metaphysics of morals that the intuition takes for granted. Imagine that Anjali and I have attempted to resolve our disagreement and failed. I have tried to persuade her that individuals should value their personal liberty above all else, and that they should therefore regard themselves as having a right to self-determination; I have argued further that the right to self-determination precludes any moral obligation to defer to one's parents, and that any social structure that attempts to enforce such an alleged obligation is unjust. But Anjali is unmoved by my arguments, and insists that the whole moral meaning of one's life is given by one's place among others, and one's duties and responsibilities toward them. In the course of our arguments, we have come to know each other better, and we have also learned more about the circumstances in which we have made our respective moral choices. Together we reason our way to the following insights: It makes sense for each of us to live by our own moral standards in our respective moral contexts; it would not really make sense for either of us to try to live by the other's moral standards in our respective moral contexts; nor would it make sense for either of us to leave our respective moral contexts and move to the other's in order to take up the life and values that would make sense there. These insights lead us to think that each of us is actually right to live by the standards that prevail in her own moral context, from which we take it to follow that each of us has made a true claim about deference to parents, in spite of the fact that our claims are contradictory. (This is where it becomes intuitively clear that the situation that advocates of the Disagreement Intuition have in mind is not merely one in Anjali and I are *not mistaken,* but is one in which we are *actually right.* The reason we cease trying to persuade each other to embrace our respective moral outlooks is that we have come to believe, positively, that it is fitting for each of us to morally live as she does, given her moral context.)

Insofar as Anjali and I are not philosophers, we are not likely to explicitly view our situation in accord with the prevailing consensus view of relativism. We do not have the requisite philosophical vocabulary with which to articulate how an antirealist metaphysics of morals might give rise to relativism-inducing disagreements in which parties who make contradictory claims are both right. Nor do we have the formal tools with which to avoid outright violations of the law of non-contradiction by portraying truth as relative. Nevertheless, we have come as close to the consensus view as it is possible to come with only vernacular terms at our disposal. Anjali and I believe that we occupy different moral contexts in which different standards of moral conduct hold; and we believe that our respective moral claims are true just in case they accord with the standards of moral conduct that hold in our respective moral contexts; and we believe on this basis that we are both right when we respectively claim that deference to parents is and is not morally obligatory.

When the Semantic Relativist portrays Anjali and me as affirming and denying the same proposition, she thereby provides for one necessary condition for disagreement—which is that the parties involved hold, and also register that they hold, contradictory beliefs. I observed earlier that this makes for an important disanalogy between what Semantic Relativists would regard as True Relativism and mere Indexical Relativism. In the latter case, where truth is relative owing to the presence of indexical pronouns, we may find an appearance of contradiction among truths, as when I say truly "I am a woman" and my husband says truly "I am not a woman." But it is clear that this is a *mere* appearance that no one who understands indexical pronouns would ever be taken in by, for my husband and I are clearly not affirming and denying the same proposition—I am saying of myself that I am a woman and my husband is saying of himself that he is not a woman. Whereas, on the present interpretation of my example, Anjali and I regard ourselves as contradicting each other by affirming and denying the very same moral proposition, that deference to parents is morally obligatory. According to the Semantic Relativist, it is reasonable for us to continue to regard ourselves in this way even after we have come to the view that both of our claims are true. That is why there is supposed to be a disanalogy with the indexical case—in True Relativism, the appearance of a contradiction among truths is to be taken seriously.

However, it is one thing to concede that it might *initially* be natural for the Indian woman and me to take the appearance of a contradiction between us seriously. It is quite another to say that we should continue to take this appearance seriously once we have reached the understanding of our situation that we are now trying to envisage, on which we have made our way to the conclusion that we are both right because we are subject to different standards of moral conduct.

Speaking just for myself, when I project myself into the example as we are now envisaging it, I would not continue to think that Anjali and I really are making contradictory claims, even though it had initially appeared that we were. I would find it more natural to reinterpret our claims to clarify that we are not really talking about the same thing, and indeed had not been from the start—for it would have become clear to me that she had been talking about what is obligatory according to the moral standards to which she is subject, namely, the standards of Indian tradition, while I had been talking about what is obligatory according to the moral standards to which I am subject, namely, the standards of American individualism. I could easily make this explicit by disambiguating two different senses of the phrase "morally obligatory": *morally-obligatory-in-the-Indian-traditionalist-sense* versus *morally-obligatory-in-the-American-individualist-sense*. Another way in which I might make this explicit is by acknowledging that our respective English and Hindi moral terms are not intertranslatable, because the meaning of the English phrase "moral obligation" is bound up with liberal conceptions of universal rights and attendant notions of contracts and promises, whereas the meaning of the Hindi term "katarvya" is bound up with a conception of the many different and highly specialized duties that members of extended families in a village setting bear to various others, depending upon their particular relations to them (as given by generational order, sibling order, wider kinship orders, and so forth).[14] Obviously, Anjali and I do not disagree if she affirms that deference to parents is a *katarvya* while I deny that such deference is a *moral obligation*. Given the quite different conceptual embeddings that her katarvya and my moral obligation have, this respective affirmation and denial do not amount to a disagreement.

This reinterpretation of the example points back to the difficulty that I raised in Section 1, which I had said is the most fundamental one confronting the Disagreement Intuition. The difficulty is that the situation that advocates of that intuition have in mind does not qualify as a disagreement at all, because there is nothing to be resolved between the parties. Resolution would require that one of the parties change her mind and come to agree with the other party about the matter over which they disagree. But since the parties to an alleged relativism-inducing disagreement already agree that they are both right, they cannot appropriately view their situation as presenting an occasion for this sort of resolution. The reinterpretation of the example that I have just given makes this intuitively clear, by showing how natural it is to portray Anjali and me as affirming and denying different propositions—thereby simultaneously removing the formal appearance of a disagreement between us, and showing that there is nothing to be resolved between us.

It might be objected that all I have really done is to show that we *can* find a way to remove the appearance of a disagreement in the example if we are determined to do so, but that this falls short of showing that we *must* do so. However, recall my earlier warning about the misuse of

---

14. "Katarvya" refers to more duties than these—aside from the special duties that one has to members of one's immediate family and community, it may also refer to special duties to one's work, to all of humankind, and to God.

example in discussions of relativism: there is always more than one way to interpret any given example, and because we cannot reasonably expect to show that any one interpretation is necessarily imposed on us, the only reasonable goal is to show that our interpretation affords philosophical progress on the issues that it is being used to illustrate. It will take the arguments of both this chapter and the next to fully bring out how my reinterpretation of the example at hand will help us to realize that goal. As a start, though, I want to explain why we should be unimpressed by some of the grounds that advocates of the Disagreement Intuition routinely invoke for retaining the appearance of a disagreement in examples like the one now under discussion. (This is only a "first pass" at the issues being raised here, which will unavoidably come up again in Chapters 3 and 4, where I will be able to address them in somewhat more satisfying detail than I can at this preliminary stage of my overall dialectic in this book.)

Evidence from empirical linguistics appears to show that ordinary speakers generally regard moral terms like "good," "right," "obligatory," and so on as univocal—that is, as having meanings that are invariant across contexts. On the basis of this evidence, we might predict that if ordinary speakers were faced with my example, they would construe Anjali and me, not as affirming and denying different propositions in the way that my reinterpretation does, but rather as affirming and denying the same proposition, and hence as disagreeing. It is sometimes suggested that this linguistic evidence suffices to rule out the reinterpretation that would disambiguate terms as unreasonable.

I have conceded that the most natural *initial* response to the example is to see it in this way, as illustrating a disagreement. That is why I began my discussion of it in the way I did, by offering an interpretation that takes the appearance of a disagreement at face value. However, when we take that appearance at face value, we naturally take it to be the appearance of an ordinary disagreement in which both parties cannot be right, and we are no longer taking that appearance at face value when we try to view it as a relativism-inducing disagreement in which the parties are both right. Furthermore, there is in any case a philosophical account of meaning that positively invites my own reinterpretive move to disambiguate terms so as to remove the appearance of disagreement, namely, the holistic account promoted by Quine and Davidson on which questions about what speakers mean by their words and speech cannot be settled independently of questions about what their psychological attitudes are. I will be discussing their work in greater detail in Chapters 3 and 4 when I take up Davidson's argumentative strategy against relativism. But let me quickly lay out their central idea in order to better clarify what drives the reinterpretation of the example that I am recommending.

Here is a quick illustration of the interdependence of meaning and belief: If I were to use the words "credit card" to refer to a small piece of plastic because I had heard them used in that way but had no supporting beliefs about what credit is, or even about what a monetary transaction is—suppose, say, I were a small child or lived in a barter economy— then I could not possibly mean what ordinary adult Americans mean when they use the words "credit card," informed as they typically are by numerous background beliefs concerning credit, monetary transactions, retail sales, lending institutions, and such. Similarly, when Anjali and I talk about what is "morally obligatory," we respectively bring to bear very different background moral beliefs, in the light of which it makes sense to suppose that we do not really mean the same thing. It makes more sense to suppose, as I have suggested, that she means "katarvya," or "what is morally-obligatory-in-the-Indian-traditionalist-sense," while I mean "morally-obligatory-in-the-American-individualist-sense."[15]

---

15. Advocates of the Disagreement Intuition might try to insist that we should take the linguistic intuitions of ordinary speakers more seriously than I am allowing, on the ground that ordinary speakers surely know what they mean when they use words, and so, insofar as the parties in an example like mine find it natural to think that they are affirming and denying the same proposition, then surely they are. This objection presupposes, quite rightly, that speakers generally *do* know what they mean. But it cannot help itself to this presupposition unless it offers an account of meaning that is consistent with it and, indeed, supports it. It will emerge in Chapter 3 that the *only* sort of account of meaning that can do full justice to the idea that speakers know what they mean is an account that takes the Quine-Davidson interpretive approach seriously, and pushes it to its logical conclusion, as Akeel Bilgrami (1992) has shown.

The Quine-Davidson approach to meaning that drives my reinterpretation of the example no longer dominates in philosophy of language in the way that it did some decades back. All the same, I shall be arguing throughout this book that we ought to take it seriously, and that it has important implications for the overall topic of relativism. For the moment, I will close my discussion of the linguistic argument in favor of preserving the appearance of a disagreement in my example with the following observations: even if we were to suppose for the sake of argument that there are hard linguistic facts (and I very much doubt that there are) that constrain us to portray Anjali and me as using *sentences* with contradictory *meanings,* this would not suffice to establish that we hold contradictory *beliefs,* and the very same normative considerations that in my view speak against interpreting us as uttering contradictory sentences speak much more directly against attributing contradictory beliefs to us—and if we do not have contradictory beliefs, then we do not disagree in any sense at all.

This brings me to a second ground that advocates of the Disagreement Intuition routinely invoke for portraying Anjali and me as having a disagreement. They claim that the appearance of a disagreement between us is not merely a linguistic one. That is, in their view, Anjali and I do not just appear to be *saying* contradictory things, but the appearance of conflict between us is also *practical* and *psychological,* because she and I appear to be committed to carrying out *opposed courses of action,* namely, deferring and not deferring to our parents; and they take these opposed courses of actions to reflect opposed beliefs about the moral obligation to defer to parents, from which they take it to follow that we really do disagree. However, although it is surely right to insist that parties who hold opposed evaluative beliefs really do disagree, it is wrong to assume that agents who appear to pursue opposed courses of action must also hold opposed evaluative beliefs—they might merely be pursuing different goals. For instance, suppose you and I are vacationing in St. Lucia, and I have decided to look for coral formations and you have decided to look for driftwood, and my choice leads me to swim out to sea and your choice leads you not to swim out to sea (but to remain on the beach). This supposition does not by itself provide reason to posit an underlying disagreement between us about the value of swimming *per se*—we can perfectly well agree about the goodness of swimming compatibly with making our respective choices to look for coral and driftwood, and therewith, to swim and not to swim. Furthermore, the appearance of "opposition" in our chosen courses of action need not indicate an underlying disagreement about the value of looking for coral and driftwood either—we can agree that they are both good things to do, even as each of us chooses one and not the other on a particular occasion. Of course, there are some disanalogies between this case, in which there is no hint of relativism, and the example about Anjali and me when it is reinterpreted to remove the appearance of a disagreement. But all the same, the case does serve to show that we cannot assume that the appearance of opposed courses of action generally indicates an underlying evaluative disagreement. The important point is, when Anjali and I appear to choose opposed courses of action, by appearing to choose for and against deferring to our parents, this does not necessarily signal that we have opposed moral attitudes, in the sense of affirming and denying the very same moral proposition (that it is morally obligatory to defer to one's parents), because it could also signal that we have different moral goals that are given by our different moral standards. There is a further point to be made here as well, which I think is even more telling about why the example is not appropriately viewed as involving a conflict of any kind: If we take sufficient care to describe the choices and actions that are respectively made by Anjali and me, so as to clearly reflect the underlying moral beliefs from which they issue, then our actions will not even appear to be opposed. For as soon we clarify that Anjali believes that deference to parents is morally-obligatory-in-the-Indian-traditionalist-sense, while I believe that deference to parents is not morally-obligatory-in-the-American-individualist sense, it becomes clear that she and I are not simply choosing for and against deferring to our parents; she is choosing to act so as to fulfill her katarvya toward her parents, while I am choosing to act so as to fulfill the individualist ideal of self-determination.

It may occur to someone to object: Even if I have shown that the grounds on which advocates of the Disagreement Intuition would reject my reinterpretation of the example, which removes *all* appearance of contradiction and conflict, are not compelling, I myself have not done enough to show that the grounds on which I favor the reinterpretation are compelling. So let me reiterate what I take to be the most powerful consideration in favor of removing that appearance. It derives from what I have said is the most fundamental difficulty confronting the Disagreement Intuition, which is that the usual normative point of registering a disagreement is entirely missing. Because Anjali and I agree that we are both right, there is nothing to be resolved between us, nothing in dispute between us and nothing we disagree about; and only if there were something to be resolved between us would there be a compelling normative point in portraying our claims, and the beliefs we thereby express, as contradictory. Neither the linguistic evidence I just considered above, nor the psychological consideration that I just discussed, adequately addresses this difficulty for interpreting us as having a disagreement of any kind.

Advocates of the Disagreement Intuition generally do accept that the *usual* normative point of registering a disagreement would be missing in the situations that they allege to be relativism-inducing disagreements. They persist in portraying the situations as disagreements anyway, because they see *another* normative point that would be served by doing so. This other normative point is to register the presence of a particular form of *exclusion* that they think relativism intuitively involves. I think this goes to the heart of the Disagreement Intuition—to why so many philosophers take it to be *the* intuition that we must capture when we aim to formulate the doctrine of relativism in a philosophically satisfactory way—for there is no doubt that relativism does intuitively involve some form of exclusion.

We can easily see that this is so by returning to the example. When we take the example to illustrate relativism, the situation is one in which Anjali and I come to agree *that* we are both right. Yet this agreement does not extend to the matter about which it had initially appeared that we disagree, for agreement requires sharing the very same beliefs, and we do not come to share the very same moral beliefs in the situation as it is now being envisaged—that is, neither of us comes to *embrace* the other's moral belief together with her own. This is a curious, and indeed problematic, aspect of the sort of situation that the relativist intuitively has in mind, insofar as it seems to commit her to holding something of the form "P is true but I don't believe it," thereby sending her to one side of Moore's paradox. It may seem unwise to portray the relativist's stance as embroiling her in this paradox. I think one important motivation for Semantic Relativism derives from a desire to avoid precisely that, by providing a more carefully qualified statement of what is true and what the relativist believes when she is faced with the situation that is alleged to give rise to a relativism-inducing disagreement. Rather than portray her as believing something of the form "P is true but I do not believe P," she is portrayed as believing something of the form "Someone else may truly affirm P even though I deny it, so long as our respective claims (and attitudes expressed) are true relative to different contexts." However, I do not see this as really *avoiding* the relativist's apparent descent into one side of Moore's paradox. When the relativist is portrayed as holding that truth is relative, this still provides for a *sense* in which she really does allow that P is true even as she herself declines to believe P. So it seems to me that, however problematic this aspect of the relativist's stance may be, it is nevertheless a basic and defining feature of it; and when I said above that relativism seems intuitively to involve a form of exclusion, this is what I was referring to—a circumstance in which we assess someone else's belief as true and yet refrain from embracing it ourselves.

As an aside, I should add that it will not do to try to avoid this feature of the relativist's stance by trying to make out that when we encounter the sort of situation that is alleged to be a relativism-inducing disagreement, we should simply *stop thinking* about whether the other party's claim (or expressed attitude) is true or not. We could not be in a position regard it as a relativism-inducing disagreement unless we had gotten so far as to see the other party as making a claim (holding an attitude) that contradicts one's own—that she denies a proposition I affirm. The *logic* of the situation does not permit us to set aside the question whether her claim (attitude) is true, but positively *invites* us to

conclude that it is *false*. If an impression of relativism arises, it is because we find reason to *resist* this logical conclusion. The resistance
does not come from thinking that it is somehow inappropriate to assess the truth of the other party's claim at all, and nor does it come
from thinking that we might be faced with a truth-value *gap* in which
her claim (attitude) is neither true nor false—as we might think if we
were faced with a case of referential failure (as in Strawson's example,
"The present king of France is bald"); the resistance comes rather from
a positive impression that the other party's claim (attitude) is *true*.

A central challenge for anyone who wishes to formulate the doctrine of relativism, then, is to make sense of this sort of case, where
we take another party's claim (attitude) to be true, even though we do
not take this as a reason to embrace it ourselves—we need to make
sense of this particular form of exclusion. One advantage that might be
claimed for the Disagreement Intuition is that it provides a way of
meeting this challenge, by supplying a reason some beliefs cannot be
embraced together even though they are both true—which is that they
are contradictory. Moreover, advocates of the Disagreement Intuition
might claim that this is the distinctive normative point that there
would be in registering a relativism-inducing disagreement, which is
different from the usual normative point of registering an ordinary
disagreement. Unlike in an ordinary disagreement, the parties to a
relativism-inducing disagreement would agree that they are both right;
but they would also be registering that nevertheless, in spite of their
both being right, neither can embrace the other's beliefs together with
her own, because their respective beliefs are contradictory and therefore logically exclude each other.

If this defense of the Disagreement Intuition seems convincing, it is
only because we cannot think of anything else, besides the presence of
a contradiction, that could possibly provide for the form of exclusion
that relativism intuitively seems to involve. But we should not be too
quick to conclude that nothing else *could* provide for such exclusion.
If that really were the case, then the effect of my reinterpretation of
the example about Anjali and me should have been to remove any
impression that the example still illustrates *relativism*, since it certainly

removed any impression of a contradiction. I want to insist that this was *not* its effect, as I shall now go on to explain.

The primary aim of the reinterpretation is to show how Anjali and I can both be right without violating the law of noncontradiction, and it accomplishes this aim by portraying us as respectively affirming and denying different propositions—what she is affirming is that deference to parents is morally-obligatory-in-the-Indian-traditionalist-sense while what I am denying is that such deference is morally-obligatory-in-the-American-individualist-sense. If it really were the case that these two attitudes do not exclude each other, then the appropriate normative response on both our parts would be to embrace both together, in which case we would have come to *agree* about the matter about which we had initially seemed to disagree concerning deference to parents—we would both have come to believe both that such deference to parents is morally-obligatory-in-the-Indian-traditionalist-sense and that it is not morally-obligatory-in-the-American-individualist-sense. (This would probably require that we come to agree on other matters as well, so as to share the same general moral outlook—an outlook that would somehow combine the standards of Indian tradition and American individualism.) But this is certainly not the situation being envisaged on my reinterpretation of the example. What is being envisaged is that each of us continues to deliberate and act exclusively on the basis of her own prior moral beliefs—I on the basis of the moral standards of American individualism and she on the basis of the moral standards of Indian tradition. This shows that we do not go so far as to embrace each other's moral beliefs even though we assess them as true. I am not suggesting that we do not acquire *any* new beliefs through our encounter. I am suggesting that what we learn from it is more appropriately viewed as a bit of informal sociology than as genuine moral instruction—in other words, each of us has learned *about* the other's moral outlook without in any way altering her own moral outlook. So it simply is not true that when we remove the appearance of a moral disagreement between Anjali and me, we thereby remove the appearance that our beliefs are mutually exclusive, and therewith the appearance of moral relativism.

To reinforce this point, it may help to compare our situation with another one that is often confused with relativism—the "When in Rome..." policy that instructs travelers to follow the standards of moral conduct that hold in the various places they visit. It is conceivable that the encounter between Anjali and me might have led us to embrace the "When in Rome..." policy, and if it did, then the outcome of our encounter would have been a moral agreement. We would both have come to believe that we should both follow the standards of American individualism whenever we are in the United States and that we should both follow the standards of Indian tradition whenever we are in India. But this is not the situation that we are envisaging when we take the example to illustrate relativism, and this is so both when we interpret it as illustrating a relativism-inducing disagreement and when we reinterpret it to remove the appearance of a disagreement. On both interpretations, the relation that Anjali and I bear to our respective moral contexts emerges as being much deeper than what it would be on the "When in Rome..." policy. Neither of us is being envisaged as thinking that it would ever be appropriate to deliberate and act upon the other's moral standards, even when we travel to the location where the other lives; what is being envisaged is that we both find it appropriate that each of us should continue to deliberate and act exclusively on the basis of her own prior moral beliefs, which stand unrevised in the wake of our encounter.

On reflection, it makes sense that my reinterpretation of the example should succeed in illustrating the particular form of exclusion that relativism intuitively involves, and that advocates of the Disagreement Intuition aim to capture, even though it removes the appearance of a disagreement between Anjali and me. For apart from the issue of whether our beliefs are contradictory or not, the two interpretations are in every other respect *metaphysically equivalent*: they both posit the same basic facts in the case, they both portray both of our claims as true, and they both give the same account of why our claims are both true. More specifically, they both agree that Anjali and I occupy different moral contexts in which different standards of moral conduct hold, and that our respective moral claims about deference to parents are true just in case they accord with the different standards of moral conduct to which we are respectively subject. *Given this metaphysical equivalence of the two interpretations, the suggestion that only one of them illustrates what the relativist intuitively has in mind, whereas the other one does not, simply is not convincing.*

I want to underscore: My complaint about the interpretation that posits a disagreement is not that it cannot plausibly be taken to *illustrate* what the relativist intuitively has in mind—after all, the Disagreement Intuition does capture *one* intuitive conception of what relativism involves. My complaint is that it does not offer a coherent way to *elaborate* the relativist's position, due to the general difficulties that I've raised for the very idea of a relativism-inducing disagreement. Insofar as we do want to elaborate the relativist's position in a coherent way, to satisfy the third desideratum for a philosophically satisfactory formulation of the doctrine of relativism, we must find another way to elaborate it. For this purpose, it is highly significant that we can plausibly interpret the example so that it does not posit a disagreement, and furthermore, that this interpretation is metaphysically equivalent to the one that does posit a disagreement. Clearly, the most reasonable way to proceed at this point is to investigate what else these two interpretations of the example have in common over and above their metaphysical equivalence.

With this aim in mind, I want to return to the suggestion I made above on behalf of the Disagreement Intuition—that there might be a distinctive normative point in registering a relativism-inducing disagreement that is different from the usual normative point of registering an ordinary disagreement, which is to register a particular and distinctive form of exclusion that relativism intuitively involves. Since making that suggestion, I have tried to convey why we do not need to portray Anjali and me as holding contradictory beliefs in order to retain the appearance that our beliefs somehow exclude each other; and in the course of conveying this, another normative peculiarity of our situation began to emerge as well, which is that we do not regard our encounter as presenting either of us with any reasons to alter our respective moral outlooks in any way. This goes well beyond the point that neither of us is prepared to embrace the other's moral belief together with her own. In addition, neither of us sees any reason to critically reexamine her own beliefs with a view to possibly finding an error in them that might lead her to revise them or give them up, and likewise, neither of us sees any reason the other should undertake such a critical reexamination in the light of our encounter. Thus, the situation emerges as being one in which our beliefs do not speak to each other at all, in the sense that it is ultimately a matter of moral indifference to each of us what the other's moral beliefs are. In short, the Indian woman and I seem to agree that the appropriate normative response to our encounter is *normative unresponsiveness*. This, I suggest, is the *distinctive normative stance of the relativist*.

The conclusion I am working up to is that when we reflect on what the two, metaphysically equivalent, interpretations of the example that I have been discussing have in common, it emerges that they both capture a situation in which the normative stance that I just described above seems appropriate. There is nothing to be gained by interpreting this situation as one of disagreement, because the normative response being called for is nothing like the response that disagreement calls for, which would be some form of *resolution,* or failing that, at least an acknowledgment that there is something *to be* resolved. In contrast, there is much to be gained by reinterpreting the situation to remove the appearance of disagreement, for doing so clarifies that there is nothing to be resolved, and it clarifies as well that there is no logical obstacle to prevent both parties from being right, as there would be if they held contradictory beliefs.

Admittedly, my reinterpretation of the example does not clarify *how* beliefs can exclude each other when they are not contradictory—that is, it does not supply a philosophical account of what this particular and distinctive form of exclusion is, which I am claiming does not give rise to a disagreement and yet does give rise to relativism. The most that can be claimed for the reinterpreted example is that it *illustrates* such exclusion, by making vivid that if the encounter between Anjali and me is not appropriately conceived as a disagreement, it is not appropriately conceived as an agreement either. So the main lesson that I draw from the example is that if there is any scope for a coherent relativism, it lies here, in the sort of situation that cannot appropriately be characterized either as a disagreement or as an agreement, and that calls for the distinctive normative stance of the relativist as I described it above—of *normative unresponsiveness,* or you might say, *normative disengagement.*

I had promised that my critical discussion of the Disagreement Intuition would bring us round to the Alternatives Intuition, and so it has. When we encounter situations in which the distinctive normative stance of the relativist would be warranted, we are not prepared to embrace the beliefs of others together with our own, even if they are true. To encounter such beliefs is to encounter *alternatives,* which I shall now define as *truths that cannot be embraced together.* According to the Alternatives Intuition, *relativism arises with the existence, or perhaps just the possibility, of alternatives in this sense.*

Note that if there could be relativism-inducing disagreements in which both parties are right, then the parties' respective beliefs would qualify as alternatives in this sense. So, part of my brief for the Alternatives Intuition is that it actually subsumes the Disagreement Intuition. Another part of my brief for it is that the particular way in which the Disagreement Intuition would have us make sense of alternatives is problematic on two counts: First, it requires us to portray the relativist as allowing exceptions to the law of noncontradiction, and second, even if Semantic Relativism provides an adequate formal solution to this problem, it still requires us to posit contradiction and disagreement where the usual normative point of positing these things is missing. Yet another part of my brief is that we can see alternativeness at work in the example about Anjali and me even when the appearance of a disagreement between us is removed.

I leave it as tasks for Chapter 2 to elaborate the Alternatives Intuition more fully, and to explore what the doctrine of relativism amounts to when it is formulated as affirming the existence (or possibility) of alternatives. Before turning to those tasks, let me round out the discussion so far in this chapter by attending to a refinement of the Semantic Relativists' basic strategy for preserving the Disagreement Intuition via the Relative Truth Intuition.[16]

---

16. This refinement owes to John MacFarlane (2005, 2007).

## 4. Assessment Relativism Does Not Rescue
## the Disagreement Intuition

In Section 3, I considered the most basic strategy by which Semantic Relativists might try to rescue the Disagreement Intuition. This basic strategy assumes that it suffices for the presence of a disagreement that the parties involved affirm and deny the same proposition, and so all we need to do in order to make sense of the idea of a relativism-inducing disagreement is to find a way to portray parties as affirming and denying the same proposition while both being right—which is supposed to be accomplished by portraying the truth of their claims as relative to the different contexts in which they make their claims.

I have objected that this is not convincing because it is missing the usual point of registering a disagreement, which is to register that the parties cannot both be right. The refined strategy that I now want to consider offers a response to this objection by imposing a further necessary condition for disagreement, which is that each party must *assess* the other's claim (and belief expressed) as false, and hence as mistaken. Here is what is required for this response to be successful: it must show how it is possible that each party to a relativism-inducing disagreement can be right to assess the other's claim as false while at the same time providing for a sense in which both their claims are true. The refined strategy proposes to show how this is possible by introducing another *way* in which truth can be portrayed as relative to context. On the basic strategy, truth is portrayed as relative to the context that a party occupies when she makes her claim (or embraces her belief)—which is commonly called a context of *use*. On the refined strategy, it is portrayed as relative to the context that a party occupies when she assesses the truth of a claim (or belief expressed)—which is called a context of *assessment*.

The distinction between contexts of use and contexts of assessment is clearest in connection with the case of indexicals. Whenever a person makes a claim involving indexical pronouns, the very proposition that she thereby expresses is determined by her context of use, because that is what fixes the reference of indexical pronouns—the reference of "I" is fixed by who uses it, the reference of "now" by when it is used, the reference of "here" by where it is used, and so forth. In contrast, the task of assessing the truth of a sentence containing indexical terms is a very different sort of task, which can be carried out only after determining what proposition it has been used to express given its context of use. The context from which such assessments are carried out is constituted by relevant normative standards, such as standards of proof and evidence.[17]

---

17. Here are some further reflections on the distinction between contexts of use and contexts of assessment as it applies to the case of indexicals. On each occasion when an indexical pronoun is used, the person who is using it is the sole and exclusive occupier of that particular context of use. This is perhaps most obvious in connection with the pronoun "I," which each person can use only to refer to herself and to no one else. But we should not confuse this exclusivity of the *reference* relation that holds between uses of "I" and its users, with the exclusivity of the *occupation* relation that holds between users of all indexical pronouns and their particular contexts of use. While only I can use the pronoun "I" in order to refer to me, lots of other people can use the pronouns "here" and "now" to refer to the very same places and times to which I refer with those pronouns. Clearly, they cannot do this without occupying the very same spatial and temporal locations that I occupy when I refer to those locations as here and now. But this does not mean that they occupy the very the context of use that I occupy when they and I refer to the very same places and times with "here" and "now." For the reference of these pronouns is not determined merely by the location of the speakers who use them; their reference to such locations is determined *reflexively* through a speaker's very use of them. Thus, "I" refers to the author of *this* thought or speech act; "now" refers to the time of *this* thought or speech act, and "here" refers to the place of *this* thought or speech act, and so on. That is why each of us is the sole occupant of the contexts in which we use indexical pronouns—because we are the sole authors of the acts in which they are used, by which their reference is determined.

In contrast, we generally are not the exclusive occupiers of our contexts of assessment, because the normative standards by which we assess truth are generally shared by others who share our context of assessment. Yet this still leaves in place a sense in which each person bears a special relation to her own context of assessment: it is impossible to apply anyone else's normative standards of assessment but one's own. If this seems possible, consider what would be involved in trying to figure out whether a given claim is true by

The distinction between contexts of use and contexts of assessment is less straightforward in the sorts of cases that are of interest to the relativist than in the case of indexicals. In the sort of moral case that is at issue in my example, a person's context of use would be constituted by her standards of moral conduct, whereas her context of assessment would be constituted by the normative standards that she employs when she assesses the truth of moral claims. In the normal course of things, we should expect to find an extremely close correspondence between these two sorts of standards. After all, the moral *truth* concerns what it is morally good and right *to do,* and so it is only natural that we would derive the normative standards by which we assess the truth of moral claims from our standards of moral conduct. This might give the impression that it would not make much difference to adopt the refined strategy—that is, to portray truth as relative to the former standards rather than to the latter. Yet we ought not to overlook the special character of the cases that intuitively give rise to moral relativism. In these cases, we are asked to suppose that there are different sets of standards of moral conduct that hold in different moral contexts. We are also asked to suppose that we may have occasion to assess the truth of claims made in other moral contexts that we do not ourselves occupy. On such occasions it will make a difference how we derive the normative standards by which we assess the truth of such claims—whether we derive them from the claimant's standards of moral conduct or from our own.

---

applying standards that belong to someone else: in the very act of applying them, one would have adopted them and made them *one's own.* At the same time, when we thus make normative standards of assessment our own by adopting them for ourselves, we do not thereby undermine their intersubjective availability. So unlike the contexts that we occupy when we use indexical pronouns, the contexts from which we assess the truth of claims containing them can be shared, and generally are. This helps to ensure that these two sorts of context are different in cases involving indexical pronouns, because as I just explained above, others cannot share the context of use that we occupy when we use such pronouns.

On the basic strategy, Semantic Relativists portray the truth of moral claims as relative to standards of moral conduct themselves—to what the refined strategy would identify as contexts of use. This leaves no scope for assessing on the basis of our own standards of moral conduct the truth of moral claims that are made in other moral contexts, but forces us to assess their truth on the basis of the claimant's standards of moral conduct instead. In my example, it forces me to assess the truth of Anjali's claim that deference to parents is morally obligatory by appealing to her Indian traditionalist standards of moral conduct, with the result that I must assess her claim as true and so fail to retain any sense that she is mistaken. When the refined strategy distinguishes contexts of assessment from contexts of use, it affords scope for assessing her moral claim by the lights of my own American individualist moral standards, thereby allowing me to assess it as false and to preserve a sense of disagreement. But that is not all. Not only does the refined strategy supply me with grounds for assessing Anjali's claim as false; it also affords grounds on which to acknowledge a sense in which her claim is true—it is true relative to her context of assessment. In this way the refined strategy seems to accomplish all that is needed in order to make sense of the Disagreement Intuition: it seems to preserve a genuine sense of disagreement, because not only does it portray the parties as affirming and denying the same proposition, but also, it portrays them in such a way that each can rightly assess the other's claim as false, because each party's claim *is* false relative to the other party's context of assessment; yet at the same time it seems to provide for a sense in which both parties are right, because each party's claim is true relative to her own context of assessment; and it seems to accomplish all of this without any outright violation of the law of noncontradiction, because there is no context of assessment relative to which a given claim (or proposition or belief or indeed any truth-value-bearer) and its negation are both true.

Can this refined strategy of the Semantic Relativist improve the formulation of relativism as understood by the Disagreement Intuition?

To respond to this question, let me bring us back to the four desiderata that any adequate formulation of the doctrine of relativism should meet: It should capture a central intuition about the doctrine's content; it should attribute to the relativist a distinctive, though also controversial, metaphysical commitment; it should allow us to see the relativist's position as coherent; and it should provide a way to live relativism. Like the basic strategy of Semantic Relativism, the refined strategy of Assessment Relativism clearly satisfies the first two desiderata just by virtue of the fact that it takes the Disagreement Intuition as its starting point. And like the basic strategy, it promises to spare the relativist from any outright violation of law of noncontradiction by portraying truth as relative, thereby going at least part of the way toward satisfying the third desideratum, of coherence, by ensuring that the doctrine of relativism emerges as at least *logically* coherent.

It is not entirely clear to me that Assessment Relativism goes all the way on this last score, of providing a logically coherent way to elaborate the Disagreement Intuition, and I have argued elsewhere—though perhaps incorrectly—that it does not.[18] Admittedly, contradictions do not *immediately* arise: if truth is relative to a context of assessment, then if Anjali and I occupy different contexts of assessment, I may without contradiction assess my own claim as true while assessing her claim to the contrary as false; and at the same time, she may assess my claim as false while assessing her own contrary claim as true. But it is hard to set aside the suspicion that contradictions would inevitably arise somewhere if she and I were to explicitly embrace Assessment Relativism. For example, each of us would be committed to regarding the other as simultaneously *mistaken* and *not mistaken*. Looking at things from my side of the encounter, insofar as I am committed to assessing Anajli's moral claim about deference to parents as false, I am committed to regarding her as mistaken, and yet insofar as I embrace Assessment Relativism, I must allow that her assessment of her own claim as true is not mistaken. It might be argued that this is not really a contradiction, because it is her *moral claim* about deference to parents that I regard as mistaken, whereas it is her *assessment* of that claim as true that I regard as not mistaken. But it seems to me that if I believe that her assessment of her own claim as true is not mistaken, then I am committed to allowing that there is a sense in which the claim itself

---

18. See Rovane 2012.

is not mistaken, and that is the ground on which I have argued elsewhere that Assessment Relativism does not fully succeed in rescuing the Disagreement Intuition from logical incoherence.[19]

On further reflection I have come to see that the philosophically interesting thing to do here is not to try to catch the Assessment Relativist out in a formal contradiction. The more interesting thing to do is to consider whether the overall proposal of Assessment Relativism fully succeeds in all respects, taking for granted that it might be able to bring the tools of formal semantics to bear in order to avoid the particular threat of contradiction that I have raised. I shall now argue that it does not fully succeed in this, because it does not provide the relativist with a fully coherent normative stance to take up in the situations that are alleged to be relativism-inducing disagreements.

The reason it does not provide this has to do with the fourth desideratum. Here is how I have come to think of it. If we attempt to *live in accord* with Assessment Relativism, we shall fail to comply with a very basic requirement of rationality. The requirement I have in mind is much discussed in contemporary philosophy of action, most especially in connection with *akrasia;* it is a requirement to arrive at and act upon *all-things-considered judgments* that take into account all of one's relevant beliefs, values, and other attitudes.[20] Usually the requirement

---

19. The reason why I am no longer sanguine about this complaint is that there is scope for portraying mistakes as relative to contexts of assessment, in parallel with the way in which truth is portrayed as relative to contexts of assessment. However, for reasons I go on to give in the text, I do not see the formal issues at stake here as being paramount. The question is whether the doctrine of relativism emerges as coherent in a broader philosophical sense as well as in a narrower formal sense.

20. It would be more natural to say that what we ought to take into account in our all-things-considered judgments is not all of our relevant *attitudes,* but rather, all of the *objective matters* of fact and value that bear on our deliberative problem. But when we are thinking of the requirement to arrive at all-things-considered judgments as a requirement of *rationality,* then we cannot suppose that we ought to take into account all such objective matters. For one thing, we are not omniscient and, so, we *cannot* take them all into account. For another, to fail to be omniscient in this way is

is understood as instructing us to take everything that we think into due account when we deliberate about *what to do,* but I want to discuss a parallel requirement, that we ought to take everything that we think into due account when we deliberate about *what is true*—including when we are deliberating about whether someone else's claim or belief is true.[21] One drawback of Assessment Relativism is that it expressly instructs us *not* to do this when it instructs us to assess the claims of others as false when we encounter relativism-inducing disagreements. To see why, let us consider again the situation being envisaged in my example. I believe that Anjali should conduct herself in accord with the standards drawn from her own Indian tradition and not in accord with my American individualist standards. Nevertheless, when she makes moral claims and professes moral beliefs that accord with her own moral standards, I am instructed to assess them as false on the ground that they do not accord with mine. At first sight this may seem appropriate: Since I embrace the standards of American individualism as true, and since they guide me when I deliberate about what it is morally right for me to think and do, why should they not also guide me when I assess the truth and falsehood of others' moral claims and beliefs? But there is a very straightforward reason this would not be appropriate. I should not assess the truth of Anjali's moral claims solely on the basis of normative standards drawn from my American individualist standards of moral conduct because, if I did so, I would fail to take into account all of my relevant beliefs that bear on the question of whether her moral claim is true. I would be fastening solely on my estimation of a discord between her moral claims and my

---

not a failure of *rationality*—it is a quite different sort of epistemic failure that, as it happens, is unavoidable for creatures like us. What *is* avoidable— and also a rational failing—is to fail to take into due account what we actually *think* about such objective matters of fact and value, insofar as they are relevant to our deliberative problem.

21. Those who think we cannot *decide* to believe may object to the idea that we ever deliberate about what is true. But it is obvious that we sometimes do this—we do it whenever we attempt to figure out the implications of what we already think for what else *to* think.

standards of moral conduct, and ignoring the evident accord between her moral claims and her standards of moral conduct, as well as my belief that her moral standards are appropriate in her moral context. *As a result, I would be in violation of the all-things-considered requirement on rationality.*

The Assessment Relativist might try to respond by rejecting the all-things-considered requirement as *too demanding.* Even granting that it is only our own thoughts that it requires us to take into account, the difficulty is that it requires us to take them *all* into account. It may be impossible to ever review all of what we think, and moreover, even if that were possible in principle, it probably would not be either feasible or practical in the context of any particular deliberation about any particular matter. So if "ought" implies "can," then it is hard to see how it could be a *requirement* that we arrive at and act upon all-things-considered judgments. This objection does not carry nearly as much force as it appears to, for two reasons. First, however hard it may be to live up to this requirement of rationality, it does seem that, as rational beings, we are implicitly *committed* to living up to it. This is shown by the forms of self-criticism that we undertake when we make bad choices as a result of having overlooked certain matters of fact and value that we do know about but somehow failed to take into account anyway. We do regard it as a rational failing in our part not to have taken them into account, and yet following the letter of Assessment Relativism would lead us to such a rational failing. Second, if anyone were to deny that our self-critical attitudes show that we are indeed committed to living up to the all-things-considered requirement, they would still have to allow that we are committed to living up to a suitably weakened version of it that does not put us in violation of "ought" implies "can"—such as a requirement to take into account those thoughts of ours which are *salient,* and *obviously relevant,* to the deliberative question before us. Assessment Relativism would put us in the way of violating even this weaker requirement. If we actually came to believe that we were confronted with a relativism-inducing disagreement in the domain of morals, then it would a salient, and obviously relevant, feature of the situation that the other party embraces different moral standards from our own, and that it is appropriate for her to take them as the basis of her own moral deliberations and actions, as well as the basis on which she should assess the truth of her own moral attitudes.

The Assessment Relativist might try to respond by claiming that when I assess the truth of Anjali's moral claims, the only relevant beliefs of mine to take into account are my specifically *moral* beliefs. The other beliefs I just mentioned—that Anjali occupies a different moral context in which different standards of moral conduct hold, and so forth, are not moral beliefs either but, instead, as I myself said earlier in order to make a quite different point, *sociological* beliefs. My point then was to explain how I can regard Anjali's moral belief as *true* while not embracing it for myself, and it was no part of my point then that my beliefs about her moral context would be irrelevant to the project of assessing the truth of her moral beliefs and claims. My point now is that I do not see how this can credibly be deemed to be irrelevant. My sociological beliefs about how Anjali occupies a different moral context from mine are certainly relevant to my understanding of what makes her moral beliefs true.

At this point the Assessment Relativist might reply that I am failing to take due account of her very proposal, which is to decouple the basis on which I should assess the truth of Anjali's moral beliefs from the basis on which *she* should do so. In other words, the Assessment Relativist might reply that imposing a rational requirement that I arrive at some sort of all-things-considered judgment when I assess the truth of Anjali's claims is tantamount to refusing to make assessments of truth relative to context in the very way that she has proposed—because the rational requirement would direct me to take into account my beliefs *about* the moral context that Anjali occupies *together* with the strictly moral beliefs that I embrace from within my own moral context, whereas Assessment Relativism instructs me to take only the latter into account. But this reply does not join my objection, which is expressly urging such a refusal precisely on the ground that it would put me in violation of the rational requirement. (To repeat: this is so even on the much weaker version of the rational requirement that no one should find controversial.)

I conclude, then, that if there is a fully rational response to the sort of situation that is alleged to give rise to relativism-inducing disagreements, Assessment Relativism does not supply it—and this is why its particular way of developing the Disagreement Intuition falls short of satisfying my fourth desideratum, that is, falls short of providing a formulation of the doctrine of relativism on which it is possible to *live* in accord with it. But we should not have expected otherwise, since as I have said all along, the fundamental difficulty is that the situation does not plausibly qualify as a disagreement, because it is missing the usual normative point of registering a disagreement, which is that the parties cannot both be right. Assessment Relativism *nominally* supplies this normative point by exploiting something true, and which is evident in the example about Anjali and me: if it *were* appropriate for me to assess the truth of her claim solely on the basis of my own American individualist standards of moral conduct, then it *would* be appropriate for me to assess it as false. But this *is not* appropriate on the fuller understanding of the situation that goes together with the Disagreement Intuition. On this fuller understanding, I believe that Anjali is not answerable to my standards of moral conduct in her actions, and if she is not answerable to my standards in her actions, then she is not answerable to them in her attitudes either, nor in her expressions of them. Assessment Relativism goes wrong, then, in suggesting that I should regard her as somehow answerable to them nonetheless, even though to do so requires that I overlook my own avowed grounds for supposing that she is not.

This returns us to my proposal in Section 3, which was to reinterpret the example so as to clarify that Anjali and I are not talking about the same thing when we respectively claim that deference to parents is and is not morally obligatory, because she is talking about what is morally-obligatory-in-the-Indian-traditionalist-sense while I am talking about what is morally-obligatory-in-the-American-individualist-sense. With our terms suitably disambiguated, I can always clarify when she is talking about what is morally obligatory in her moral context and when she is talking about what is morally obligatory in mine, and then it will always be clear to me *whose* moral standards it would be appropriate to appeal to when I assess the truth of her moral claims, and I shall never be put in the position of having to make such assessments without following the rational requirement to take due account of all that I think.

As I emphasized in the last section, although this reinterpretation does not posit a disagreement between Anjali and me, it does not posit an agreement between us either, and it is important that it not do so, since if it did, then the example could no longer be taken to illustrate the sort of situation that the relativist intuitively has in mind, which involves a particular and distinctive form of exclusion. I conceded there that one advantage that might be claimed for the Disagreement Intuition is that it expressly provides for such exclusion by construing it as the form of logical exclusion that arises through contradiction. Similarly, one main advantage that might be claimed for Assessment Relativism is that it does a more convincing job of providing for this form of logical exclusion than the more basic strategy of the Semantic Relativist. Although the latter does posit a contradiction, her strategy for formally accommodating the contradiction by portraying truth as relative to so-called contexts of use leaves the parties no option but to assess each other's beliefs as true, and this might seem to place normative pressure on them to embrace each other's beliefs together with their own—at any rate, the Semantic Relativist has not offered a positive account of what form of exclusion remains once the parties to an allegedly relativism-inducing disagreement have assessed each other's moral beliefs as true relative to their respective moral contexts. In contrast, the Assessment Relativist's more refined strategy for formally accommodating the contradiction is specifically designed to give each party normative grounds on which to assess the other's beliefs as false, and this would clearly preclude agreement.

But ultimately, neither strategy is convincing. The basic strategy inappropriately posits a "contradiction" that lacks the logical significance of a contradiction because the law of noncontradiction does not apply, with the result that the parties involved can agree that their apparently contradictory claims are both true. Similarly, the refined strategy of Assessment Relativism posits a "falsehood" that lacks the epistemological significance of a falsehood because there is no error on either party's part that stands in need of correction, and here too this is something that the parties themselves can agree on. In the case at hand, when Anjali and I each assess the other's belief as false, we cannot regard these assessments as implying that either of us ought to give up her allegedly "false" belief, for if we did, then we would take ourselves to face an ordinary disagreement in which we cannot both be right, and then there would be something to be resolved between us—something actually in dispute between us and something we disagree about. If Assessment Relativists wish to keep in place the difference between such ordinary disagreements and the situations that they propose to characterize as relativism-inducing disagreements, and if they wish to be clear about the distinctive normative significance that attaches to the latter, then they should—just as Semantic Relativists who employ the basic strategy should, and indeed, just as all other advocates of the Disagreement Intuition should—give up their determination to see these situations as disagreements of any kind. What they should do instead is concentrate their attention on trying to describe the distinctive normative significance of the situations that they are envisaging without trying to exploit normative concepts—those of contradiction, disagreement, falsehood, mistake—that do not apply in those situations because their normative point is missing.

This is the express purpose for which I have introduced the concept of alternatives—of truths that cannot be embraced together. In the situations that relativists intuitively have in mind, the parties are prepared to assess each other's beliefs as true and yet for some reason they refrain from embracing each other's beliefs together with their own beliefs. This is a striking and distinctive normative aspect of such situations, and it remains in place when we remove the appearance of contradiction and disagreement. So let me now, finally, turn to the task of formulating what the doctrine of relativism amounts to when it affirms the existence of alternatives.

# 2

## Relativism as Multimundialism

What, then, would a philosophically satisfactory formulation of the doctrine of relativism—satisfactory, that is, in meeting all four desiderata—look like? In this chapter I will approach an answer to this question by further elaborating and defending the Alternatives Intuition.

The arguments of Chapter 1 show that the Alternatives Intuition is worth taking seriously, because it does better justice to the very sort of situation that advocates of the Disagreement Intuition have in mind than their own intuition does. However, somewhat more argument is needed to establish that the Alternatives Intuition is central to elaborating the doctrine of relativism, as the first desideratum demands. That is the task of Section 1. In Section 2, I will spell out in some detail what the doctrine of relativism amounts to when it is formulated as affirming the possibility of alternatives, and these details will show that the doctrine, so formulated, meets the other three desiderata I have set. Section 3 gives a brief account of how the formulation I am proposing differs from one that Bernard Williams proposed in his important and influential article "The Truth in Relativism." Section 4 will address some methodological issues that I will need to bear in mind as I turn in Part Two to the task of evaluating what grounds there are to accept or reject the doctrine of relativism when it is formulated in a way that does justice to the Alternatives Intuition.

## 1. The Prevalence of the Alternatives Intuition

I observed in the Introduction that the Alternatives Intuition is *the* intuition that predominated in the main debates about relativism in the last century. A number of disciplines and intellectual projects of that period were commonly thought to harbor potentially relativistic implications, including cultural anthropology, logical positivism, Kuhnian history and sociology of science, Feyerabend's appropriation and extension of Kuhn's ideas, Goodman's suggestion that there were "ways of worldmaking," some varieties of pragmatism—most especially, the position advocated by Rorty. *None* of these twentieth-century projects characterized the threat (in some cases it was regarded more as a promise) of relativism in terms of a special kind of irresoluble disagreement in which the parties are both right. It was characterized in terms of another kind of *difference,* one that was supposed to arise because different languages or theories, purportedly about the same subject matter, fail to share the meanings of their central terms.

Take Kuhn, for example. Although there are good reasons not to classify him as a relativist, his account of theoretical paradigms and the revolutionary character of scientific change was widely regarded by his contemporaries as having relativistic implications.[1] This was not because he characterized competing theoretical paradigms as giving rise to relativism-inducing disagreements in which both parties are right. The relativistic implications were thought to flow from a quite different aspect of them, which is that they do not share meanings at all, and moreover, that this so even when they appear to employ the same theoretical terms. Kuhn's idea was that when theories belonging to different paradigms appear to employ the same theoretical terms,

---

1. Kuhn 1962.

they nevertheless apply those terms in completely different ways, with the result the terms do not refer to the same theoretical entities. It follows that such paradigms could not, strictly speaking, contradict each other, in the sense of affirming and denying the same proposition. Thus, disagreement between the theories was not the thing at stake; it was more that these theories, without a commonly shared semantics for their terms, were to be characterized as *alternatives* to each other. In his early work in philosophy of science, Feyerabend took Kuhn's claim that there is no meaning invariance across theory change as his starting point.[2] Similar claims were made by cultural anthropologists, who argued that different social settings determine meanings within a culture that are not available to those who live outside them and cannot be adequately translated into the languages of other cultures.[3] Some philosophers of language—or perhaps I should say, some philosophers interested in language—also held that not all languages have the same expressive power, and that consequently they are not all intertranslatable. That is how Carnap viewed his "linguistic frameworks," and it is how Goodman viewed "languages of art" and other symbol systems, as he eventually made clear in his relativist tract, *Ways of Worldmaking*.[4] Although Rorty seemed to take Davidson's antirelativistic side when he supported his anti-conceptual-schemes argument,[5] he nevertheless claimed himself to be a relativist on the ground that we are all situated in different conversational practices—and he certainly did not view the situation that we confront when we encounter conversational practices different from our own as a situation of disagreement.[6]

Thus, a pervasive tendency in writing about relativism in the twentieth century was that there are different theoretical and linguistic

------

2. Feyerabend's most interesting piece in this regard is an early one entitled "Problems of Empiricism" (1965), though we will see in Chapter 3 that his position there does not count as a relativist position by my lights.

3. Whorf 1956.

4. Carnap 1947; Goodman 1978.

5. Rorty 1972.

6. Rorty 1989.

schemes that in some sense exclude one another even though they cannot contradict one another because they do not share the relevant meanings and conceptual repertory. This thought was very much on Davidson's mind when he set out to refute the doctrine of relativism in his presidential address to the APA-, "On the Very Idea of a Conceptual Scheme."[7] It was *alternative* conceptual schemes that were his target, and he defined them in terms that made no reference to logical conflict, but referred only to differences in meaning. According to his definition, alternative conceptual schemes are *true but not translatable*, and this is a good approximation of my definition of alternatives as truths that cannot be embraced together.[8]

Bernard Williams's contribution to twentieth-century discussions of relativism stands out in two respects. First, he made a very deliberated and considered attempt to formulate the doctrine of relativism in a satisfactory way.[9] Second, he departed from the consensus view of the twentieth century that I have just expounded by insisting, as the current consensus does, that the presence of logical conflict is a necessary condition for relativism. He incorporated this condition on a satisfactory formulation, because he could not see any other way in which different systems of belief could exclude one another except through logical conflict. Although his insistence on this condition would seem to align him with the Disagreement Intuition, we will see that his detailed positive suggestion about how we might capture "the truth in relativism" did not actually exploit the idea of logical conflict in any significant way—and so he was not really out of line with the twentieth-century consensus that focused on the idea of alternatives.

Many philosophers share Williams's doubt about whether the particular form of exclusion that the relativist intuitively has in mind can possibly be captured without appealing to the idea of logical exclusion, which is to say, contradiction. As I noted in Chapter 1, some of these philosophers are moved by examples that illustrate so-called "disputes of inclination" in which both parties are said to be right—as

---

7. Davidson 1973.

8. See section 3 of Chapter 3 for further explanation.

9. Williams 1981.

when I affirm that snails are delicious while my interlocutor affirms that they are not. But they have a philosophical point to make as well, which is that when they raise the question, what *else* could possibly stand in the way of embracing truth-value-bearers together, aside from contradiction, they find themselves at a loss for an answer. Perhaps the best explanation of why the Disagreement Intuition continues to have such a grip on our collective philosophical imagination lies in the fact that this question has proved hard to answer.

The despair in finding an answer to this crucial question is implicit in a standard form of objection that is commonly raised against the very possibility of formulating a coherent conception of relativism. The objection is raised specifically against the Alternatives Intuition, so I will label it the *Dilemma for Alternativeness.* The dilemma is supposed to be this: Any pair of truth-value-bearers is either inconsistent or consistent; if the two truth-value-bearers are inconsistent, then by the law of noncontradiction they cannot both be true; if they are consistent, then they are conjoinable; in neither case do we have alternatives in the sense that is supposed to be required for relativism according to the Alternatives Intuition—that is, truths that cannot be embraced together.

When I first introduced the Alternatives Intuition, I noted that there is a sense in which it subsumes the Disagreement Intuition: if there *could* be relativism-inducing disagreements in which both parties are right, then their beliefs would qualify as alternatives in the sense in which I have defined them, as truths that cannot be embraced together. Yet there is one point on which the Disagreement Intuition sides with the Dilemma for Alternativeness, and against the Alternatives Intuition as I aim to elaborate it. It takes for granted that the Dilemma correctly identifies all of the logical possibilities—any pair of truth-value-bearers must be either inconsistent or consistent—and accordingly, it tries to provide for alternativeness by rejecting the reasoning of the Dilemma's first horn and asserting instead that a pair of inconsistent truth-value-bearers can both be true.

One main thrust of my arguments in Chapter 1 against the Disagreement Intuition is that the Dilemma's first horn is right: If truth-value-bearers are inconsistent, then they cannot both be true. But the second horn is also undeniably right: If truth-value-bearers are both true and consistent, then they can be embraced together. This may seem to suggest that there is no realistic prospect of formulating the doctrine of relativism in terms of the idea of alternativeness. This is precisely what prompts the standard and common objection I am considering, the objection that relativism is not false but that it cannot be coherently formulated.

The Dilemma for Alternativeness is, explicitly or implicitly, ubiquitous. It surfaces in some form or other in almost any argument about relativism, whether in informal philosophical discussion or the detailed discussions of specialists. The question is immediately (and usually impatiently) posed: What makes alternative conceptual schemes or incommensurable theories *competitors*? Is it that they are inconsistent? If so, then they cannot both be true and the parties who hold them simply disagree. If not, then they are both true and nothing should prevent the parties who hold them from coming to agree, in the sense of embracing them both together. Where, then, is the supposed relativism?

The fact that the Dilemma for Alternativeness surfaces so routinely in arguments about relativism is a clear sign that the Alternatives Intuition is indeed a central one and is widely associated with the very idea of relativism, and the historical record of the twentieth-century debates about relativism simply adds support for this conclusion. So if we take the Alternatives Intuition as our starting point for formulating the doctrine of relativism, we can at least be assured that we will satisfy the first desideratum that any satisfactory formulation must meet. There is all the more reason to adopt it as our starting point, because, as the arguments of Chapter 1 brought out, there are serious difficulties for the competitor intuitions in which relativism might be grounded—the Disagreement Intuition, along with the Relative Truth Intuition that is often wheeled in to prop it up.

## 2. The Real Dividing Issue: Unimundialism versus Multimundialism

If we take the Alternatives Intuition as our starting point, then our first step must be to find a way out of the Dilemma for Alternativeness.

Furthermore, if we grant, as I think we should grant, that both horns of the Dilemma are correct, then our second step is already laid out: we must look for a third possibility that the Dilemma overlooks.

The briefest reflection serves to show that there is exactly one remaining possibility to consider, which is that in some cases *truth-value-bearers are neither inconsistent nor consistent.* I will want to make something of this possibility, so let me begin to explore it.

When truth-value-bearers are neither inconsistent nor consistent, and are true, they arguably do qualify as "alternatives" as I have defined that term—they are truths that cannot be embraced together. The point here can be put initially and tersely as follows: When truth-value-bearers are not inconsistent, the law of noncontradiction does not rule out that they are both true, and when they are not consistent, then the law of conjunction does not entitle us to conjoin them. This latter part of the point needs some explanation, for I use the expression "law of conjunction" in a somewhat nonstandard way and it may be confusing on that account. In formal languages, there is usually a syntactic rule for constructing sentences using the conjunction operator, which allows us to conjoin *any* well-formed sentences, *including* sentences that are inconsistent with each other. This is obviously not the rule to which I am referring when I say that the law of conjunction would not allow us to conjoin sentences that are not consistent. I am referring to a rule of inference that would govern *belief* formation rather than sentence construction, and that would take us from truths to further truths. The point, then, is that when we take two truth-value-bearers to be true but not consistent, we are not licensed by the law of conjunction to believe their conjunction. To put the point in another way that more effectively directs our attention away from merely syntactic considerations, this law of conjunction constrains us to recognize that truths are *co-tenable* only if they are consistent.

The possibility that some truth-value-bearers may be neither inconsistent nor consistent is a strange possibility to contemplate, and considered in the abstract it is not immediately clear what it involves. Yet this is precisely the possibility that I was implicitly raising in Chapter 1 when I reinterpreted the example about Anjali and me so as to remove the appearance of a disagreement between us. What we learned there was that once we disambiguate terms so that there is no inconsistency between her belief and mine (that is, so that we do not respectively believe that deference to parents is morally obligatory and that it is not, but rather, she believes that such deference is morally-obligatory-in-the-Indian-traditionalist-sense while I believe that it is not morally-obligatory-in-the-American-individualist-sense), there still appears to be a form of exclusion present in the example, insofar as neither of us is prepared to embrace the other's moral belief together with her own, in spite of being prepared to grant both that it is true and that it is not inconsistent with her own. I am now suggesting that if such beliefs cannot be embraced together even though they are *not inconsistent,* then it must also be the case they are *not consistent,* because if they were consistent, then the law of conjunction would entitle us to embrace them together.

To repeat the warning I gave in Chapter 1: Examples cannot bear the burden of proof in discussions of relativism. So the immediately foregoing remarks are not intended to convince anyone that when the example about Anjali and me is taken to illustrate alternativeness, we have conclusive grounds on which to formulate the doctrine of relativism as involving alternativeness. Moreover, even if we were convinced by the example that we should *formulate* the doctrine along these lines, we ought not to regard the example as providing conclusive grounds on which to *embrace* the doctrine so formulated. No such convictions on our part can prevent others from interpreting the same example in other ways, so as to illustrate other positions—not only other formulations of the doctrine of relativism, but an antirelativist position as well. So, if we cannot reasonably expect the power of example to serve as a substitute for philosophical investigation, the work of this chapter is to commence such a philosophical investigation. But here I shall not be trying to establish whether or not there *are* any alternatives; I shall concentrate my efforts instead on critically examining the idea of alternativeness and exploring what it would mean to formulate relativism in terms of the idea, proceeding from the assumption that if there is any logical room for alternativeness at all, it lies in the third possibility that the Dilemma for Alternativeness overlooks—that a pair of truth-value-bearers may be neither inconsistent nor consistent.

It does not take much reflection to see that when truth-value-bearers are neither inconsistent nor consistent, they fail to stand in any logical relations at all. They are, as I shall put it, *normatively insulated* from one another. It follows that, according to the Alternatives Intuition that I am elaborating, *the most fundamental dividing issue between relativists and their opponents is really a logical one.* It concerns whether there is any such thing as normative insularity, or equivalently, it concerns whether logical relations run everywhere among all truth-value-bearers. Relativists deny this, while their opponents insist upon it.

The goal, given my initial setup of desiderata for a satisfactory formulation of relativism, is to establish that when we frame the dividing issue between relativists and their opponents in these logical terms, all of the three remaining desiderata are fulfilled: within such a framing, relativism emerges as possessing a distinctive but nevertheless controversial metaphysical significance, and as coherent, and as having clear practical implications so that it becomes clear what it would mean to *live* relativism.

Let me proceed negatively first. When we formulate the doctrine of relativism along these lines, it incorporates a negative claim, that logical relations do not run everywhere among all truth-value-bearers. The best way to understand this negative claim is by contrast with the positive claim that the doctrine denies.

### 2.a. Unimundialism

If logical relations do run everywhere among all truth-value-bearers, then all of the true ones must be consistent and conjoinable. It follows that there is a *single, consistent, and comprehensive body of truths,* and this amounts to a metaphysical commitment to the *oneness* of the world, or *Unimundialism.*

Perhaps by some philosophical measures, precisely because Unimundialism is derived from logical considerations, it should not be counted as a strictly metaphysical thesis. But if the conception of the world as one is not to be counted as a metaphysical conception, then neither should the vision that Wittgenstein offered with the opening words of the *Tractatus Logico-Philosophicus:* "The world is all that is the case." His position was also explicitly derived from logical considerations, so much so that he was methodologically committed to remaining neutral on all metaphysical issues that cannot be settled on the basis of logic alone. Yet in spite of his careful neutrality on a wide range of metaphysical issues, Tractarian realism certainly does qualify as a metaphysical conception by the criterion I gave in the Introduction, on which the important contrast is between metaphysics and epistemology, so that a claim counts as metaphysical if it is a highly general one concerning what is the case, or what there is, or the nature of the things there are, as opposed to being a claim about what we can or cannot *know* about such things. By that criterion, Unimundialism is also a metaphysical thesis: in claiming that there is just one world, it makes no particular claims about the character and/or limits of our knowledge of it. This is so in spite of the fact that it employs logical notions like consistency and conjoinability, and even in spite of the fact that these logical notions implicitly introduce the idea of a point of view from which consistent and conjoinable truths can be embraced together. I will return to this last aspect of the metaphysical significance of Unimundialism below, but first I want to address the matter of its coherence.

Prima facie, if there is any threat to the coherence of the doctrine of Unimundialism, it seems likely that it would be a threat of logical incoherence. Since I am not a logician, I shall have to leave it to others to verify that the doctrine is logically coherent. Yet I do want to raise one potential logical difficulty and explain why I think we may reasonably set it aside. The explanation will help both to convey the practical significance of Unimundialism and to further elaborate its general metaphysical significance—even though, like Tractarian realism, it is neutral on a great many metaphysical issues that are not settled by its logical basis.

Before raising the potential logical difficulty for Unimundialism that I have in mind, two quick clarifications about its logical content are in order. When I characterize it as affirming that there is a single, consistent, and *comprehensive* body of truths, it is natural to think of it as being in some sense *complete*. Yet it need not be complete in the logician's sense. A formal language is logically complete just in case it can be proven that whenever sentences of the language are semantic consequences of other sentences, they are also syntactically derivable from them. As far as I can see, the Unimundialist need not take a stand on whether it is possible to express all of the truths in a formal language that is complete in this logical sense; but whether or not I am right about this, I am not referring to the logicians' notion of completeness when I say that the Unimundialist holds that there is a single, consistent, and *comprehensive* body of truths—I am only saying that this body of truths is *all-inclusive*. Similarly, as far as I can see, the Unimundialist need not commit herself to the principle of bivalence that characterizes classical logic, according to which every sentence is either true or false. There are well-known reasons that philosophical logicians have given for allowing that some sentences are neither true nor false, which have to do with various familiar phenomena such as reference failure or threatened paradox, and I do not see why a Unimundialist should be disallowed from being moved by those reasons to allow truth-value gaps, because this need not affect her point that all truth-value-*bearers* stand in logical relations.[10]

If there is a logical difficulty confronting the Unimundialist's idea of a single, consistent, and comprehensive body of truths, it seems likely that it would be the sort of difficulty that tends to arise in connection with the idea of a totality that threatens to be too large to be formally tractable.[11] I do not know how grave this difficulty really is,

---

10. In Rovane 2002 I misleadingly used the word "complete" rather than "comprehensive" to characterize the Unimundialist's idea of a single, consistent, and *all-inclusive* body of truths. I also attempted to spell out the idea of comprehensiveness (which I then called "completeness") in such a way as to leave room for the possibility of such truth-value gaps. I suggested that a body of truths is complete (read "comprehensive") if, for every well-formed proposition, either it or its negation figures in it. What I meant by "well-formed" is truth-value-bearing—so that a truth-value-bearer is ill-formed if it gives rise to a truth-value gap. I should have added the qualification that if a well-formed proposition is not true, and so does not belong to the single, consistent, and comprehensive body of truths, then its negation does, *provided* that its negation is well-formed.

11. Several of my colleagues have expressed reservations about this, but interestingly, the colleagues who are actually practicing logicians do not share those reservations.

because, as I have already noted, the doctrine of relativism can be conceived as holding in a domain-specific way, and in that case the doctrine to which it is opposed can also be conceived in a domain-specific way. Then the question whether there is a single, consistent, and comprehensive body of truths would not be one that we raise just once and for all, but one that we raise and consider separately with respect to different domains—so for example, we could separately consider whether there is such a body of truths in the domain of natural facts studied by science, or in the domain of moral value, or in the domain of mathematics, and so on. But I want to concede for the sake of argument that the difficulty that I have just raised might still arise even when we construe the doctrine of Unimundialism in this domain-specific way—that the doctrine will typically make reference to a totality that is too large to be formally tractable. The point of stressing the possible persistence of such a difficulty for restricted domains is that it brings out something about the aspiration that lies behind the doctrine. Even if the difficulty should persist within a specific domain, the idea of an all-inclusive body of truths can still function as a regulative ideal that governs our logical, and more broadly epistemic, practices within that domain—the *Unimundial Ideal*.

When we conceive the idea of a single, consistent, and comprehensive body of truths as a regulative ideal, Unimundialism takes on the following practical significance: It instructs us that we must not take anything to be true without taking it to be consistent and conjoinable with everything else we take to be true. This means that, for any truth-value-bearer that we might happen to come across, we can accept it as true only if it is consistent with what we already believe; and if it is inconsistent with what we already believe, then we must choose one of the following options: either we must reject it as false, or we must revise our prior beliefs to accommodate its truth, or we must suspend belief on it along with the subset of our prior beliefs that are inconsistent with it. Thus the Unimundial view requires us to take this normative stance toward each and every truth-value-bearer that we come across, and any effort to characterize this normative stance will employ a universal quantifier whose scope seems to be unbounded. We find it natural to think of this quantifier as ranging over the totality of all of the possible truth-value-bearers, and to think of the true ones as a subset of those. My point is that even if we cannot arrive at a formally adequate conception of that totality, we can still *conceive* it, and furthermore, we can always conceive our inquiries in normative relation to it. When we do this we are embracing the Unimundial Ideal.

As I have said, Unimundialism resembles the Tractarian position in the respect of remaining metaphysically neutral except insofar as such neutrality is precluded by its logical commitments. So when we embrace the Unimundial Ideal, we need not think of ourselves as directly embracing any other, more substantive metaphysical commitment, except to the oneness of the world. Yet this is not to say that we shall never find any interesting connections and disconnections between the issue of Unimundialism and other metaphysical issues. It is only to say that if there are such connections and disconnections, they do not immediately intrude when we state the doctrine and embrace its immediate normative implications.

In particular, Unimundialism makes no mention of the issue that divides realists and antirealists concerning whether the world is or is not mind-independent. It does not affirm its mind-independence as realists do; it also does not reduce truth to any epistemic conditions (verification conditions, assertibility conditions, and so on) as antirealists typically do; and it does not affirm the weaker form of mind-dependence that Kant proposed with his transcendental idealism. All it does is impose logical constraints on truth that ensure the oneness of the world.

When we turn to the task of evaluating the doctrine of relativism, we shall have occasion to consider whether and how arguments for and against realism might nevertheless provide us with reasons to accept or reject relativism, and in the course of considering this we shall also be considering the extent to which such arguments provide us with reasons to accept or reject the Unimundial view that relativists oppose. I shall leave further discussion of how Unimundialism relates to realism for Chapters 3 and 4, except to register just one preliminary point now: The realist idea that the world is mind-independent does not by itself suffice to establish the oneness of the world in the sense affirmed by Unimundialism. It is easy to be misled on this matter by the fact that realists can easily conceive the world as one in a different sense: they can conceive all of the mind-independent facts as constituting a single totality in the sense of comprising a single *set*. But this conception clearly falls short of the Unimundial Ideal on account of the fact that it makes no mention of the normative constraints that would follow upon the logical relatedness of all truth-value-bearers. This normative constraint is part of what I mean to convey by referring to a single *body* of truths rather than to a single *set* of them.

Though it is relatively independent in these ways from the metaphysical commitments of realism, there is one fairly substantial metaphysical commitment that Unimundialism does clearly carry, which goes beyond its bare logical content. This commitment concerns the idea of a point of view, and it is a sort of Unimundial counterpart to Thomas Nagel's "View from Nowhere."[12] According to Nagel, the realist conception of reality as radically mind-independent invites us to try to transcend our subjective viewpoints so as to conceive reality as it is in itself, and even though we cannot conceive anything except from a particular subjective point of view, we must nevertheless do the best we can to try to conceive reality as if from no point of view at all. Because Unimundialism does not directly incorporate a commitment to realism, it does not necessarily bring in train an aspiration to this perspectiveless form of objectivity. But it does commit us to a highly ambitious conception of what might be achieved from within a single perspective, for when we embrace the Unimundial Ideal and suppose that all of the truths are consistent and conjoinable, we implicitly make reference to a point of view from which all of the truths could in principle be apprehended and embraced together. This would have to be a universal and all-encompassing point of view from which it is possible to apprehend and embrace every truth that can be known from every other point of view. Thus, what Unimundialism invites us to conceive is not a View from Nowhere, but a *View from Everywhere;* and we could not be fully justified in affirming Unimundialism if we came to doubt that such a View from Everywhere is a real metaphysical pos-

---

12. Nagel 1986.

sibility. It might seem to be a foregone conclusion that it is not a real metaphysical possibility—insofar as we are prepared to grant that the very idea of a single, consistent, and comprehensive body of truths may be formally intractable. But in Part Two we shall see that there are other, philosophically more interesting, ways to approach the question whether and why a View from Everywhere is possible. In any case, what I want to emphasize at this juncture is that Unimundialism does bring in train this one metaphysical corollary, over and above its logically driven commitment to the oneness of the world, and that otherwise the doctrine is metaphysically neutral.

It may seem that Unimundialism cannot be as neutral as I am claiming with respect to the metaphysical issue of realism and its various antirealist contraries. For when we construe the idea of a single, consistent, and comprehensive body of truths as I just suggested above, as a regulative ideal with normative implications for inquiry, it may seem that we are restricting its metaphysical significance to its practical significance, and this looks very much like the characteristic move of pragmatism, which is to reduce the meaning of any conception to its potential practical bearing. It is certainly true that I have framed Unimundialism in such a way that it is compatible with a pragmatist outlook. In fact, I take it to be a *virtue* of my approach to formulating the doctrine of relativism that it affords room for pragmatists to oppose it by affirming Unimundialism—as I think Peirce implicitly did. Nevertheless, I want to emphasize that Unimundialism and pragmatism are quite distinct doctrines, and this can be seen from the fact that the former is metaphysically neutral on matters about which pragmatists most definitely are not neutral.

It is worth navigating in some detail through these relations that Unimundialism bears to pragmatism, in order to take in various points of convergence as well as divergence.

The pragmatist position that Unimundialism seems to resemble most closely is that of Peirce. When he defined truth as what would be believed by the community of investigators at the end of inquiry, Peirce offered us an idealized conception that goes beyond any actual state of knowledge that we are capable of attaining, much as I have claimed that the Unimundial ideal of a single, consistent, and comprehensive body of truths does. Moreover, just as I have refused to attribute to Unimundialism any further metaphysical commitments that are not necessary for making sense of the Unimundial Ideal, likewise Peirce refused to take on any additional metaphysical commitments that are not necessary for making sense of his ideal limit of inquiry. It naturally goes together with such metaphysical neutrality to connect the meaning of an ideal with its regulative function. Unimundialism invites us to conceive whatever we hold to be true as part of the single, consistent, and comprehensive body of truths, and Peirce invites us to conceive whatever we hold true as part of what would be believed at the ideal limit of inquiry. Each ideal also invites us to conceive any changes that we might make in our body of beliefs as bringing us closer to it, either by removing false beliefs from our body of beliefs so that it contains nothing that is not in the ideal, or by adding new beliefs to it so that it contains more of what is in the ideal.

Perhaps there are more similarities than these between Unimundialism and Peirce's pragmatism. But the ones I have mentioned suffice to give the impression that Unimundialism is a form of pragmatism. So let me now explain why the impression is wrong. I will first explain why Unimundialism is distinct from Peirce's position, and then generalize the point to all versions of pragmatism.

Peirce held that as actual inquiry proceeds over time, it will bring us progressively closer to its ideal limit. In contrast, no such notion of cumulative progress is built into the Unimundial Ideal. This may seem hard to reconcile with the claim I just made about how we are to conceive any changes of mind that we might make as bringing us closer to it. But that was a claim about how we must view our changes of mind from within, at the times that we are making them. In this regard, it is of a piece with one side of Moore's paradox, on which we cannot assert that we believe something and simultaneously assert that it is not true. (It is the other side of the paradox that I have claimed relativists fall into, by allowing that something is true while refraining from believing it.) Nothing follows from the necessity of taking our beliefs to be true at the times we hold them about how they will appear from the perspective of temporal distance, for we are always free to disagree with our past beliefs, and even our anticipated future beliefs (though this is more controversial, because it may make us vulnerable to Dutch booking). Similarly, nothing follows from the necessity of taking our changes of mind to be epistemic improvements at the times we make them about how they will appear from the perspective of temporal distance, for we are always free to regard what we once took to be improvements as mistakes that landed us in losses of true beliefs and/or acquisitions of false ones. In principle, such lessons from the past could lead us to rate the probability of continuous improvement over time as low. This is not to say that the Unimundial Ideal definitely speaks against the possibility of epistemic progress. It is silent on the issue. It is silent because it never asks us to step back and view our beliefs from any temporal perspective besides the present. The practical stance that follows upon it is a stance that we take *in* time, in which we relate our current epistemic states and activities to the logical constraints that it imposes. Insofar as it seems to refer to *all* times and *all* possible epistemic states, it is only in order to affirm that this logical constraint is completely general. But it can be general without carrying any instruction to apply it cross-temporally in the course of inquiry. It does tell us that any set of beliefs cannot all be true unless those beliefs are all consistent with one another, and this logical constraint does apply to the beliefs that we hold at different times. But it does not tell us that we must *evaluate* the truth of the beliefs that we hold at different times from any perspective but the present, and this means that it leaves us free *not* to be consistent over time so long as we are prepared to assess the beliefs that we held at earlier times as false when they are inconsistent with our present beliefs. Furthermore, just as it does not tell us that we must be consistent over time, it does not tell us whether the cumulative impact of our various changes of mind will bring us closer to the single, consistent, and comprehensive body of truths.

The silence of Unimundialism on the question of our epistemic progress goes together with another important point of divergence from Peirce. I said earlier that Unimundialism does not aim to reduce truth to epistemic conditions in the ways that various antirealists have attempted to do, and let me now clarify that this includes Peirce's definition of truth as what would be believed at the end of inquiry. Even though the epistemic condition to which this definition refers is highly idealized—because we shall never reach the end of inquiry—it is nevertheless an epistemic condition. If it were not, then Peirce would not have been making a philosophically significant or controversial claim when he claimed that there can be no more to the truth than what would be believed at the end of inquiry. But Unimundialism does not assert that there is nothing more to the truth than this, but instead it leaves conceptual room for a skeptical possibility that Peirce dismissed as incoherent; that is, it leaves room for the thought that what would be believed at the end of inquiry—our "best" theory of the world—might fail to be true.

Similarly, the Unimundial Ideal allows that what counts as true according to any other pragmatist definition of truth might also fail to be true—for example, something might satisfy James's definition of the truth as what works and yet fail to be true. This is the most fundamental difference between Unimundialism and all pragmatist positions. Unlike pragmatism, Unimundialism makes no claim about the essential knowability of reality. This is bound to make it seem as though Unimundialism is much closer to realism than to pragmatism. But I have already taken pains to explain that Unimundialism is not positively committed to the mind-independence of reality either. As such, Unimundialism is neither realist nor pragmatist nor antirealist in any other sense; it is, as I have emphasized all along, metaphysically neutral on the issue of mind-independence. This may seem to reinvite a perhaps persistent impression that Unimundialism should not really be counted as a metaphysical doctrine at all, but only as a logical one. But that impression is quite mistaken, as I have already explained. Its claim that the world is *one* is a very general claim about *what is the case,* and that puts it squarely within metaphysics as opposed to epistemology.

I want to close my discussion of Unimundialism by briefly addressing the question, What would it mean to *live* as a Unimundialist? To a large extent this question has already been answered. We have seen that the Unimundial Ideal of a single, consistent, and comprehensive body of truths imposes normative constraints on inquiry, in the form of various permissions and constraints on how we may normatively respond to any truth-value-bearers that we come across in the light of their logical relations to other truth-value-bearers. We have also seen that these permissions and constraints do not usually dictate one uniquely appropriate normative response but instead leave open a range of normatively acceptable epistemic options from which to choose. Nevertheless, Unimundialism does force a choice among these options, because logical relations always carry a normative signifi-cance that we are never free to completely ignore—we *must* respond to their normative force in one way or another.

Everything I just said about the normative implications of the Unimundial Ideal for pure theoretical inquiry carries over to our in-terpersonal dealings with others in conversation and argument. As Unimundialists, we are never free to be completely indifferent to what others believe, because everything that they believe stands in logical relations to everything that we believe, and there are always normative implications that need to be thought through. If their beliefs are con-sistent with our own, they are candidates for belief by us too, though we might choose to suspend belief instead; and if their beliefs are in-consistent with our own, then they are not candidates for belief by us unless we are prepared to change our minds in some way or other to accommodate their truth, though in this case too we might choose to suspend belief on the entire matter instead. In all of these cases, there is potential for *learning* from others, either by acquiring new beliefs that leave our prior beliefs unaltered, or by acquiring grounds on which to reject, or revise, or suspend our prior beliefs. And of course, the learning need not always be on our side rather than theirs, since when others fail to hold our beliefs, this may be an occasion on which we are able to impart new beliefs to them, or to correct their prior beliefs.

My claim that Unimundialists can never be wholly indifferent to the beliefs of others may seem exaggerated in the light of my discus-sion of the possibility of irresoluble disagreements in Chapter 1. There I had described a self-confident internalist who generally does not re-gard her disagreements with others as occasions on which to learn from them because she is always sure that they are the ones who are mistaken and not she. It is easy to imagine that such a self-confident internalist might be extraordinarily indifferent to the beliefs of others, to the point of functioning nearly as an epistemic solipsist. All we need to imagine is the following: First, in addition to the fact that she is self-confident, she is also uncurious and, so, just as she never questions the truth of her own beliefs, she also does not wish to acquire any new beliefs on matters that she has not already considered herself, with the result that she never takes her encounters with others as occasions on which to change her mind about anything, even when their beliefs are consistent with hers; second, she is also epistemically ungenerous, in the sense that she is completely uninterested in getting others to change their minds about anything, even when she sees them as mistaken or ignorant because they do not share her beliefs. It may seem that this internalist would be as indifferent as anyone ever could be to the beliefs of others. Yet I have not described her in such a way that she could not embrace the Unimundial Ideal of a single, consistent, and comprehensive body of truths. On the contrary, my description of her took for granted that she does embrace that ideal, for I have allowed that she generally sees the beliefs of others as being either inconsistent or consistent with her own. So in spite of her antisocial epistemic stance, she is not free to ignore the normative implications of these logical relations—specifically, she is not free *not* to pronounce the beliefs of others false when they are inconsistent with hers and she is sure she is right, and she is not free *not* to view the beliefs of others that are consistent with hers as candidates for belief by her even though she is not interested in acquiring any new beliefs.

Admittedly, the doctrine of Unimundialism has epistemic attractions that would be lost on someone who functioned in the antisocial way I just described, and refused either to learn from others or to try to teach them. But I have taken pains to consider just how epistemically indifferent a Unimundialist could in principle be in order to bring out that her epistemic indifference could never be completely thoroughgoing, and this marks an important contrast with the much more thoroughgoing epistemic indifference that follows upon relativism as I am proposing to formulate it.

### 2.b. Multimundialism

When we take the Alternatives Intuition as our starting point for formulating the doctrine of relativism, it emerges first and foremost as a
negative doctrine that rejects Unimundialism. I have defined alternatives as truths that cannot be embraced together, and I have noted
that if there are alternatives in this sense, then there must be a third
possibility that the Dilemma for Alternativeness overlooks, which is
that some truth-value-bearers are neither inconsistent nor consistent.
Insofar as such truth-value-bearers are not inconsistent, they can both
be true, and yet insofar they are not consistent, they cannot be conjoined even when they are true, and so they qualify as alternatives in
the requisite sense. But insofar as alternatives are neither inconsistent
nor consistent, they fail to stand in any logical relations at all, and this
means that when relativists affirm the existence (or possibility) of alternatives, they deny all of the central claims of Unimundialism—that
logical relations run everywhere among all truth-value-bearers,
that there is a single, consistent, and comprehensive body of truths,
that there is one world. Relativists affirm instead that some truth-
value-bearers do not stand in logical relations to one another, that
there are many noncomprehensive bodies of truths that cannot be
conjoined, that there are many worlds rather than one. In a word, they
affirm *Multimundialism*.

The main work of this subsection is to clarify what the doctrine of
relativism amounts to when it is formulated as Multimundialism, and
to establish that it meets all four of the desiderata for a philosophically satisfactory formulation of the doctrine.

The arguments of Section 1 have already established that the first
desideratum is satisfied: the Alternatives Intuition which is at the
heart of Multimundialism captures an important intuition about the
doctrine's content that figured centrally in the main twentieth-century
debates about it.

The second desideratum asks that we formulate the doctrine of relativism in such a way that it attributes to the relativist a metaphysical
commitment that is at once distinctive and controversial. Since Multimundialism is a denial of Unimundialism, and I have just made clear

that the latter does indeed hold metaphysical significance, it stands to reason that the former does too. While the latter affirms that there is just one world, the former affirms that there are many worlds. This *many-worlds thesis* should not be confused the modal realist's claim, that there are many *possible* worlds. Although modal realism does count as a distinctive and controversial metaphysical thesis in its own right, it is perfectly compatible with Unimundialism—with there being just one consistent and comprehensive body of truths, which comprehends all of the truths concerning what is possible as well as what is actual. The Multimundialist's claim is a quite different claim, insofar as it posits many distinct bodies of truths that are not comprehensive, and are not consistent and conjoinable with one another, but instead normatively insulated from one another. This counts as a *metaphysical* claim for the same reason that Unimundialism does—it is a general claim about what is the case, as opposed to being an epistemological claim about what we can or cannot know about what is the case.

Like Unimundialism, Multimundialism is metaphysically neutral on matters that are not directly settled by its fundamental logical commitment, and this neutrality extends to the issue that divides realists and antirealists, concerning the mind-independence of reality. When we raise the question whether or not logical relations run everywhere among all truth-value-bearers, we are not directly and automatically raising a question about whether reality is or is not mind-independent. In the eyes of some philosophers, the very separability of these two dividing issues—one world versus many, and mind-independence versus mind-dependence—might seem to speak against my proposal to formulate relativism as Multimundialism. For as I noted in the Introduction, it is a very widespread and deeply entrenched assumption, that realism and relativism are mutually opposed issues, and that any argument for relativism must therefore begin with an antirealist premise—so much so that I found it necessary to let the assumption stand without question in Chapter 1, for the purpose of giving a sympathetic exposition of the prevailing consensus view of relativism that combines the Disagreement Intuition and the Relative Truth Intuition. However, since then we have found powerful reasons to regard the Alternatives Intuition as a more promising starting point for formulating the doctrine of relativism, and to construe alternativeness in terms of normative insularity. Those reasons are not overturned by this somewhat surprising implication—I would even call it an important *insight*—that relativism and realism are not mutually opposed doctrines.

We saw that although Unimundialism is officially neutral with respect to the issue of realism, its basic logical commitment does bring in train one additional metaphysical commitment beyond a commitment to the oneness of the world, insofar as it is committed to the possibility of a View from Everywhere, which is a point of view from which every truth that can be known from every other point of view could in principle be apprehended and embraced together. Since Multimundialists deny that all truths can be embraced together, they obviously do not need to make sense of this metaphysical possibility.

Beyond what I have said so far, the broader metaphysical significance of the Multimundialist's fundamental logical commitment—what it means to posit many worlds rather than one—is really best understood in connection with the practical implications of that logical commitment. So let me now try to address all of these aspects of Multimundialism together, and in doing so, establish that it fully satisfies the third and fourth desiderata as well as the first and second—by showing that it is coherent, and by bringing out what it would mean to live in accord with it.

I want to repeat that I am not a logician, and so I shall have to leave it to others to confirm that the doctrine of Multimundialism is logically coherent. However, there are just three matters worth noting, that are visible even from a nonexpert perspective.

First, it seems to me that the main threat to the logical coherence of Unimundialism may not carry over to Multimundialism, which is that the idea of a single, consistent, and comprehensive body of logical truths makes reference to a totality that threatens to be formally unmanageable. At the very least, Multimundialism is no worse off in this regard, and it might well be better off insofar as the many, noncomprehensive bodies of truths that it posits may be smaller, and may therefore be formally more tractable, than the single and comprehensive body of truths that Unimundialism posits.

Second, if Multimundialism faces special logical difficulties of its own, they are bound to follow upon and be related to the idea of normative insularity. I suspect that many logicians may find the very idea of normative insularity unattractive, and some may even regard it as logically impossible. But a lot depends on what we mean by a logical relation. Here is what I mean: *It is in the nature of a logical relation to possess a distinctive normative force, by virtue of which it mandates, licenses, or prohibits inferences among truth-value-bearers.* For example, if a given truth-value-bearer stands in the logical relation of consistency to everything else I believe, the normative force of that logical relation does not mandate that I infer anything at all about the truth-value of that truth-value-bearer, though if I regard it as true, then the normative force of that relation does permit me to conjoin it with the rest of my beliefs; whereas, if a given truth-value-bearer stands in the logical relation of inconsistency to something I already believe, the normative force of that logical relation mandates that I infer that the truth-value-bearer is false or else change my mind so as to accommodate its truth consistently with everything else I believe. *Insofar as we conceive logical relations as relations that exert normative force in these ways, then when they fail to hold between truth-value-bearers, no inferences between them are mandated, licensed, or prohibited.* Thus, when truth-value-bearers fail to stand in logical relations, there is literally a boundary between them across which no normative force reaches, and that is why I find it fitting to describe this condition as one of "normative insularity"— because what is true or false on one side of the boundary has no normative force that reaches to the other side of the boundary, which is to say, it has no normative significance for what may be true or false on the other side of the boundary.

I shall take it for granted that it is possible to devise a formal system through which we could represent the boundaries of normative insularity. In such a system, truth-value-bearers that fall within the same boundaries would stand in the usual sorts of logical relations that sanction inferences in the usual sorts of ways; and yet these logical relations and inferences would always be confined within boundaries and never reach across them. It should be obvious that such a system would enable us to represent the many worlds that Multimundialism posits, in the form of many, noncomprehensive bodies of truths that cannot be conjoined, owing to the presence of normative boundaries between them.

I have sometimes been asked, Why should my notion of normative insularity be conceived as an *absence* of logical relations, rather than as an *additional* logical relation to be defined as one that does not sanction any inferences? Perhaps such a conception would be more in keeping with the way in which logicians think of logical relations. But I find it more natural to conceive normative insularity in terms of an absence of logical relations, for two reasons: First, in order to preserve the idea that logical relations carry a normative force that is registered by the laws of logic—a force that we are able to track through our inferential practice when we follow those laws; second, in order to make vivid just how distinctive the situation that relativists are asking us to envisage is, because when we encounter alternatives, we are encountering truth-value-bearers that carry no normative significance for us at all, in the sense that they have no implications at all for what else we may or may not believe. However, all this being said, as far as I can see, no intolerable harm would be done if logicians proposed to portray normative insularity as an additional logical relation rather than as an absence of logical relations—so long as the portrayal provided for the confinement of inferential practice within boundaries, so as to generate many, noncomprehensive bodies of truths that cannot be conjoined, as Multimundialism requires.[13]

The third matter that I want to raise in connection with the fundamental logical commitment of Multimundialism is one that I raised when I first introduced the Alternatives Intuition: If we ever were to encounter alternatives, in the form of truths that are normatively insulated from everything else we believe, then we would be put in the position of believing something of the form "*P* is true but I don't believe *P*," thereby landing us on one side of Moore's paradox. I observed in Chapter 1 that this problem arises for the Disagreement Intuition as well as the Alternatives Intuition, because in the sort of situation that is alleged to be a relativism-inducing disagreement, we are supposed to

---

13. I thank John Collins for raising this possibility.

concede that the other party is right even though we disagree with her—which is to say, we are supposed to concede that her claim is true even though we do not ourselves believe it. When I made this observation, I did not take this as a reason to set aside either of these intuitive conceptions of relativism, but rather inferred that it is a very basic feature of the relativists' distinctive normative stance that it allows for this sort of exclusion among truths, even though allowing for it lands us on one side of Moore's paradox. I am now in a position to explain why landing on the relativists' side of the paradox is not nearly so problematic as it would be to land on the other side, the side on which we would believe things without holding them true. The idea that we could believe something without holding it true defies intelligibility, because it is unclear what else believing something could possibly consist in. Whereas the idea that we might allow that something is true without believing it ourselves does not similarly defy intelligibility, because we clearly can make room in our concept of truth for this possibility. All we need to do is to allow that truths can fail to be *universal* in the social sense of being *truths for everyone,* and allow instead that some truths are *true for others* while not being *true for us.*

This idea of *true for* is not quite the same as the Semantic Relativist's idea of relative truth, on which the truth-predicate is conceived as having the binary form "__ is true relative to __." The point of introducing this binary truth-predicate is to show how sentences of the form P and not-P can both be true, how such truths can be embraced together without violating the law of noncontradiction—insofar as P is true relative to one context and not-P is true relative to another. In contrast, the point of introducing the idea of *true for* is to flag that what is true for the inhabitants of one world *cannot be embraced together* with what is true for the inhabitants of another world. The relativists' position is often characterized as involving this idea of *true for,* and although it is often rejected on this very count by critics who declare that they cannot comprehend it,[14] the above account of normative insularity provides a straightforward account of it. The failure of some

---

14. See Boghossian 2006a.

truths to be universal is simply the social corollary of the failure of some truth-value-bearers to stand in logical relation, for, by definition, such normatively insulated truth-value-bearers cannot be conjoined even when they are true; and so it follows that they cannot be embraced together from the same point of view even when they are true—and that is how they can be true for some while not being true for others.

Relativism's most dismissive opponents will not likely be appeased by my suggestion that we can make sense of the relativists' idea that some truths are not universal by invoking the idea that some truth-value-bearers are normatively insulated from one another. On the contrary, insofar as they are already inclined to reject the latter idea, of normative insulary, on the ground that the Dilemma for Alternativeness exhausts the logical possibilities, they will likewise be inclined to reject the former idea, that some truths are not universal, on Kantian grounds. Kant claimed that whenever I reason, I must regard myself as an exemplar of all rational beings, and there is no doubt that when I do this I must regard the truths that I embrace as truths for everyone. But as I see it, if we intuitively conceive the doctrine of relativism as involving some form of exclusion among truths—that is, alternatives—then one question that is being raised by the relativist is whether this Kantian universalist attitude is always mandated, or even always permissible. This question is clearly being raised when we construe alternativeness in terms of normative insulary, for if some truth-value-bearers are normatively insulated from one another, then reasoning must take place within boundaries—boundaries within which logical relations hold and across which they do not hold. Speaking for myself, if I came to believe that there are such boundaries, then I would no longer regard it as appropriate to think of myself as reasoning for *everyone,* but would think of myself as reasoning only for those who are located within the same boundaries as I; and if such reasoning led me to embrace certain truths, then I would not think of them as truths for everyone, but only as truths for those who are located within the same boundaries as I. It has been remarked to me that if I were thus to fail to regard the truths that I embrace as truths for everyone, the effect would be that I would be alienated from my own rational nature and thereby from my very self.[15] But this seems to me to be both a wrong and an excessive conclusion to come to. What would be true—and I think it is what relativists have probably always intended to suggest—is that I would be alienated from *certain others,* namely, those who are not located within the same boundaries as I, and for whom the truths that I embrace are alternatives. Once this becomes clear, I think that terms such as "indifference" or, better yet, "normative disengagement" are more apt terms than "alienation" to capture the phenomenon.

To join this point about the social significance of normative insularity with its metaphysical significance: To discover that certain others are located on the other side of a boundary of normative insularity, so that what is true (or false) on their side has no normative implications for what is true (or false) on my side, would be to apprehend that they occupy a different world. The point gives phenomenological significance to the doctrine of relativism as well: If we were to find ourselves epistemically indifferent to, in the sense of being normatively disengaged from, certain others because they occupy different worlds from ours, this would amount to an *experience* of Multimundialism.

I do not offer these reflections in order to try to make the relativist's position attractive when it is formulated as Multimundialism. The task of formulating the doctrine of relativism is not one of making it attractive. It is, among others, the task of capturing a central and important intuition about the doctrine's content, which attributes to the doctrine a distinctive and *controversial* metaphysical commitment. The social corollary that follows upon my account of alternativeness merely provides another perspective on what it is that makes the doctrine metaphysically controversial when it is formulated as a doctrine that is committed to the existence of alternatives. I think it should be clear by now that the doctrine can be controversial in this way without falling into incoherence.

I have already said something about the practical implications of the doctrine of Multimundialism—what it would mean to *live* in accord with it—and I will close my exposition with some remarks that pull some of these strands together and unify them.

---

15. Michael Friedman has made this argument to me.

Because logical relations always hold a normative significance that we are never free to disregard, I have claimed that the relativist displays a form of epistemic indifference that is more thoroughgoing than the forms of epistemic indifference that are open to the Unimundialist. To drive this point home, I contrasted this indifference with another—the indifference of an antisocial internalist who functions virtually as an epistemic solipsist: she prefers never to learn from others or to teach them, because she has decided in advance of any interaction with others that if they have beliefs on matters she has not yet considered, she does not want to embrace them for herself even if they are true, and furthermore, if they disagree with her, then they are the ones who are wrong and not she, and yet she has no wish to correct what she sees as their mistakes. Although this antisocial internalist would exhibit what appears to be a fairly profound epistemic indifference toward others, it is not as thoroughgoing as the epistemic indifference that follows upon relativism. As I have described this solipsist, she does accept the Unimundial view that logical relations run everywhere among all truth-value-bearers, and she is therefore bound to acknowledge the normative force of these logical relations wherever they hold—in particular, whenever she views the beliefs of others as consistent with her own, she *must* admit that they are candidates for belief by her and that it is willful ignorance on her part not to consider them; and whenever she views the beliefs of others as inconsistent with her own, she *must* pronounce them mistaken or change her mind. Another way to put the point is that, in spite of her antisocial attitudes, she is still bound to think of herself and other inquirers as inquiring into the *same world* in a normatively laden sense that presupposes that truths are *universal* in the social sense that I just explained above. Something cannot be true for others without being true for her, and that is why she must confess to willful ignorance when she refuses to consider whether the beliefs of others that are consistent with her own are also true; likewise, something cannot be true for her without being true for others, and that is why she must pronounce others as mistaken when they disagree with her. By contrast, as Multimundialists, we would have occasion to display a much more thoroughgoing epistemic indifference. To encounter alternatives would be to face a boundary that completely insulates our own proper epistemic concerns from what lies on the other side of that boundary. The truth-value-bearers that lie there would not be candidates for belief by us even when they are true; and what is more, the truth of our own beliefs would not rule the truth of any such truth-value-bearer in or out, because owing to the absence of any logical relations that reach from our beliefs to them, there are no such implications. This means that if we were to encounter alternatives, there would be no prospect of learning from those on the other side of the boundary that we face, or of teaching them. Our attitude would strongly resemble the attitude of the antisocial internalist *except* in two crucial respects. First, unlike her, we could not view ourselves as potentially ignorant when we refrain from embracing the beliefs of those on the other side of the boundary; and second, we could never appropriately view ourselves as being in disagreement with them either. The reason is that the truth of our own beliefs would not have any implications for what they may or may not truly believe, and vice versa.

To recapitulate. To *live* relativism when it is construed as Multimundialism is to view one's own inquiries as taking place within boundaries, and to view what lies outside of them as not a proper object for one's own inquiries, even though it may be a proper object for someone else's inquiries. Correlatively, it is to have the most profound epistemic indifference imaginable toward certain others, which involves believing that we have nothing to learn from them or to teach them—because their true beliefs are true for them but not true for us (and vice versa). Finally, it is to occupy a particular world from the perspective of which there are other worlds whose inhabitants resemble us in the respect of being subjects of belief, and yet our encounters with them are not occasions for normative engagement with them.

In Chapter 1, I claimed that the example about Anjali and me can still be taken to illustrate the particular form of exclusion that the relativist intuitively has in mind even after the appearance of a relativism-inducing disagreement between us has been removed, because it can still be taken to illustrate alternativeness. Let me now revisit that reinterpretation of the example in the light of my elaboration of the Alternatives Intuition—so as to take the example to illustrate Multimundialism.

I had emphasized that, on this reinterpretation, not only do the Indian woman and I refrain from embracing each other's moral beliefs, but also we do not regard our encounter as an occasion for moral learning or teaching in either direction. Perhaps this was implicitly so even when we had interpreted the example to illustrate the Disagreement Intuition. But that interpretation did not afford a convincing account of *why* the Indian woman and I have nothing to learn from or teach one another concerning morals. When we formulate the doctrine of relativism in accord with the Alternatives Intuition, as Multimundialism, we can gain insight into why this is so. It is because our respective moral beliefs are normatively insulated from each other and, as a result, they simply do not speak to each other at all. Thus, neither Anjali nor I regards the truth of her own moral beliefs as providing any sort of critical perspective in the light of which the other should change her mind about any moral matter, either by revising or giving up her prior moral beliefs, or by taking on new ones; conversely, neither of us regards the truth of the other's moral beliefs as providing any sort of critical perspective in the light of which we should change our own minds either. Insofar as Anjali and I do take this view of our situation, we are taking up the stance of the Multimundialist whose inquiries are circumscribed by boundaries, where what lies on the other side of those boundaries is of no epistemic concern to us at all. She and I are to be conceived as inhabiting different moral worlds, from the perspective of which what is morally true and false in one has no implications for what can be morally true and false in the other, and so is a matter of the most profound epistemic indifference.

If anyone is tempted to conceive these different moral worlds that we occupy in terms of our different physical locations—the United States and India, respectively—they need only recall how different our view of our situation is supposed to be from the "When in Rome . . ." view. The latter view posits physical boundaries across which we could in principle move so as to become subject to the other's moral standards, and as a result the view allows that we could in principle come to a moral agreement in the sense of sharing exactly the same moral outlook, which would include beliefs about how we are both conditionally subject to the moral standards of Indian tradition and American individualism, depending upon where we are. But according to the Multimundial view, the boundaries of our respective moral worlds are not physical boundaries across which we might move so as to become subject to the other's moral standards; the boundaries that confine us are normative boundaries across which there is no opportunity to move as we each proceed in our respective moral inquiries. This goes together with the common characterization of relativism as undermining or denying the universality of truth. If I would not become subject to the standards of Indian tradition by traveling to India, and if Anjali would not become subject to the standards of American individualism by traveling to the States, it is because the moral truths that follow upon those moral standards are not truths for everyone. Thus, even after she and I have come to learn *about* one another's moral beliefs, we have not arrived at anything that could be called a shared moral outlook—morally speaking, we neither agree nor disagree, because we inhabit different moral worlds.

A reminder about how we should see the significance of the example about Anjali and me at this point in the dialectic: I am using the example merely to illustrate a particular intuition about the content of the doctrine of relativism, in order to give a somewhat more concrete sense of what I aim to capture when I formulate relativism as Multimundialism. It should not be thought that I am attempting to persuade anyone to accept the doctrine on the force of this, or indeed any other, illustrative example.

Before going on, I want to concede that even when I expressly aim to reinterpret the example so as to illustrate Multimundialism, it may seem that I do not fully succeed in capturing all that I have said so far about Multimundialism—in particular, what I have said about its neutrality on the issue of realism. It is exceedingly difficult to dislodge the general assumption that relativism and realism are mutually opposed doctrines—and more specifically, that if there really were distinct moral worlds in the sense I have been elaborating, it could only be because we *make* those worlds by setting up different moral standards in different social contexts—in which case, the moral "facts" would *not* be mind-independent in the way that realism requires. Nothing I have said in this chapter precludes the possibility of an argument for moral relativism along these antirealist lines. But likewise, nothing I have said in this chapter precludes the possibility of an argument for moral relativism that does *not* proceed along these antirealist lines either. I leave further discussion of this matter for Chapter 4, where I explore what reasons there are for and against moral relativism. But to anticipate just a bit: It would be preposterous to suggest that we might make sense of morality in a way that abstracts altogether from all aspects of the human condition, including human history as well as human nature. So if there is any room for a "realist" conception of moral "facts" as genuinely mind-independent, it had better not be allied with that preposterous suggestion. A sane moral realism should be conceived rather along the following lines: Whatever the moral truths may be— the truths about how we should live, and the right basis of our moral choices—it is not up to us to just *decide* what they are, we must instead *discover* what they are. If we were to allow that this can be so even when moral truths are bound to particular social contexts, then we would have cleared a conceptual space in which moral relativism and moral realism do not automatically rule each other out.

### 3. A Brief Digression about Merely Notional Confrontations

The foregoing account of how the example about Anjali and me might roughly illustrate Multimundialism brings to mind Bernard Williams's idea of a "merely notional confrontation," which he introduced as part of an effort to capture what he saw as "the truth in relativism."[16] His effort stands out as one of the few attempts made in the twentieth century to formulate the doctrine of relativism in a philosophically satisfactory way, and for this reason alone it would be worth pausing to review it. But as it happens, reviewing his proposal will help me to further clarify my own.

According to Williams, the "first condition" of what he called the "problem" of relativism is that there must be systems of belief that

---

16. Williams 1981.

somehow *exclude* one another. His account of this condition of the problem was very much in keeping with what is now the prevailing consensus view, which sees relativism as arising with a certain kind of disagreement. He argued that there is only one way in which systems of belief can possibly exclude one another, which is by logically conflicting with one another.[17] This argument was mainly directed against Kuhn's picture of incommensurability, according to which scientific theories that belong to different theoretical paradigms do not share any meanings, and because they do not share meanings there are no points of logical contact at which they can conflict. Kuhn regarded such theories as somehow excluding one another, and Williams objected that they cannot exclude one another unless there are some points of logical contact, such as common points of reference, or a common evidence base, at which they conflict.

Obviously Williams's first condition cannot by itself suffice to capture what is distinctive about the relativists' position, because *no one*, whether relativist or not, could possibly deny that systems of belief may exclude one another by virtue of logically conflicting with one another. The real innovation on his part was to try to capture the particular kind of exclusivity that he thought relativists have in mind by turning to the practical aspects of their position. It was for this purpose that he introduced his second condition, the idea of a *merely notional confrontation,* which he defined as follows: The holders of one system cannot *go over* to another system without *losing their grip on reality.*

The terms of this definition are not typical terms for a philosopher to use, and they stand in need of further clarification. The first bit of

---

17. There is a minor qualification. He said they need not actually conflict, so long as they have conflicting consequences. But I do not see any interesting distinction here. Systems of belief are distinguished by their *contents,* and if two systems of belief have conflicting consequences, then their contents are such as to rule one another out—and I take this to suffice for *actual* conflict. However, this presupposes a holistic picture of content that absorbs, within the content of a given belief, its various implications. Those who reject this holistic picture should bear Williams's qualification in mind.

clarification that Williams provided was to contrast merely notional confrontations with *real* confrontations, which are marked by the fact that it is a *real option* for the holders of one system to go over to another. Although this contrast does not make everything suddenly clear, it is clear enough to show that his first and second conditions taken together do not serve to isolate the right kind of exclusion—the kind that only relativists, but not their opponents, would want us to acknowledge. As he himself noted, our confrontation with phlogiston theory meets both conditions—that is, phlogiston theory conflicts with our current theories and, moreover, we could not go over to it without losing our grip on reality. Yet the reason phlogiston theory is not a real option for us is that we regard it as seriously mistaken, and it is not a particularly relativist suggestion that we would lose our grip on reality if we went over to a theory that, by our current lights, seriously misrepresents it.

At this juncture, advocates of the prevailing consensus view would be tempted to invoke their idea of a relativism-inducing disagreement in which both parties are right. But Williams had very little to say about *truth* in his effort to capture the "truth in relativism," and he never went so far as to say that both parties in a merely notional confrontation are actually right. Instead, he introduced a third condition on the problem of relativism. In addition to being confronted with a system of beliefs that conflicts with our own, and in addition to finding that it is not a real option for us to go over to that system while retaining our grip on reality, we would have to find as well that any attempt on our part to rationally appraise that system would be either inappropriate or pointless. The intuition here is that, according to relativists, some systems of belief may be profoundly unavailable to us, not because we view them as mistaken, but because we do not stand in any significant rational relation to them at all.

I have been arguing that this is *the* intuition about relativism that we ought to make central and develop, which I have done by introducing the idea of alternativeness, and then elaborating that idea in terms of the idea of normative insularity, and formulating the doctrine of relativism accordingly as Multimundialism. This may seem to be very close indeed to what Williams was suggesting with his third and final condition on the problem of relativism. But there are significant problems of interpretation here, and addressing them will bring to light that his formulation of the doctrine of relativism is really quite different from the one I am proposing.

One glaring problem of interpretation is that Williams's third condition appears to be ruled out by his first. As I explained in the first chapter, the usual point of registering the presence of a logical conflict (and hence a disagreement) is to register the normative constraints that are imposed by the law of noncontradiction. I have since said repeatedly that no matter how we might choose to respond to these normative constraints—whether it be by rejecting the other party's beliefs as false or giving up our own, or by embracing suitably revised versions of both parties' beliefs together, or by suspending our beliefs on the matters under dispute—we shall be engaged in a form of rational appraisal. This means that rational appraisal is never pointless where there is logical conflict, but on the contrary always appropriate; it *must* be appropriate, because it is unavoidable.

Williams could not have failed to see this, so a charitable reading of him requires us to infer that he must have had some other form of rational appraisal in mind. That is, he must have had in mind a form of rational appraisal that might be pointless or inappropriate even as we engage in the minimal form of rational appraisal that goes together with apprehending logical conflict. In most cases of logical conflict, many other forms of rational appraisal are available—for instance, we can appraise whether one or the other side of a conflict is susceptible of a formal proof, or is better supported by empirical evidence, or has some theoretical advantage such as that it affords greater unity of explanation. From an epistemological point of view it is highly advantageous that these other forms of rational appraisal generally are available, because it is only through them that the parties involved can discover which of them is mistaken and which (if either) is right, thereby resolving the conflict between them—which would of course involve one of them "going over" to the other's view. But as I made clear in my discussion of irresoluble disagreements in Chapter 1, there is no guarantee that the parties to a conflict will always be able to find such a rational basis for resolving it. So perhaps this is what Williams had in mind when he raised the possibility that in some cases of conflict rational appraisal is either pointless or inappropriate—namely, that in such cases there is no prospect of finding a rational basis on which to resolve the conflict. Note that this interpretation would provide an explanation of how our confrontation with phlogiston theory can qualify as a merely notional confrontation in the sense that he defined, without providing any support for relativism. As I observed earlier, the reason we cannot go over to phlogiston theory without losing our grip on reality is that the theory is *mistaken* by our best current lights; and insofar as this assessment of phlogiston theory is backed by *further* rational appraisal—such as that it does not meet the standards of scientific evidence and explanation that it would have to meet in order for us to deem it true (or even probable)—the situation would not be of the sort that Williams was claiming the relativist has in mind. It will come as no surprise that I think he was on to something important here: when these further forms of rational appraisal are appropriate, we are adopting a stance that is definitely quite unlike the stance of the relativist as I have characterized it. The question is, did Williams manage to fully capture what is distinctive about the relativist's stance by raising the possibility of notional confrontations in which these further forms of rational appraisal would not be appropriate?

The answer to this question depends in part on our attitude toward a particular way of "going over" to another system of beliefs, namely, *conversion*. The occasion and need for conversion arises precisely when we are faced with a conflict and there is no rational basis on which we could resolve it. Williams certainly would not have denied that conversion is sometimes a real option, and hence is not always an occasion for a merely notional confrontation. In our own place and time, it is a real option to convert to Christianity or Islam, insofar as we would not say that someone had lost their grip on reality by coming to have faith in these religions. (Some narrow-minded atheists say so, but they would be wrong. Religious conversion is a recognizable human phenomenon that has often been highly valued, and in fact it is part of the very content of the Christian and Muslim religious doctrines that the path to believing them may have to go via conversion.) Since conversion may be a real option, Williams owed us an account of the difference between the sorts of cases in which it is a real option and the sorts of cases in which it is not, so as to isolate the cases where we would have an instance of relativism as he was asking us to conceive it, in terms of merely notional confrontations.

Some philosophers would seek to explain the difference between these cases by appealing to the issue of realism. Suppose we face a conflict that we believe we will never have a rational basis for resolving, and this leads us to believe that we could never change our minds about what is at issue in the conflict without undergoing a conversion. And suppose we also believe, as many realists are supposed to, that there are mind-independent facts in the light of which only one side in the conflict can be right. Then we might attach great importance to the idea that it is a real option to go over to the other side, because otherwise we would be stuck with a dogmatic commitment to whatever view we happened to have arrived at first. (This is one way of summarizing William James's preoccupation in "The Will to Believe," and also of Feyerabend's preoccupation when he proposed "methodological pluralism" as an antidote to dogmatism.)[18] But there is little sign that Williams would have exploited realism in this way in order to support unforced decisions to believe. What is more, given his understanding of the issue of realism, it is not obvious how he could have exploited realism in order to explain why conversion is sometimes a real option, since he endorsed the scientific realist picture on which we need reasons of a particular kind to take realism seriously. These would be reasons for believing that we are in epistemic touch with mind-independent facts in something like the way that scientific realists hold. According to them, scientific methods afford such epistemic touch by providing a rational basis for changing and improving our scientific theories in order to arrive at progressively better, in the sense of more accurate, depictions of such mind-independent facts. Clearly, any domain in which we have such a rational basis for improving our theories so as to track the mind-independent facts will be a domain in which there is no opportunity or need for conversion. That is why I say

18. See James (1897) 1979; Feyerabend 1965.

that it is unclear how Williams could have exploited his understanding of realism in order to explain why conversion is sometimes a real option.

Richard Rorty would have proposed to explain the difference between cases in which conversion is and is not a real option by pointing out that there are social contexts in which conversion is *regarded* as a real option, and that there are other social contexts in which it is *not* so regarded.[19] But Williams clearly did not embrace Rorty's brand of relativism. Rorty's was an across-the-board relativism that derived from a generally antimetaphysical stance in philosophy, and what he substituted for metaphysics—his account of community and conversation—was supposed to apply in all domains, including science.[20] By contrast, Williams's philosophical orientation was not thoroughgoingly antimetaphysical, insofar as he viewed scientific realism as providing our main positive model for objectivity. This need not have prevented him from adopting Rorty's position in domains outside science, where Williams thought we do not have the sorts of grounds for realism that we have in the case of scientific realism. If that was his position, then perhaps he could have explained why conversion sometimes is and sometimes is not a real option in Rorty's way, by making it a matter of our attitudes, as they are dictated by our social conditions.

I am not sure whether it would be right to attribute this Rorty-like view to Williams in domains like ethics, politics, and aesthetics. But

---

19. This theme runs through many of Rorty's writings on relativism, some of which are collected in Rorty 1982, 1989.

20. This is a point about Rorty that I underscored in the Introduction. I noted there that his opposition to metaphysics was really an opposition to what he viewed as *the wrong kind* of metaphysics, which centers on, and finds a problem in, the mind–world relation. Now that I have formulated relativism as Multimundialism, it may have become apparent that Rorty's way of being antimetaphysical does not really lay to rest the metaphysical issue that I claim divides relativists from their opponents—which concerns whether there are many worlds or just one, by virtue of the presence or absence of normative insularity. In fact, it seems to me that the source of Rorty's "antimetaphysical" relativism—his picture of inquiry as always situated in conversational practices—implicitly commits him to Multimundialism.

even if he did hold such a view, that would not have enabled him to provide a satisfactory formulation of the doctrine of relativism. That project simply cannot leave the issue of *truth* to the side in the way that Williams tried to do. (To Rorty's credit, he did not leave that issue to the side, but recognized that he needed to say something about it.) After all, consider how his first condition for relativism—that there must be *logical conflict*—inevitably raises the question whether both parties in a conflict can be right. I have already observed that he never came out and *said* that he thought that this is possible, and precisely because he did not, it does not make sense to interpret him as advocating the Disagreement Intuition according to which relativism arises with a certain kind of disagreement in which both parties are (or can be) right.

If Williams thought that the parties to a conflict can*not* both be right, then it is completely unclear how he was proposing to capture a distinctively *relativist* stance. Such conflicts are just ordinary disagreements in the sense I discussed in Chapter 1. This is so even if they give rise to merely notional confrontations, as we saw with phlogiston theory; and it is so even if they cannot be rationally resolved, as we saw in connection with religious conversion. If such conflicts cannot be rationally resolved, all that follows is that they are irresoluble owing to epistemic limitations on someone's part; and if this what Williams had in mind, then all he accomplished was to formulate a doctrine of epistemic relativism, and not the metaphysical doctrine that I aim to formulate and evaluate in this book.

On the other hand, if Williams thought that the parties to a conflict *can* both be right (even though he never said so), then he was implicitly committed to the Disagreement Intuition that governs the prevailing consensus view of relativism. I have said what I have to say about why it is better to turn our backs on that intuitive conception of relativism, and to take the Alternatives Intuition as our starting point instead.

## 4. Some Methodological Issues

I will conclude with some methodological issues that emerge from the argument so far, issues that it will be important to keep in mind when we turn in Part Two to the task of evaluating what reasons there are to accept or reject the doctrine of relativism when it is formulated as Multimundialism.

I raised one such issue when I first introduced the Relative Truth Intuition. I noted that objections are often raised against the formulation of relativism as a doctrine with universal application, according to which *all* truth is relative, and that in the contemporary literature these objections are generally set aside as soon as they are raised, on the ground that relativism is best conceived *not* as a universal doctrine but as a domain-specific doctrine—a doctrine that holds in some domains and not others. As I approach the task of evaluating Multimundialism, that is precisely how I propose to conceive it, at least initially. I shall not raise the question just once and for all: Is it or is it not the case that logical relations run everywhere among all truth-value-bearers? Rather, I will raise and consider the question in two broad but separate domains, with respect to which philosophers have traditionally been most intensely interested in the issue of relativism—in the domain of natural facts that are appropriate objects of scientific investigation and in the domain of morals.

It may seem that the very act of distinguishing different domains in which this question can be raised would already settle the question against Unimundialism—that if there are many domains, then there must be many worlds as well. But that is not so. Different domains are distinguished by their different subject matters, and we may raise the question whether or not logical relations run everywhere within certain domains while leaving open the question whether or not such relations also hold between those domains. Of course, we may find that we cannot leave the latter question open very long, because the process of settling whether logical relations do or do not hold among all truth-value-bearers within a given domain may uncover reasons why logical relations do or do not hold among the truth-value-bearers belonging to that domain and truth-value-bearers belonging to other domains as well. So one possible outcome of a domain-specific approach might be to learn that relativism qua Multimundialism is indeed a universal doctrine, because *all* truth-value-bearers stand in logical relations no matter what their subject matter; in other words, we might learn that there is no normative insularity anywhere, not within any specific domains and not between them. But a second possible outcome might be that some domains are normatively insulated from each other without containing any normative insularity within them; and a third possible outcome might be that there is normative insularity within some domains that are also normatively insulated from one another. It seems to me that the second of these is not altogether out of keeping with a familiar philosophical attitude. Although the idea of normative insularity may itself be new and unfamiliar, it is certainly a familiar enough suggestion that there is a sharp fact–value distinction, and one good way to conceive that distinction is by conceiving the domains of fact and value as normatively insulated from one another. Furthermore, many philosophers who are open-minded about relativism are predisposed to think that it would not hold in the domain of scientific facts but might hold in the domain of values, and my proposal to formulate the doctrine of relativism as Multimundialism simply puts a particular gloss on what it is that they are predisposed to think—namely, that there is only one logically unified world for science to inquire into but many worlds of value.

Another, more delicate, methodological issue concerns who bears the burden of proof in debates about relativism, and why. All along I have urged that we formulate relativism so that it emerges as a controversial metaphysical doctrine, and it may seem fairly obvious that if a metaphysical doctrine is controversial, then only its advocates should have to bear the burden of proof and not its opponents. However, once we have formulated relativism as Multimundialism, and reflect on the nature of the dispute between relativists and their Unimundialist opponents, this is far from obvious.

It *is* obvious is that we should place *some* burden of proof on Multimundialists. But what is *not* obvious is whether it would be reasonable to place the *entire* burden of proof *exclusively* on them. That would have the effect of awarding default status to the Unimundialists' position, and once that is done, then the only way Multimundialists could successfully carry the burden that has been placed on them would be by finding reasons in favor of their position that would rationally *compel* a precommitted Unimundialist to change her mind and give up her view in favor of Multimundialism. But it is foreseeable from the start that this is not possible. At least, this is not possible if I have been correct in granting that Unimundialism is logically coherent—that there is nothing logically incoherent in the claim that logical relations run everywhere among all truth-value-bearers. If that is so, then Multimundialists will certainly never be able to produce internal reasons of a *logical* nature as to why Unimundialists ought to give up their view.[21]

This aspect of the dispute sheds light on my claim, in Chapter 1, that examples cannot carry the burden of proof in philosophical debates about relativism. I said there that whenever we offer an example to illustrate the doctrine of relativism, the example will always admit of multiple interpretations, including a *nonrelativist* interpretation. So even if some of us find it plausible to interpret my example about Anjali and me as illustrating the Multimundial view, on which our claims are alternatives—allowing that both our claims are true and yet insisting that they cannot be conjoined because they are normatively insulated from each other—this does not mean that the example cannot also be interpreted in line with the Unimundial view that would invoke the Dilemma for Alternativeness to rule out such normative insularity—insisting that either our claims are inconsistent and so

---

21. Let me reiterate that even if I am wrong about this—because, say, the corollary that there is a single, consistent, and complete body of truths faces special logical difficulties owing to its size and universal character—I have urged that we ought not to reject Unimundialism on that account, any more than Russell should have rejected the idea of a set owing to difficulties with the idea of a universal set, or than Kripke should have rejected the idea of universal truth owing to the semantic paradoxes that are generated by a universal truth predicate (or, I would add, than certain relativists should reject the universal claim that all truth is relative owing to the difficulty of stating their doctrine). We are accustomed to find that when we reach the further reaches of the application of certain concepts, especially recursive concepts that invite us to apply them universally, we run into formal difficulties, and the reasonable response has never been to reject those concepts outright, or their open-ended character, but rather to respond constructively by viewing the formal difficulties that attend them as problems to be solved.

cannot both be true, or they are consistent and conjoinable. One important reason such a nonrelativist interpretation is always available is that it would not incur any logical incoherence.

It seems to me, then, that *neither* the power of example *nor* purely logical considerations can ever rationally compel a precommitted Unimundialist to give up her view, and that is why it is foreseeable that a Multimundialist could not successfully carry the burden of proof if the *entire* burden were to be placed exclusively on her. But consider what would happen if the tables were turned, and Multimundialism were accorded default status, thereby shifting the entire burden of proof to the Unimundialist. It is just as foreseeable that the Unimundialist could never offer reasons that would rationally compel the Multimundialist to give up her view in favor of Unimundialism—for neither the power of example nor purely logical considerations speak decisively against Multimundialism.

This reflection serves to bring out that when we formulate the dividing issue between relativists and their opponents in the way that I am proposing, in terms of whether logical relations run everywhere among all truth-value-bearers, there is a real danger that the debate between them might degenerate into a standoff. The issue in dispute is a radically disjunctive issue with respect to which there is no neutral place to stand, and once we have taken a stand, we can always successfully beg the question in our own favor, by insisting that anyone who attempts to push us off of our stand will necessarily have begged the question in their own favor from the other side. The resulting standoff can lead to a tiresome, though not unfamiliar, form of philosophical debate, in which each side tries to claim default status, thereby shifting the entire burden of proof to the other side. What is so frustrating—and even irritating—about this dialectical strategy is that it is foreseeable in advance *from both sides* that neither can convince the other. Not only does this mean that the strategy will never offer a satisfying resolution of the issue, but it also means that both parties are bound to seem disingenuous. Each tries to create an appearance that the other side cannot be justified, even though she can do no better in showing that her own side is better justified. Philosophy is done no favors when we proceed in this way.

The dialectical situation would be vastly different—and much improved—if we were prepared to *distribute* the burden of proof to both Multimundialists and Unimundialists. The delicate methodological question is, on what basis should we do this?

It is surely relevant that the dialectical situation we face here is similar to the one that I described in Chapter 1 when I was trying to identify conditions in which an ordinary disagreement might be irresoluble. I said that if each of two supremely self-confident internalists have opposed views in the light of which the other is mistaken, then even though they will agree that one of them must be mistaken, there are no prospects for their coming to agree about which one of them that is, thereby resolving their disagreement to their mutual satisfaction. I noted then that if we shared Mill's attitude toward the epistemic significance of disagreement, then our inability to persuade others should undermine our confidence in our own views. In the case at hand, if Multimundialists and Unimundialists should find themselves in a disagreement that they cannot resolve for the reasons I just gave above, then the Millian attitude would dictate that they should both suspend belief on the matter in dispute between them, concerning whether logical relations run everywhere among all truth-value-bearers. Once they have done so, then perhaps they might seek *other* grounds on which to prefer one view over the other—grounds that do *more* than merely claim default status for their own view so as to beg the question on their own behalf and shift an unbearable burden of proof to the other side. Thus, the effect of adopting Mill's attitude toward disagreement in this situation would be to *distribute* the burden of proof to both parties, in the way that I have suggested would improve the dialectical situation.

However, although I do want to recommend that we distribute the burden of proof in the philosophical debate about relativism, I do not think we should do so on general Millian grounds. This is because it would be quite wrong to suggest that it is never appropriate to adopt the attitude of self-confident internalism, which would have us cleave to our own views even in the face of what appear to be irresoluble disagreements with others. This latter attitude is the one that the pragmatists recommended when they argued that we ought not to be

moved by skeptical worries but only by what Peirce called "living"
doubt—by which he meant *internal* grounds for doubt that may arise
even as we take it for granted that our settled and well-working opin-
ions are all true. It seems to me that this attitude is generally sensible
in the normal course of things. That is, in the normal course of things,
we ought to take it for granted that our settled and well-working opin-
ions are true, and to use them as our measure of what *else* is or can be
true, our not entirely settled conjectures and hypotheses, for instance;
and when we do this, we will not be moved by skeptical possibilities
such as that ordinary experiences might be mere dreams, or that we
might be brains in vats, or even that others whom we regard as less
well informed than we might actually be right about the matters over
which we disagree. If this attitude might sometimes get us into situations where we cannot resolve our disagreements with certain others
by persuading them to agree with us, it is not any the less rational on
that account—rationality does not rule out the possibility that others
may remain mistaken and even incorrigibly so. Thus, it seems to me that
if there are good reasons to distribute the burden of proof in the debate
between Multimundialists and Unimundialists, it is not because we
ought never to shift the burden of proof to others when we are confi-
dent that we are right. So, if there are good reasons here, it can only be
because *neither side qualifies as having a settled and well-working opinion
about which anyone should have such confidence.* And that is what I contend
is the case.

Matters might be different if common sense were clearly and exclusively committed to either the Multimundial or the Unimundial view.
No doubt, many philosophers are inclined to think that common
sense is implicitly antirelativist, and these philosophers will propose
that if I am right to formulate relativism as Multimundialism, then
common sense must implicitly be Unimundialist. But if that really
were so, then we should find that ordinary folk (nonphilosophers, I
mean) *never* regard it as appropriate to respond to the different viewpoints that they attribute to others with the sort of epistemic indifference and normative disengagement that I have described in these
pages—whereby they feel that they cannot dismiss those viewpoints as
false exactly and yet feel that they cannot take them on board for

themselves. To put it another way, it would have to be the case that human beings have always responded to such different viewpoints in accord with the Dilemma for Alternativeness, by supposing that either they have encountered a disagreement in which one or other party is mistaken, or that they have encountered an opportunity for learning new truths that can be embraced together with their current views. Although there is much evidence of this antirelativist attitude in human responses to "difference"—including missionary zeal, imperialist intervention, and "experiments in living"—it would be going too far to say that the historical record gives no evidence of other attitudes as well, which are more in line with the relativist's Multimundial stance as I have described it.

Just as it is unimpressive when philosophers claim victory by claiming default status for their views and begging the question on their own behalf, it is equally unimpressive when they do so on the ground that they can find *some* support for their view in common sense while *disregarding* the fact that their opponents can *also* find some support for their view in common sense.

It might be useful and illuminating to conduct a comparison here. I have argued elsewhere that this attitude has impeded philosophical progress toward resolving the dispute over personal identity, in which so-called animalists rightly point out that common sense does provide some support for their equation of personal identity with human identity, but blatantly disregard the obvious support that common sense also provides for Locke's idea that the life of a person could in principle come apart from the biological life span of a given human being. It hardly needs mentioning that many religions would have us believe, with him, that our lives will continue after the death of our biological bodies. In addition, science and science fiction have offered us other ways to conceive the possibility that our individual lives might come apart from the life of a given human animal, which are compatible with atheism—such as if our brains were transplanted into new and different bodies, or if another brain were "reprogrammed" so as to realize our own total psychology, or if our brains and bodies were duplicated molecule-for-molecule, and so forth. But finally, even if we should find that we cannot take these possibilities entirely seriously, the important point for my purposes is that it is not common sense that prevents us from doing so. On the contrary, the ease with which we understand Locke's original thought experiment about personal identity, in which the consciousnesses of a prince and a cobbler are switched, each into the other's body, shows that we *do* conceive persons primarily as subjects of thought, and that we do not necessarily equate the concept of a subject of thought with the concept of a suitably endowed animal—because we find it very natural to say that after the switch the prince and the cobbler each wake up to find himself in the other's original body. So although common sense certainly does provide significant support for the animalists' vision of our selves, it is not *all* on their side. Because it provides for Locke's side as well, we can only conclude that our commonsense beliefs about personal identity are conflicted, and so, if philosophers wish to arrive at a coherent view, they have no choice but to make and defend a *revisionist* recommendation that will provide good reasons for retaining and developing some aspects of our commonsense outlook while giving up others.

There is *some* scope for thinking that our commonsense outlook is similarly conflicted with respect to the logical issue that divides Multimundialists and Unimundialists. On the one hand, we find it natural to think of truth as universal, and that suggests that our commonsense view precludes the relativist's Multimundial stance; yet on the other hand, common sense also seems to leave scope for that very stance on the part of explorers, anthropologists, and others who have sometimes responded to the different views they encountered by refusing either to reject them as false or to embrace them for themselves.

Admittedly, the conflict here is not as clear and stark as it is in the case of our commonsense outlook with respect to personal identity, which is fairly explicit in both accepting and rejecting Locke's distinction between personal and human (animal) identity. But if it cannot plausibly be said that common sense *explicitly* rejects the possibility that Multimundialists affirm and Unimundialists deny—of normative insularity—it seems to me that the reason is that it does not really incorporate the concept of normative insularity within its repertoire. I think the same is true of the philosophers of the twentieth century who came closest to doing so, by construing relativism in line with the Alternatives Intuition rather than the Disagreement or Relative Truth Intuitions—*they* did not explicitly raise the possibility of normative insularity either. The concept of normative insularity is a concept that *I* have articulated and exploited in an effort to provide a satisfactory formulation of their position. Precisely because the doctrine of relativism has not previously been formulated as Multimundialism, it is hard to make a convincing case that there is any firm or definite *opposition* to it in our commonsense view. To insist that there is would not only require us to overlook what evidence there is from history and the social sciences that human beings have *in fact* responded to different viewpoints with the sort of normative disengagement that bespeaks normative insularity (albeit while lacking the philosophical vocabulary with which to articulate it); it would also require us to suppose that common sense is at least implicitly committed to the idea that logical relations must run *everywhere* among *all* truth-value-bearers. This is a philosophical issue that goes well beyond the concerns of common sense—which is to say, it is an issue that we can reasonably expect that common sense would *not* have settled for us.

Even if we were prepared to allow that common sense is at least predisposed in favor of Unimundialism, it would be unreasonable to award it default status on that ground alone, thereby sparing it from all burden of proof. Its claims reach so much farther than common sense, and are so ambitious, that they do not deserve to stand in advance of receiving any critical examination or positive support. After all, if I am right, its fundamental logical commitment brings in train a very substantial metaphysical commitment, to the possibility of a View from Everywhere—and this is not a commitment that we should automatically take on board as if it were more straightforwardly tenable and correct than the Multimundialist's commitment to the possibility of normative insularity.

My methodological recommendation, therefore, is to adopt a position of *suspense* between the two views, Unimundialism and Multimundialism, thereby *distributing* the burden of proof to both, and to commence an investigation into the reasons there are to affirm one or the other, bearing the following in mind:

First, we should allow that each side in this debate can, if they are determined to do so, beg the question on the logical issue that divides them in her own favor.

Second, we should therefore require that each side should do more than *merely* beg the question on the logical issue that divides them—where to require this is to prevent either side from trying to proceed simply by shifting the entire burden of proof to the other side.

Third, when we allow that it is possible for both sides to successfully beg the question in their favor, we are adopting an optimistic attitude on which any formal problems that would arise for either side will have adequate formal solutions, and we are also allowing that there is more than one adequate system of logic, one of which does not provide for normative insularity and one of which does provide for it.

Fourth, if the above attitudes toward logic are well placed, then we cannot expect to find purely logical grounds on which to settle the logical issue that divides Unimundialists and Multimundialists, but rather, the decision about what sort of logic to adopt—whether to adopt one that does or does not posit normative insularity—will have to be driven by *nonlogical* considerations. Thus, as we look for grounds on which to take a stand in this debate, which would enable us to do better than *merely* beg the question, we should look beyond narrowly logical issues, to broader issues in metaphysics, philosophy of science, philosophy of language and mind, value theory, and such. We need to investigate whether the stands that we have reason to take in these other areas of philosophical concern might provide us with reasons to adopt one logical vision or the other, along with its metaphysical and normative implications.

Fifth, whenever we do find nonlogical grounds on which to take a stand on the underlying logical issue, we must still concede that that underlying logical issue is a radically disjunctive issue with respect to which there is no neutral place to stand. This means that any negative consideration that weighs against one side is bound to weigh in favor of the other even if it does not seem to offer any direct argument in favor of it; likewise, any positive consideration that seems to weigh in favor of one side is bound to weigh against the other even if it does not seem to offer any direct argument against it.

Finally, if we find that we are moved by any reason, of any kind, to take a stand on the logical issue that divides Unimundialists and Multimundialists, we must admit that our reason shall not have met the sort of standard of proof that philosophers like to impose, that would guarantee that our opponents have been *refuted*. Anyone who wishes to retain that high standard is free to do so. But if they are honest, then they must declare this debate over before it begins, as the sort of stand-off that it will foreseeably be. Similarly, if anyone is predisposed to one side or the other, they should not pretend to have gained a victory just by virtue of the fact that they can stand unrefuted by the other side. That is too easy a way to get one's way in philosophical debate. It is also a way that cuts us off from an interesting and potentially fertile investigation, through which we might learn much about how and why other, more substantive philosophical considerations might invite us to adopt one logical vision or the other, of the Unimundialist or the Multimundialist.

# PART TWO

# Evaluating the Doctrine of Relativism

# 3

## Relativism concerning Natural Facts

W hat reasons are there to reject or accept Multimundialism—or equivalently, to accept or reject Unimundialism—in the domain of natural facts that are appropriate objects of scientific investigation?

There is some controversy among philosophers about how inclusive the domain of natural facts might prove to be. Some are inclined to the view that it comprehends everything that is real, on the ground that nothing should be counted as real unless it is an appropriate object of scientific investigation. These scientistically minded philosophers all agree that if matters of *value* concern anything real, then they must reduce to matters of natural fact, but they do not all agree about whether such a naturalistic reduction of value is possible—which is to say, they do not all agree about whether there are any real or objective matters of value. Other philosophers claim that moral values are irreducible to matters of natural fact and yet are perfectly real and objective nonetheless. I think the latter philosophers are right, but my arguments in this chapter are neutral with respect to this issue. I will be exploring what reasons there are to accept or reject Multimundialism in the domain of natural facts without prejudging whether that domain comprehends everything that is real.

As I proceed, I will bear in mind the methodological issues that I raised at the close of Chapter 2, most especially that: it is possible to beg the question either way on the logical issue that divides Multimundialists and Unimundialists, concerning whether or not logical relations run everywhere among all truth-value-bearers; the reasons we seek are therefore substantive reasons that do not merely or directly beg that logical question, but bring to bear considerations drawn from other areas of philosophical study such as metaphysics, philosophy of mind and language, and philosophy of science; and these reasons will predictably fall short of strict proof in the sense that would provide a non-question-begging refutation of the opposed view.

I will begin my discussion in Section 1 by considering a view that would, if it were true, entail Multimundialism—namely, the radically empiricist view of meaning and confirmation that Quine attributed to Carnap when he argued against it in "Two Dogmas of Empiricism."

In Section 2 I will go on to offer a Davidsonian argument against Multimundialism, which elaborates the argument he gave in "On the Very Idea of a Conceptual Scheme." His argument relied on a principle of charity that he took over from Quine, and the question arises, What justifies that principle? One very powerful answer is *holism*. We will see that the interest of holism goes well beyond the support that it supplies for charity, because it speaks much more directly than charity does to the underlying logical issue that divides Multimundialists and Unimundialists. On a holistic picture, concepts and beliefs are holistically interconnected, and in the main these holistic interconnections rest on *logical relations*, broadly construed. So, insofar as holism is uncontained—insofar as it is all-encompassing—it leaves no room for normative insularity, and no occasion for adopting the normative stance of the Multimundialist. From here on, I shall refer to this as the Argument from Holism Against Normative Insularity.

When Kuhn argued for incommensurability in science, he seemed to be suggesting that holism is not uncontained, because each scientific theory is an interrelated whole unto itself that is normatively insulated from other competing theories. Although this result would fall short of establishing Multimundialism (that would require arguing that some incommensurable theories are equally true—something for which Kuhn did not argue), it would suffice to undermine the Argument from Holism Against Normative Insularity. In Section 3 I will argue that the holistic constraints that Davidson emphasized in his work *do* constrain us to adopt the normative stance of the Unimundialist for the purposes of scientific inquiry. What does this show about Kuhn's notion of incommensurability? As far as I can see, it does not necessarily dislodge the core epistemological challenges that Kuhn posed for scientific methodology. But it does show that the sort of incommensurability for which he argued is better understood as leaving us with disagreements that are intractable, potentially even to the point of being irresoluble, rather than as issuing in normative insularity, or the thoroughgoing epistemic indifference of the Multimundial stance that would follow upon an encounter with normative insularity. This is something that Feyerabend seems to have understood in his early work on empiricism, for although he agreed with Kuhn that different scientific theories generally fail to share meanings, he explicitly described incommensurability as involving *conflict*. Thus, in spite of the highly radical tendency of his thought overall, there are clear indications in his early response to Kuhn that he took it for granted that there is no option but to adopt the Unimundial stance in science, and that this would remain so even if we were to embrace his recommended *pluralist* methodology. I will conclude Section 3 by considering why, for reasons that are quite independent of the Argument from Holism Against Normative Insularity, the Unimundial stance seems so fundamental to the scientific outlook—and why this seems so even in the face of various reasons that might be put forward in favor of a pluralist conception of scientific methods.

This leaves us with a remaining question that I will discuss in Section 4. Does the Argument from Holism Against Normative Insularity close off all plausible avenues of argument for Multimundialism in the domain of natural facts as they are studied by natural science? Does it leave any room for alternatives at all—even as a possibility that lies beyond the scope of human knowledge? Of course, we cannot so much as make sense of such a possibility without invoking the realist view that *we* are not the measure of *things,* and so in this concluding section I will explore the extent to which a commitment to realism—a doctrine that is usually assumed to be opposed to relativism—might actually give us reasons to take the possibility of alternatives-unknowable-by-us seriously. If there are such reasons to take that possibility seriously, they will have to establish more than a mere logical possibility; and they will also have to establish more than the sort of mere conceptual possibility that is raised in the flights of fancy and science fiction that give rise to skepticism. If there are reasons to take the possibility of alternatives-unknowable-by-us *seriously,* they should establish a metaphysical possibility in a much stronger sense, of being entailed by our actual scientific beliefs.

It is not immediately obvious how realism could give us such reasons to take this metaphysical possibility seriously, since its defining commitment is to the mind-independence of reality and, as I emphasized in Chapter 2, that commitment does not speak directly to the logical issue of concern to Multimundialists regarding whether logical relations run everywhere. Yet in spite of this apparent mutual irrelevance of the two doctrines, there is much to be gained by revisiting the question of their relations in the wake of my other arguments in this chapter. Doing so will allow me to clarify why nothing in Davidson's armory of arguments suffices to rule out the possibility of alternatives-unknowable-by-us—not his original charity-based argument against the very idea of a conceptual scheme, not my elaboration of it in terms of holism, not his subsequent arguments against skepticism, and not his positive account of the directness of mind–world relation, which he claimed follows once we give up the "scheme–content" distinction. Davidson apart, some scientific realists have tried to provide a more direct response from within philosophy of science to the challenges that Kuhn and Feyerabend leveled against scientific methods, and I shall also make clear in Section 4 that even if their responses were fully effective, that would not entirely settle the issue of Multimundialism versus Unimundialism, but would leave some aspects of it for *science* to settle. I will close the section and the chapter by considering a quite distinct position present in one current scientific theory that potentially does have implications for the issue of Multimundialism versus Unimundialism, namely, Chomsky's account of human cognitive abilities. It provides us with substantive reasons for dismissing the possibility of the sort of View from Everywhere that Unimundialism requires us to conceive, and for regarding the possibility of alternatives-unknowable-by-us as a serious metaphysical possibility. My conclusion, then, is that even though we are constrained to function as Unimundialists in our scientific investigations, we cannot rule out the possibility that there may nevertheless be many worlds-to-be-investigated-by-someone.

Before proceeding, I should mention as an aside that there is one very natural conception of what a scientific theory is, on which it seems there is no philosophically interesting obstacle to embracing all of the scientific truths together. On this highly *discursivist* conception, a scientific theory is just a string of *sentences* (these might be sentences of a natural human language or of an artificial language expressly devised by human beings for scientific purposes), and what it means to embrace theories together is just to *syntactically conjoin* all of the sentences that constitute them. If we assume that any sentences that are not overtly inconsistent can be conjoined, then the only obstacle to embracing all of the true scientific theories together would be having insufficient space and time to articulate and conjoin all of the sentences that constitute them. However, I hope it is clear that if we were to make this last assumption, we would really be invoking the terms of the Dilemma for Alternativeness against Multimundialism in a way that begs the question. So let me clarify again, that when I say that I am seeking substantive reasons to settle the issue of Unimundialism versus Multimundialism in the domain of natural facts, I am saying that we should go further, or deeper, than just uncritically adopting this discursivist conception of what a scientific theory is. As the arguments of the chapter proceed, we will have occasion to revisit the conception, and to situate it in relation to other, more substantive reasons for supposing that nature is *one*.

## 1. The Carnapian Argument for Multimundialism

The Carnapian argument for Multimundialism follows the standard pattern of argument for relativism in the twentieth century that was inspired by Kant's transcendental idealism. As I briefly described in the Introduction, the first step of such arguments aims to establish some respect in which the world is mind-dependent, the second aims to establish that there is more than one kind of mind on which a world might depend, and their conclusion is that there is more than one world. Since Carnap self-consciously drew upon and also departed from Kant, it will be helpful to review some details from Kant's own work, in order to see how it provided for this pattern of argument so as to deliver a Multimundial conclusion.[1] This will also be helpful in Section 4 when I discuss the transcendental character of Davidson's arguments against skepticism.

Kant claimed that knowledge of objects is possible only if they can be given to us in experience, and only if we can make truth-value-bearing judgments about them; and he claimed that this is not possible unless they meet certain *subjective* conditions, from which it follows that they are mind-dependent. Specifically, if an object can be given to us in experience, then it must conform to our particular forms of sensibility, which he identified as space and time; and if an object is one about which we can frame truth-value-bearing judgments, then it must conform to the particular forms of our understanding, which he derived from a table of "logical categories." After he posited these subjective conditions on human knowledge, he went on to argue that because the exercise of our understanding unavoidably involves the application of our own logical categories, we cannot exercise it in order to conceive other forms of understanding besides our own. Yet he did allow that we can exercise our understanding in order to conceive other forms of sensibility besides our own, and this is what generates the Multimundial implications of his transcendental idealism. If there were subjects with forms of sensibility different from ours, they would know worlds different from the one that we know—not the spatio-temporal world of our experience, but worlds that conform to their particular forms of sensibility.

Perhaps it is not immediately obvious that this "many-worlds" implication of Kant's transcendental idealism amounts to the Multimundial doctrine that I have formulated. Whether it does depends

---

1. These details are all drawn from Kant (1781) 1998.

upon whether the truths that would be known by subjects with different forms of sensibility would qualify as alternatives in the specific sense that I have defined, on which they would be normatively insulated from one another and hence not embraceable together from any point of view. If this is not immediately obvious, it is because Kant claimed that we must conceive subjects who inhabit different sensory worlds as employing the very same logical categories. But he also claimed that these categories are meaningful only insofar as they have empirical application, and he took it to be a serious problem how this is possible. His solution was to posit an a priori "synthesis" of the logical categories of the understanding with a priori representations of the forms of sensibility. In our case, these latter representations take the form of a priori "intuitions" of space and time—thus the word "idealism" in Kant's "transcendental idealism" refers to his peculiar suggestion that space and time are literally *in* us. The point about his account of "synthetic a priori" knowledge that matters for my purposes is this: Any given subject of experience can apply logical categories only *in combination* with the forms of her sensibility, and there simply is not any meaningful use of those categories that would bridge across the world that she knows through her sensibility and the different worlds that would be known by subjects with forms of sensibility different from hers. That is why Kant's transcendental idealism really does provide for normative insularity, and so really does entail Multimundialism.[2]

---

2. The only way in which we might try to resist the Multimundial implications of Kant's transcendental idealism would be by arguing that his overall framework can somehow provide for the Unimundialists' View from Everywhere, even though no subject of experience could ever achieve it, owing to the essentially limiting character of sensibility. Kant did raise the possibility of a kind of nonempirical knowledge that would not be mediated by sensibility, but would consist rather in direct *intellectual intuition*. But I do not see how his conception of direct intellectual intuition helps us to conceive a View from Everywhere, since it makes no more sense to suppose that a subject of intellectual intuition could come to apprehend and embrace the very same truths that we know through our forms of sensibility than it does to suppose that we can apprehend and embrace the very same

The Kantian argument for Multimundialism is of only limited interest, because it does not provide for the possibility of our ever encountering alternatives—that is, it does not provide for the possibility of *living* relativism by adopting the Multimundial stance in our inquiries and interpersonal relations. This is one major point of difference between Kant and Carnap, whose view does provide for this possibility. Yet Carnap drew upon Kant in many ways. He agreed with Kant that we can have objective knowledge only insofar as objects are given to us in experience; he also concurred with the view that empirical knowledge must take the form of truth-value-bearing judgments; and he accepted Kant's claim that such judgments are not possible unless certain a priori concepts can be brought to bear on what is given in experience, including most especially a set of logical concepts. Let me now situate these points of agreement within his early account of meaning and truth.

One of Carnap's central projects was to regiment natural language for the purposes of exact science, which involved specifying the meanings of scientific terms in such a way that there would be clear rules for confirming (or disconfirming) sentences containing them as true (or false) on the basis of experience.[3] In his view, the importance of this project went beyond exhibiting what empirical evidence we have for our scientific claims, for he also espoused the "empiricist criterion of cognitive significance" that was shared by many members of the Vienna Circle, according to which *no* use of language is objectively meaningful unless it involves a use of sentences with clear confirmation (and disconfirmation) conditions in experience.[4] In this project of regimentation, Carnap drew upon the work of Frege and Russell, who both saw natural language as full of unclarity, and even nonsense, and also as unfit to express the particular logical concepts that they had

----

truths that other subjects of experience would know if they had different forms of sensibility.

3. See Carnap (1928) 2003.

4. See Hempel 1950 for a thorough review of the logical positivists' efforts to develop the "empiricist criterion of cognitive significance," as well as an anticipation of Quine's arguments against it in Quine 1953—arguments that were anticipated by Carnap himself (1947).

introduced as part of what was then the "new" logic. This led them to devise artificial languages to suit their logical purposes, in which they introduced new logical terms whose meanings they stipulated with explicit definitions. Carnap held that science requires something similar—the introduction of a more exact scientific language, whose terms would be explicitly defined so as to clarify their objective empirical content as well as their logical form.

Carnap referred to all of these artificial and regimented languages as "linguistic frameworks," and he viewed all issues of meaning within such linguistic frameworks as matters of convention. He also viewed such linguistic conventions as the sole source of a priori truths, including the truths of logic and mathematics. Adopting Kant's terminology, he counted such truths by convention as "analytic," which is to say, true by virtue of meaning alone. The only "synthetic" truths that he recognized were a posteriori truths known through experience, thus leaving no room for Kant's category of the "synthetic a priori." But the more important point for my purposes is that in his view there are many different linguistic frameworks that we could devise, and that it is up to us to devise them and choose among them.

That Multimundialism follows from Carnap's account of linguistic frameworks can be established in three quick steps.

First, truth-value-bearers that belong to distinct linguistic frameworks are normatively insulated from one another. This follows because every logical truth is a consequence of the particular linguistic conventions that govern the use of logical terms *within* a given linguistic framework, and there is no provision for logical relations holding *between* truth-value-bearers belonging to distinct linguistic frameworks, thus ensuring that they are always normatively insulated from one another.

Second, normatively insulated truth-value-bearers that belong to distinct linguistic frameworks may be equally true, thereby qualifying as alternatives. That this follows can be seen in Carnap's well-known discussion of two sorts of ontological questions—*internal* questions versus *external* questions.[5] Internal questions are raised from within a

---

5. See Carnap 1947.

given linguistic framework by employing its terms, and such questions can be objectively settled on the basis of experience because there are linguistic conventions that specify the empirical conditions in which existentially quantified sentences containing those terms are true—examples of such sentences might be "Electrons exist" or "Emperors exist." External questions concern whether to employ a whole set of terms (both logical and nonlogical) that belong to, and also constitute, a given linguistic framework—for example, we can ask ourselves whether we should adopt a linguistic framework that contains terms for enduring physical objects or whether we should adopt one that contains terms only for momentary existents as contemporary "stage theorists" propose we do. Although each such linguistic framework will include rules for confirming (or disconfirming) various ontological claims on the basis of experience, there is no similar empirical basis on which to say that any one framework is somehow more "accurate" or "true" than another. Carnap concluded that there is no objective basis on which to settle external questions, and that they must be settled on purely practical grounds such as convenience, elegance, and so on. However, he did not see this conclusion as compromising the objectivity of internal questions, for the answers to such questions can be expressed by us in synthetic sentences that have clear confirmation (or disconfirmation) conditions in experience, and they therefore qualify as true (or false) in the only sense in which anything can be objectively true (or false) according to his radical empiricism.

It clearly follows that each linguistic framework provides a vantage point on a separate world, in the sense that it allows those who adopt it to know a *separate* body of truths—where by "separate" I mean that it cannot be conjoined with the truths that are knowable from the vantage point of any other linguistic framework, owing to the normative insularity of all such frameworks from one another. Yet Carnap saw no bar to our understanding and recognizing the truths that would be apprehended from within other linguistic frameworks. In fact, his view positively requires that other linguistic frameworks are in some sense epistemically accessible to us, because that is a precondition for our ever facing the sort of choice among them that he thought we clearly do face. This ensures that if we took Carnap's view seriously, we would have to take Multimundialism seriously as well—and not merely as a conceptual possibility as a Kantian might, but as something that we must actually *live* when we are confronted with the multiplicity of alternative linguistic frameworks. The reasons that Carnap's view thus supplies for embracing Multimundialism clearly qualify as substantive reasons of the sort I am seeking, that do not merely beg the logical question at issue—because they are derived from a set of systematically related philosophical commitments concerning logic, meaning, confirmation, and truth.

It should be evident that the Carnapian argument for Multimundialism conforms to the standard pattern of twentieth-century arguments for relativism. The first premise, that reality is mind-dependent, is secured through two related aspects of his view: his insistence that having a linguistic framework in place is a necessary condition for knowledge through experience, along with his insistence that linguistic frameworks themselves are supplied not by experience but by our own choices, and so are products of our minds. The second premise, that there is more than one kind of mind on which reality might depend, follows upon the plurality of possible linguistic frameworks from which we might choose. The conclusion that different kinds of minds would know different worlds follows fairly straightforwardly. If this seems an excessively metaphysical conclusion that does not really follow from these premises, we need only recall three related aspects of Carnap's empiricism: (1) Given his empiricist criterion of meaningfulness, we cannot speak meaningfully about any alleged reality that is distinct from what is confirmable (or disconfirmable) in experience from the vantage point of one linguistic framework or another; (2) it would therefore be wrong to suppose that different linguistic frameworks must somehow "answer" to such a reality in order that their claims be true; and (3) it would likewise be wrong to deny that such claims are both objective and true when they are confirmed by experience—which is just to say, there is no basis on which to deny that they correctly describe a world. We may conclude, then, that if Carnap's empiricist account of meaning and truth within linguistic frameworks is correct, and if there is more than one linguistic framework in his sense, then there is more than one set of objectively true sentences that correctly describe different worlds.

In many ways, the Carnapian argument for Multimundialism can serve as a frameworking model for the arguments of Goodman, Whorf, Rorty, and other twentieth-century thinkers who argued for relativism along roughly Kantian lines. There were some differences: Goodman offered a *constructivist* account of language and meaning that dispensed with Carnap's early empiricist commitments, and explicitly claimed that we literally *make* different worlds by devising different linguistic conventions. Although Whorf and Rorty were also in some sense "conventionalists" about meaning, they saw linguistic conventions not as the products of deliberate choice but rather as organic outcomes of history and culture. They all agreed with Carnap that languages are human creations that may differ from place to place and time to time, and that they supply crucial necessary conditions for the possibility of truth-value-bearing thought and talk about a world. This was especially clear in the cases of the three thinkers I have mentioned, all of whom may appropriately be regarded as Multimundialists.

## 2. A Davidsonian Argument against the Multimundial Stance

When Davidson argued against relativism in "On the Very Idea of a Conceptual Scheme," he argued at the broadest level of generality, without specifying any particular domain of application.[6] Yet I shall proceed as if his argument were confined to the domain of my concern here, which is the domain of natural facts open to scientific investigation. This approach makes sense for several related reasons: First, all of the illustrative cases that he discussed have to do with matters of fact as opposed to value; second, with just one exception these illustrative cases fall within the narrower domain of my concern (the one exception is the case of "mental" facts, which he did not regard as scientifically tractable, but if he was right about this, it is because the mental displays an irreducibly normative character that places it on the value side of the fact–value dichotomy); third, there are significant

---

6. Davidson 1973.

obstacles that he did not appreciate, that stand in the way of carrying his argument over to the case of values in a convincing way. I will argue for this last point in Chapter 4, and I will continue to confine my focus in the present chapter to the domain of natural facts—though I shall also continue to leave it open how inclusive that domain may or may not prove to be.

Quite apart from questions about the domain of its application, we should expect that Davidson's argument in "On the Very Idea of a Conceptual Scheme" would speak to the issue of Multimundialism. His main target was *alternative* conceptual schemes, which he explicitly defined as schemes that are *true but not translatable,* and it does not take much reflection to see that alternative conceptual schemes, so defined, would contain alternatives in the sense required by Multimundialism— truths that cannot be embraced together because they are normatively insulated from one another, which is to say, because they are neither inconsistent nor consistent. That truth-value-bearers belonging to Davidson's alternative conceptual schemes are not inconsistent follows upon their untranslatability, for if truth-value-bearers belonging to different schemes are not translatable, then they cannot be understood as affirming or denying the very same proposition. That such truth-value-bearers are not consistent either is provided for by Davidson's clear, though unstated, presumption that they cannot be embraced together even when true—that was the whole point of his labeling the different schemes to which they belong as "alternatives."

However, there are several distinct strands in Davidson's argument against relativism, and it must be admitted that not all of them speak very directly to the issue of relativism qua Multimundialism. The most prominent strands are (1) the conceptual connection between truth and translation that figured in Tarski's semantical definition of truth, (2) the principle of charity that Quine recommended as a guide to belief attribution, and (3) the rejection of the "scheme–content" distinction. In many ways Davidson saw this last strand of his argument as the most important one, because in his view it points to a correct, positive account of the mind-world relation as *direct*—an account that he continued to develop in subsequent work, bringing it to bear in efforts to undermine skepticism and to establish the social character of intentionality and meaning. Yet although these themes were important ones in Davidson's work, they do not bear on the task of evaluating Multimundialism, and I will postpone discussion of them until Section 4 when I take up the question how Multimundialism relates to realism. Of the other two strands of the anti-conceptual-schemes argument, the first speaks more directly against alternatives as Davidson himself defined them, as true but not translatable, while the second speaks more directly against alternatives as I have defined them—indeed, it provides a breathtakingly quick argument to show that there is no scope at all for adopting the distinctive normative stance of the Multimundialist.

Here is the quick argument: The Multimundial stance is supposed to be one from which we can attribute beliefs to others, and regard those beliefs as in some sense true—namely, *true for them*—while *refraining* from embracing those beliefs ourselves. But the principle of charity, a principle that we cannot avoid wielding in interpretation, according to Davidson, instructs us that whenever we attribute beliefs to others, we should attribute to them beliefs that are (by and large) true by our own lights. This directly rules out our ever having occasion to attribute beliefs to others unless they are (for the most part) ones that we *already embrace ourselves.*

If this quick argument is to be compelling, it needs to be supplemented. We need to consider why Davidson thinks the principle of charity is unavoidable in interpretation, what sort of justification can be supplied for the principle so that we can be sure that a charitable approach would not amount to an *unwarranted* projection of our own beliefs onto others; and we need to consider whether and why such a justification might illuminate the underlying logical issue that divides Multimundialists from Unimundialists, so that when we recognize what grounds we have for taking a charitable approach to belief attribution, we may not only take them as grounds on which to expect that others share our beliefs, but grounds on which to suppose that logical relations do indeed run everywhere, among all truth-value-bearers, as Unimundialists contend.

Davidson took the principle of charity over from Quine, so it makes sense to start with Quine's own understanding of its role and importance. Going back to Quine makes all the more sense given that Davidson portrayed his anti-conceptual-schemes argument as undermining a third dogma of empiricism to be placed alongside the other two dogmas against which Quine had argued in "Two Dogmas of Empiricism."[7] But the real advantage to be gained by returning to Quine's arguments is that they draw on another consideration aside from charity, one that played a central role in all of Davidson's work in philosophy of language and mind—namely, *holism*. It is fair to say that Davidson went further than Quine himself did in his efforts to fully elaborate the significance of holism, for he showed us that when charity is driven by holism, it *is* well justified, indeed required—that it does not amount to an unwarranted projection of our own beliefs onto others. I will be elaborating the significance of holism perhaps even further than Davidson, in order to bring out how powerfully it speaks against the idea that we could find someone intelligible if their beliefs were normatively insulated from ours—a quite different claim from the conclusion of the quick argument from charity above, which does not mention normative insulary all, nor its opposite, logical relatedness.

All of this will require some patient exposition.

In the first half of his seminal article, Quine argued against the analytic-synthetic distinction on the ground that it is impossible to give a noncircular account of analyticity—his specific complaint was that every attempt to give such an account appeals to terms that are too proximate to the idea of analyticity itself, such as meaning, definition, necessity, and synonymy. This argument is not particularly impressive. At most it shows that the concept of analyticity belongs to a small family of concepts that are connected together in a fairly tight circle, and we might well grant this without feeling any pressure to give any of them up—indeed, we may grant this while retaining a high level of philosophical interest in them. The real difficulty with analyticity becomes clear in the much deeper second half of the article where Quine attacked the second dogma of empiricism, according to which each sentence of a language can be separately confirmed (or disconfirmed) by experience.

---

7. Quine (1953) 1980.

He portrayed his opposition to this dogma as deriving from a commitment to a holistic picture of empirical confirmation. According to confirmation holism, theories meet the tribunal of experience as wholes, in the sense that when we meet an unexpected or recalcitrant experience, there are many different ways in which we might adjust our beliefs so as to accommodate it—and, as a result, nothing is immune from revision in the light of experience, not even the terms of our linguistic framework, including our logic. This means that there is a sense in which everything is empirical, and yet nothing is purely empirical, because there is no clear distinction between what follows from semantical rules alone as opposed to what we learn from experience.

Since the Carnapian argument for Multimundialism rests squarely on the two dogmas of empiricism, it was already undermined by Quine's invocation of holism against those dogmas, quite independently of Davidson's later argument that invoked charity against the very idea of a conceptual scheme. Yet it would be quite wrong to say that the "very idea" of Multimundialism is bound up with the two dogmas of empiricism, and so it requires further argument to show how and why holism might speak against it—either directly, or by supplementing the quick Davidsonian argument against it from charity. I will continue to work my way toward such further argument by reviewing some further aspects of Quine's work on which Davidson drew.

The aspect of holism that Quine emphasized in "Two Dogmas of Empiricism"—its implications for empirical confirmation in science—is best understood in terms of changes of mind. An unexpected and recalcitrant experience may require us to change our minds. But any change of mind that we make can get one of two quite distinct descriptions. It can be described as a change of belief, but it can equally be described as a change of meaning, and this is symptomatic of the fact that there is no way to isolate what belongs to meaning alone in the way that the analytic-synthetic distinction would provide for. To the extent that that distinction was undermined by Quine, so was the possibility of such an isolation. Take, for example, the word "star." It has probably always been used to refer to the things that look bright and small in the night sky. But over time we have learned to use the term in new ways so as to distinguish stars from planets, to think of them as much larger and much farther away, and to classify the sun as being among them. Quine's point is that we can describe all of these changes as acquisitions of new beliefs about the stars as a result of ongoing empirical investigation, or we can describe them as decisions to use the term "star" differently. (Anyone who doubts Quine's confirmation holism and its negative implications for the analytic-synthetic distinction should reflect on the debate a few years back about whether Pluto is a planet. Lots of empirical evidence about the nature of Pluto was of course brought into the debate. But the debate also involved clarifying and reevaluating various criteria for planethood. As the debate proceeded, it became abundantly clear that the issue being debated was both empirical and nonempirical at the same time: the conclusion that Pluto is not a planet was in part an empirical discovery and in part a matter for decision, and those who led us to this conclusion had the wisdom *not* to portray it as definitely and exclusively one or the other, as Carnap would have been committed to portraying it, at least in the first phase of his regimenting project.)

Quine further developed his understanding of the interrelations between meaning and belief in chapter 2 of *Word and Object.*[8] His focus there was the situation of "radical translation," in which we must try to understand another's language with nothing else to go on but what we can observe about the conditions in which users of the language say what they say, whether on their own or as a result of elicitations of assent and dissent to sentences from them. When we reflect on this situation, it quickly becomes apparent that the process of figuring out what the words of a language mean is bound up with the process of trying to figure out what beliefs are reflected in uses of those words, and indeed govern their use. For example, as soon as we take a particular word in the language under study to express a certain concept, we must suppose that speakers of the language are prepared to apply the word to instances of that concept; and when we suppose that this is what they are doing, we must also suppose that their uses of the word

---

8. Quine 1960.

are guided by relevant beliefs about which things count as instances of the concept, and about what the common aspects of those things are by virtue of which they count as instances of the concept. Quine first introduced the principle of charity as a standard by which to assess translations, given that they must go together with belief attributions. The principle instructs us that we should translate others' words so that their uses of those words can be seen as guided by beliefs that are true by our own lights.

But if this is the purpose for which Quine invoked the principle of charity, it does not quite explain what justifies charity—explain, that is, why we can be sure that it does not amount to an unwarranted projection of our own beliefs onto others. As I have said, it is holism that provides an explanation, and it was Davidson who explicitly made that connection and brought it out in the open.

It was already clear in "Two Dogmas of Empiricism" that Quine's confirmation holism was really a doctrine about the nature of belief, on which beliefs owe their identities—that is, their contents—to their positions within a larger system of beliefs, which Quine later referred to as "the web of belief."[9] Attributing any belief—say, a belief someone has about a tree in their backyard—would require attributing to the person various surrounding beliefs that would establish that it is indeed a *tree* that he has a belief about, beliefs such as: that a tree is a growing but inanimate thing—a plant and not an animal; that trees, unlike grasses and bushes, lie at the tall and large end of the size scale for plants; the belief that each tree has a single main shoot or trunk (or just a few) from which smaller shoots or branches grow; the belief that trees have either leaves or needles and, also, roots; the belief that trees are living things that reproduce; the belief that trees cannot live without air, light, soil, and water. I could go on, and that is very much the point. The point, given the denial of analyticity, is that it is not compulsory to attribute any particular subset of beliefs such as these, so long as there are sufficiently many of them to establish what it is (trees) that he has beliefs about. And the holism is without check because each of these surrounding beliefs will contain concepts (of a

---

9. Quine and Ullian 1978.

branch, say, or roots, or another of any unspecified number of further concepts . . . ) that will require their own surrounding beliefs to make it clear that it is indeed that concept (branch, roots, or some other . . . ) that the beliefs are beliefs about. According to belief holism, then, both the contents of beliefs, as well as their constituent concepts—which themselves owe their individuation as those concepts to clusters of beliefs—are identified by their particular positions within an entire system of beliefs. If the constituent concepts in our beliefs owe their individuation in this way to clusters of beliefs, each of which contains constituent concepts similarly individuated, generating an overall psychological economy that consists in a system of a virtually indefinite number of beliefs, then, given the interdependence of meaning and belief, this must be reflected at the level of meaning as well. Thus, the meaning of any given term consists in the systematic role the term plays in an entire language, where that entire language cannot itself be understood without coming to understand how its overall use is governed by, and expresses, an overall system of beliefs. This is the real lesson of Quine's "Two Dogmas of Empiricism," and it informs all of his other work on language as well as Davidson's.

It is an interesting and striking outcome of such a holism that it does not allow the notion of charity to merely degenerate into the idea (sometimes wrongly attributed to Davidson) that in interpretation we must project our own beliefs onto those we interpret, because it allows us to attribute to others beliefs that we do not share, beliefs that are false by our lights. But the fact that we do not have to project our beliefs onto others raises a further question about what prevents us from attributing beliefs to others that are massively off the mark by our lights. Clearly these two things—nonprojection of our beliefs onto those we interpret, and not finding them to be mistaken—pull in different directions, and we need to say more to reconcile them. The holism in Quine and Davidson is geared precisely to make such a reconciliation and to have both things sit comfortably together in interpretation.

Davidson famously held that we can intelligibly attribute false beliefs to someone only if can we find a background of beliefs that are true by our lights, which allow us to individuate (by the holistic constraints described above) the concepts that figure in the false beliefs.

So, for instance, if we are to attribute to someone the false belief that trees grow on Mars, we need grounds on which to attribute such a falsehood. And we shall have such grounds only if we also have grounds on which to attribute enough background beliefs about trees and growing and Mars that are true by our lights—for example: that a tree has a main trunk or shoot from which smaller branches grow, and that it has leaves or needles as well as roots, and so forth; that when living things grow they generally increase in size, and this change is only one among many characteristic changes that take place in their life cycle from birth through maturation to death, and such; that Mars is a planet and not a star, and so on. Absent these (by our lights) true background beliefs, *we* would have no grounds on which to suppose that it is really *trees* that are at issue, or that trees are believed to be *growing*, or that trees are believed to grow on *Mars*. So one reason we might view such holistically constrained attributions of *false* beliefs as also *charitable* is that they are always backed by attributions of accompanying true beliefs. As Davidson often put it, intelligible disagreements are always outrun by agreements.

However, Davidson's preferred way of putting the point is unduly negative. What it emphasizes is that, given the constraints imposed by holism, we could never have grounds on which to attribute more false beliefs to someone than true ones. What it fails to emphasize is the related positive point, that those very constraints may actually invite us to attribute false beliefs to others, insofar as doing so would improve overall intelligibility. Thus, if someone seems to have largely true beliefs about trees and growing and Mars, and seems to consistently use certain words to refer to trees and growing and Mars, and goes on to use those very words in order to say, "Trees grow on Mars," the most charitable interpretation will attribute the false belief that those words seem to express. To see why this is so, consider what would happen if we were determined to see that utterance as expressing a true belief instead. Not only would we would be deliberately ignoring the holistic constraints that invited the attribution of the false belief to begin with, but it would be completely unclear what true belief we could intelligibly attribute in that case. If we believe that there is no life on Mars, then either we must suppose that the person is talking about Mars but not about trees and growing, or we must suppose that she is talking about trees and growing but not about Mars. Neither supposition would be warranted unless we could find a surround of true beliefs that would nail down what the person *is* talking about, and as the case had been described, there simply is not any. We could imagine the case differently, of course—we could imagine, for example, that there is a remote place on Earth that the person sometimes calls "Mars" and that trees grow there. But then the person would have to be prepared to affirm related true beliefs, such as "Mars is not a planet," "Mars is located at a particular latitude and longitude on Earth," and so on, whereas we are envisaging a case in which the person's other claims about Mars express true beliefs about the fourth planet from the sun. So to reiterate the positive point about the case so envisaged: It would indeed be more charitable to attribute true beliefs about trees and growing and Mars along with the false belief that trees grow on Mars than any other combination of attitudes.

The charge that charity might amount to an unwarranted projection of our own beliefs onto others is fully laid to rest by this positive articulation. I have rehearsed these familiar themes only in order to make the broader point that needs to be made for my purpose in this chapter, namely, that holistic constraints seem to force us to adopt the normative stance of the Unimundialist. Why is this? Because given holism, truth-value-bearers derive their identities from the positions they occupy in an overall system of concepts and beliefs, and what makes it a *system*—or as Quine put it, a *web*—is a *ubiquity of logical relations*. I say this is a *broader* point because it draws our attention to the fact that when we find that someone believes something that we do not already believe ourselves, we face a broader array of interpretive possibilities than I have so far considered. Rejecting their belief as false is only one such possibility. We might also revise our standing beliefs to accommodate its truth, as I myself might if I happened to encounter an expert from NASA who reports that the space rover *Curiosity* has indeed discovered life on Mars. Although this is something I do not presently believe, I could much more readily take it on board consistently with my other beliefs than the more specific belief that trees grow on Mars—because I happen to believe that if there were trees on Mars, then our explorations over the last decades would already have revealed that this is so, and they have not, whereas if there are smaller and simpler life forms on Mars, these would have been harder to detect and might have escaped our observation. In other cases, we might not be able to understand someone's belief without coming to acquire a new concept along with various surrounding beliefs in which it figures, as I in fact did when I encountered a physicist who believes that there is dark matter. But note that it was possible for me to acquire this concept, along with the surrounding beliefs that individuate it, without being required to accept the existential belief that dark matter exists—I was still free to suspend belief, or to deny it. What does this array of interpretive possibilities have in common? Not that holism constrains us to attribute to others only beliefs that we already hold ourselves, as the quick argument from charity above had suggested, nor that when we encounter beliefs that we do not already hold we must reject them as false, but rather this: In all cases where we can make sense of what others believe, we will find not only that they by and large agree with us about many matters in just the way that Davidson contended, but also that, at the points at which others diverge from us, their beliefs still stand in myriad logical relations to what we already believe, and as a result we shall not find any occasion for the thoroughgoing epistemic indifference of the Multimundialist that would follow upon an encounter with normative insularity; on the contrary, we shall have no choice but to be epistemically engaged in the ways that go together with the Unimundial stance. This completes my exposition of what I have called the Argument from Holism Against Normative Insularity.

Someone who was already convinced that the Dilemma for Alternativeness exhausts the logical possibilities might protest that we do not need this Argument from Holism Against Normative Insularity in order to rule out the Multimundial stance. But that protest would reflect a willingness to directly beg the logical question against Multimundialism without offering any supporting reasons of a more substantive kind. What I have shown is that considerations drawn from philosophy of language and mind having to do with holism provide such substantive reasons—reasons to accept (rather than to merely assert question-beggingly) that the terms of the Dilemma do indeed exhaust the logical possibilities, at least in domains where holism holds and constrains our efforts to communicate with and understand one another.

Like Davidson's own arguments in "On the Very Idea of a Conceptual Scheme," the Argument from Holism Against Normative Insularity is presented here at such a high level of generality that it does not seem clearly confined to the domain of my concern in this chapter, the domain of natural facts open to scientific investigation. But again, like Davidson's own arguments, it has focused on cases drawn from that domain. So let me qualify its conclusion accordingly in two related ways: The argument goes through only in domains where holism clearly holds and, moreover, only if holism is uncontained in such a way that no self-standing systems of belief can arise that fail to be logically related to one another. We shall see in Chapter 4 that it is unclear how to establish that this latter condition holds in the domain of moral values. As I have already indicated, there is also a good prima facie case to be made that Kuhn's account of incommensurability in science entails that the condition does not even hold in the domain of natural facts open to scientific investigation—for it would seem that on his account, incommensurable scientific theories are self-standing systems of beliefs that bear no logical relations to one another.

Before taking up either of these issues, I want to consider some objections against the doctrine of holism itself, considered apart from these questions concerning the domains of its application and the extent of its reach within those domains. It is important to do so, since those who have raised these objections will naturally be unpersuaded by my claims on behalf of Unimundialism that Davidson's position (which assumes such a holism) seems to provide.

The most obvious such objection derives from the very sort of atomistic conception of content that Quine was opposing in "Two Dogmas of Empiricism," which was shared not only by the radically empiricist wing of logical positivism but also by the longer tradition of British empiricism that included Locke, Berkeley, Hume, Russell, and more recently Jerry Fodor. Hume was particularly clear that he viewed the basic "atoms" of experience—sensory impressions—as wholly independent of one another, so that they could in principle occur in any order and in any combination.[10] This almost invites us to view such atoms as if they were all normatively insulated from one another, because the presence of any one of them in our experience would place no logically significant constraints on what else we might or might not experience together with them. But the more accurate way to portray the situation as Hume envisaged it is that the requirements for consistency are exceedingly low—that *everything* is co-tenable except for what is overtly contradictory. This means that Hume implicitly took for granted that the terms of the Dilemma for Alternativeness exhaust the logical possibilities: any pair of truth-value-bearers that is not overtly inconsistent is consistent and co-tenable. So if we were to accept his atomistic empiricism, Multimundialism would not follow; rather, we would be deprived of one interesting substantive ground on which to reject it, in the form of holism.

Yet we should not presume that Hume's vision is completely out of step at every point with the sort of holism that drives the Quine-Davidson picture of content—even if Hume could never himself be classified as a holist. As I have emphasized, once we give up the analytic-synthetic distinction, it makes sense to adopt a broad conception of "logical" relations that includes inductively based relations as well as deductive ones and those owing to material relations between concepts as given in the example above about the concept of a tree; and although Hume did insist that sensory impressions can *in principle* come in any order and combination, he also insisted that they *in fact* exhibit a great many "constant conjunctions" or "regular successions"—so much so that we are within our rights to adopt a deterministic worldview in which it makes sense to ask of each and every event what was its cause, where the answer to that question points to an inductively known general "law" under which it falls. These inductive regularities or "laws" supply many of the interconnections that I drew upon in my examples above in order to illustrate the holistic character of concepts and beliefs. So it seems to me that we would have reason to forsake holism in the face of arguments for atomistic empiricism only if we had reason

---

10. Hume (1740) 1978.

to doubt that experience is inductively tractable in the very ways that Hume (and all other sensible empiricists) allowed, so as to exhibit itself as a massively interconnected system.

Another objection to holism claims that there simply is not any argument for it.[11] If what is meant by "argument" is an a priori argument from first principles, then the contention of this objection is quite correct, for the only way I can see to become convinced of holism is through sustained observation. We need to take up specific beliefs, and to observe how their contents reflect their logical relations to other beliefs (construing "logic" broadly, so as to include some a posteriori as well as a priori relations), and how the contents of those beliefs in turn reflect their logical relations to still further beliefs, and so on indefinitely.[12] But there is no compromise to the truth of holism if it can be established only on the basis of such sustained observation and not through a priori argument from first principles.

A far more serious objection is that holism has the following problematic implication: If the content of any particular belief is individuated just by its position within a system of interrelated beliefs, it would appear to follow that no two subjects can share any beliefs without agreeing on *everything;* and what is more, it would also appear to follow that a single subject can never think the same thought twice if she undergoes any changes of mind in the intervening time. Sometimes this implication is taken to show that we cannot make sense of the possibility of acquiring concepts and beliefs, because some of them would have to be acquired in advance of acquiring others, and this appears to be impossible given that the former cannot be what they are until the latter are also in place. The implication has also been taken to show

---

11. This is one of the many complaints that Jerry Fodor has lodged against holism. See Fodor and LePore 1992.

12. There is no worry that I am going against my own methodological recommendation *not* to rest any conclusions about relativism on the power of example, as opposed to philosophical argument. My point here is that holism is an empirical claim that we might come to believe on the basis of extensive observation of many cases—not by reflecting on the nature of one or two illustrative examples.

that holism precludes a science of the mind, because if concepts and beliefs generally cannot be shared across subjects, or across time within a single subject, then they cannot figure in psychological laws.[13]

My general response to all of these worries is that if holism is true, then we must simply find a way to accommodate its problematic implication. This was William James's response, who openly embraced holism, together with this implication, as an empirically well-confirmed aspect of mental life that any adequate science of the mind must accommodate.[14] He took it for granted that one goal of such a science is to make sense of the mind–body relation, and he was satisfied that holism poses no difficulty on that front, because he took the brain to be the seat of consciousness and he pointed out that if a single subject can never think exactly the same thought twice, this is mirrored in the fact that the subject's brain can never be in exactly the same (total) neurological state twice either. It may be that he was wrong about the nature of mind–brain relation, and indeed wrong to suppose that holism leaves scope for a science of the mind. But even if he was wrong about all of this, we would not be entitled to disregard what empirical evidence there is for holism. That evidence leaves us no choice but to accept it, along with its apparently problematic implication. Both Davidson and Chomsky have had the good sense to do just that—the former inferring that a science of the mind is not feasible at all, and the latter inferring that although syntax is scientifically tractable, semantics is not.[15]

However, since the empirical evidence for the doctrine of holism is drawn from our everyday practices of interpersonal communication and psychological attribution, something would be very much amiss if we could not reconcile the doctrine with our ordinary, unscientific understanding of these practices, and this presents a prima facie difficulty, insofar as these practices do seem to take it for granted that subjects can share the very same concepts and beliefs, even when they

---

13. All of the objections just raised can be found in Fodor and LePore 1992.

14. James (1897) 1979.

15. See Davidson's "Psychology as Philosophy" in Davidson 1980; and Chomsky 2000.

are not in perfect agreement about everything—contrary to what the objection I have raised contends.

A natural first response to the difficulty is to suppose that the sharing of concepts and beliefs is a matter of degree. On this supposition, we do not need to be in perfect agreement with others (or our past selves) in order to share concepts and beliefs with them (or our past selves), because some very substantial amount of agreement short of that would suffice to provide the necessary holistic underpinnings. This was Davidson's own view of the matter, and we find it articulated in his claim that there is room for intelligible disagreement so long as there is a *sufficient* background of agreement to nail down the terms of the disagreement. Although this first response seems entirely reasonable, it leaves us with an outstanding issue concerning *how much* agreement would suffice for intelligibility, and a worry that there is no *principled* way to settle that issue.

A second response to the objection concedes that there is indeed no principled way of settling the issue.[16] In fact, this response also concedes that, strictly speaking, there is a sense in which subjects do not share exactly the same concepts and beliefs unless they agree about everything. But at the same time, it identifies another sense in which such subjects may share concepts and beliefs nonetheless, which owes to the fact that the twin tasks of communication and psychological attribution are *purpose-driven*. What the response underscores is that in many contexts these purposes render the differences in subjects' background concepts and beliefs *irrelevant*—so with respect to those purposes it makes sense to suppose that the subjects can and do think the very same thoughts in spite of their differences. Thus, the reason there is no general way of settling the issue of how much background agreement suffices for the sharing of concepts and beliefs is that the nature and extent of the agreement required will vary from context to context, depending upon the purposes at hand.

As we typically find with issues having to do with holism, reflection on cases will help to make this one clearer. Consider two people, one of whom is a trained research chemist and one of whom is scientifically

---

16. See Bilgrami 1992.

illiterate. The chemist's concepts and beliefs concerning water are informed by an understanding of its chemical composition of water as $H_2O$, and related chemical facts concerning the elements, their atomic structure, the principles of their bonding, and so forth, while the scientific illiterate's concepts and beliefs concerning water are not informed by such an understanding, but focus on the colorless, odorless liquid that fills rivers and oceans, rains from the sky, and quenches thirst. Given these differences between them, there is a clear sense in which they do not share the same concept of, or beliefs about, water. Yet it should not be hard to see that they may have purposes that render these differences irrelevant, and that with respect to those purposes there is a sense in which they can entertain the very same thoughts about water. If they are dining together at a restaurant and discussing whether to order plain tap water or bottled mineral water, their background differences do not prevent them from *agreeing,* or for that matter *disagreeing,* about whether plain tap is better than mineral.

Some philosophers would explain this in realist terms, by supposing that there is a natural kind—$H_2O$—to which they both may refer through a form of direct reference that is not mediated by their different conceptions of it. But this explanation misses the point that in this context they are *not* bringing their different conceptions to bear, and furthermore, the shared conception of water that they *are* bringing to bear is precisely *not* the natural kind that scientists study but rather the broader kind to which we all refer in everyday contexts when we want to quench our thirsts. The idea of direct reference is equally unhelpful in the context of the lab, where it may be crucial for the chemist's experimental purposes that a given beaker contains pure $H_2O$ and *not* the various impure mixtures and solutions that the scientific illiterate would classify as water, including plain tap as well as bottled mineral water. Here the differences in their background concepts and beliefs clearly do prevent the scientific illiterate from sharing the chemist's thought that the stuff in the beaker is *water*—and this point would be missed if we focused on the realist suggestion that the scientific illiterate is still, nevertheless, directly referring to $H_2O$ even though she lacks the chemical concept. The point to focus on is the latter one, that she does *not* share the chemist's chemical concept, and that this is a difference that is made relevant by the purposes of scientific experimentation.

When we concede that there are purposes in regard to which the chemist and the scientific illiterate do not entertain the same thoughts, because the differences in their background concepts and beliefs are relevant to those purposes, there is no suggestion that they cannot overcome those differences so as to come to think the very same thoughts. In other words, nothing stands in the way of the scientific illiterate becoming literate. But until she does so, there are purposes for which she is not yet in a position either to agree or to disagree with the scientist about whether the beaker contains $H_2O$—because unlike the purpose of ordering water in the restaurant, the purpose of filling beakers with $H_2O$ would require her to make distinctions that her current background concepts and beliefs do not allow her to make.

What do all these subtle points about the relation between context, purpose, belief, and meaning have to do with our subject? When we concede that there are purposes in regard to which the chemist and the scientific illiterate do not entertain the same thoughts, we ought not to infer that their distinct thoughts are somehow normatively insulated from one another, because all of the points that I made above in connection with holism, before raising the objection now under discussion, still stand. Given holism, intelligibility requires a background of overall agreement, and when we find intelligible divergences, we must still find logical relations to that shared background of agreement, and *these various logical relations ensure that encounters between the chemist and the scientific illiterate will invite epistemic engagement, and not the sort of epistemic disengagement that follows upon the recognition of normative insularity.* To put it another way, it is a *live issue* for the scientific illiterate whether to embrace or reject the scientific concepts and beliefs that she does not (yet) share—it is what Bernard Williams would have called a "real option" to go over to the scientist's view. But let us not lose sight of the general lesson that I aim to draw from this case, which is that the question whether the scientific illiterate's beliefs *as they stand* (before any effort to become literate) make it possible for her to entertain the very same thoughts as the scientist—and thereby either agree or disagree with her—will depend upon what purposes are stake.[17]

It should now be clear that holism does not pose any insuperable difficulty for making sense of our everyday practices of communication and psychological ascription. Furthermore, the particular way round the difficulty that I have just reviewed does not compromise the Argument from Holism Against Normative Insularity. Even if purposes allow us to see the effects of holism as mitigated, in the sense that subjects who possess different background concepts and beliefs may still think the very same thoughts in relation to certain purposes (provided that those purposes make their background differences irrelevant), this does not undermine Davidson's basic claim that holistic interconnections among concepts and beliefs must nevertheless be present if we are to find others intelligible, or my further claim that this rules out our ever encountering normative insularity, at least in domains where holism holds and is uncontained.

However, it must be admitted that my proposed way of handling the apparently problematic implication of holism does not particularly help us to see how a science of the mind is possible—how we might frame psychological laws, or how in particular we might give a scientific account of the initial acquisition of concepts and beliefs. With respect to the latter, the most it accomplishes is this: it helps to make clear that there may be purposes with respect to which the vast differences in the background concepts and beliefs of neophytes and experts are irrelevant, thereby providing contexts in which it makes sense to suppose that they can think the very same thoughts. But my working position remains that the empirical evidence in favor of holism is substantial enough to warrant credence, regardless of the consequences

---

17. The issue of self-knowledge drives Bilgrami's whole account of meaning in Bilgrami 1992, and it provides an effective response to the un-thought-out appeal to linguistic intuitions that I discussed in Chapter 1, on which some advocates of the Disagreement Intuition base their insistence that the situations that relativists intuitively have in mind are situations of agreement.

for a science of the mind, and so the Argument from Holism Against Normative Insularity stands in the face of the apparently problematic implications of holism.

## 3. Why Kuhn and Feyerabend Are to Be Counted as Unimundialists

My primary aim in this section is to show that Kuhnian incommensurability does not bring normative insularity in train, and so does not invite the Multimundial stance in science.[18] A secondary aim is to bring out what the real significance of Kuhnian incommensurability would be, assuming for the sake of argument that his empirical claims about scientific practice are correct. A tertiary aim is to explore various related reasons why the Unimundial stance seems so fundamental to the scientific outlook.

I should clarify as an aside that it is no part of my aim to evaluate Kuhn's arguments for incommensurability. That task is better left to those who have more detailed knowledge than I of the history and sociology of science. My concern is with what follows from his picture for the task at hand, which is to explore what substantive reasons there might be either to affirm or to reject Multimundialism in the domain of natural facts that are appropriate targets of scientific investigation.

There is a strong temptation to suppose that Kuhnian incommensurability would bring normative insularity in train, thereby supporting Multimundialism. After all, Kuhn's central claim was that incommensurable scientific theories do not share meanings, and if they do not share meanings then they cannot logically conflict with one another, and so it would appear that the only other way in which they could be *rival* theories that exclude one another is by being normatively insulated from one another. Yet we shall see that the considerations that support the thesis of what I have been calling "uncontained holism" are not undermined by the considerations that Kuhn brought to bear

18. My entire discussion of Kuhn will focus exclusively on his arguments in Kuhn 1962.

in his arguments for incommensurability in science, and as a result his arguments leave the Argument from Holism *Against* Normative Insularity in place. How can this be? Because even if the scientific theories that he portrayed as incommensurable fail to share the meanings of their crucial theoretical terms, the thesis of uncontained holism ensures that they are all logically related at least *indirectly,* by virtue of their many complicated relations to a mass of shared agreement— relations in the light of which they emerge as being *in conflict.*

But if, as I will show, my Argument from Holism Against Normative Insularity can stand in the face of Kuhn's arguments, then conversely we will also see that much of the significance that he attached to his arguments can stand in the face of my argument. His main challenge to science was that there is no objective, in the sense of *theory-neutral,* basis on which to choose among rival scientific theories and, therefore, the course of science has not been a progress of rational transitions in which later theories have retained what was correct in earlier ones while jettisoning or revising the rest, but rather a series of revolutions in which new theoretical paradigms simply overthrew and supplanted earlier ones. The Argument from Holism Against Normative Insularity does not provide an answer to this challenge, so much as require us to qualify our understanding of it. We must see scientists who advocate incommensurable theories as *disagreeing,* and we must see incommensurability as signaling the absence of any rational basis on which to *resolve* those disagreements, which is not the same thing at all as normative insularity. On my reading, then, and indeed on most readings, the real significance of Kuhn's arguments is epistemological rather than metaphysical. That is, if he can be said to have argued for any form of relativism at all, it is a form of epistemic relativism that does not call the oneness of reality into question, but rather our picture of scientific methods as objective.

Unlike Kuhn, Feyerabend explicitly characterized incommensurability as involving conflict. This is something that we might find somewhat surprising, because he accepted all of Kuhn's other claims about incommensurability, including those that seem to entail that incommensurable theories cannot conflict with one another because they do not share meanings. However, what most interested Feyerabend in his early and sympathetic responses to Kuhn's arguments was not whether incommensurability should be defined as involving conflict; what most interested him was whether Kuhn's arguments leave us with any meaningful way to make sense of science's claims to objectivity, insofar as they derive from a commitment to employing so-called empirical methods. We normally take it for granted that if our theories are empirically well confirmed, then we are within our rights to regard them as true and to demand that any future theoretical developments preserve our current theories *unless* they provide direct empirical evidence against them. There is an obvious similarity between this conservative orientation of empiricism and the attitude of self-confident internalism that I discussed in Part One, which I noted may lead (internally) rational inquirers into irresoluble disagreements. On our standard picture of scientific methods, there is not supposed to be any such threat of irresolubility in science, because scientists are supposed always to have recourse to further empirical investigation and testing, whose results they are all committed to accepting no matter what their other theoretical differences might happen to be. But obviously, such a commitment would be warranted only if these further empirical investigations and their results were genuinely theory-neutral. That is what Kuhn argued is *not* the case, and *en suite,* Feyerabend argued further that the explicitly conservative orientation of empirical methods is therefore highly problematic. He saw it as problematic for two related reasons: not only does it threaten to land scientists in irresoluble scientific disagreements, but worse yet, it amounts to *dogmatism*—an attitude that would inure them to potential grounds for regarding their current theories as false. As I elaborate further below, Feyerabend's recommended solution to the problem of dogmatism actually *exploits* the Unimundial stance, and this brings me to my tertiary aim in this section, which is to identify several ways in which the Unimundial stance is basic to the scientific outlook, indeed so basic that neither Kuhn nor Feyerabend could call it into question, even as they called into question so many other aspects of it.

First, a slightly more elaborated account of Kuhn.

Kuhn took as his starting point the sort of confirmation holism that Quine advocated at the end of "Two Dogmas," which had come to be accepted by many philosophers of science after the ebbing of the initial appeal of logical positivism. These philosophers held that there is no sharp distinction between theory and observation, because what counts as observable is largely a function of one's theoretical commitments—observation is, as they put it, "theory-laden."

I turn again to astronomy to illustrate this point, as I did before in my exposition of Quine on the interdependence of meaning and belief: If one believes, as the ancients did, that the earth is flat and that the sky is a dome, then observation will confirm that the sun is smaller than the earth, and that it moves across the sky and quite literally rises and sets on the horizon line; observation will also confirm that the sun is very different from the stars that one sees at night, being a source of light and also much larger than they; finally, observation will confirm that some stars, like Venus and Mars, though they are very small, are nevertheless much larger than other stars. But if one believes various propositions of post-Copernican and post-Newtonian astronomy—that the earth is round, that it rotates on its axis, that it revolves around the sun as part of a solar system that includes other planets that also revolve around the sun, that the sun is a star among other stars, many of which are much larger than it, and so on, then observation will in various ways confirm all of these things. To observe the sun "set" is to lose sight of the sun from a vantage point on the surface of the earth owing to the rotation of the earth on its axis; to observe the night sky is to see a vast space containing enormous stars that are both brighter and larger than the sun, and that lie at the center of other solar systems; it is also to see a few planets within our own solar system that are much smaller than any star, such as Venus and Mars; and finally, much of what we observe about all of these astronomical bodies is done with the help of telescopes. These latter observations are supported by a theoretical understanding of why what appears through a telescope qualifies as accurate information that is not directly available to the senses. Kuhn was particularly convincing in his account of how scientific observation often involves the use of instruments whose "readings" cannot so much as be described without taking the truth of one's theoretical viewpoint for granted, and how the same holds for the design of experiments and tests.

These details vividly illustrate Quine's claim that theories meet the "tribunal of experience" as wholes. But while Quine tended to emphasize that everything is in some sense empirical because nothing is immune from revision in the light of experience, Kuhn emphasized that everything is in some sense theoretical because observation is always theory-laden. It was largely on this ground that Kuhn rejected the standard picture of science as enjoying a special epistemic status owing to its reliance on so-called empirical methods.

This difficulty for the standard picture is compounded by the meaning-theoretic implications of holism, which I discussed in the last section and flagged as potentially problematic. Kuhn did not press the radical holist's claim that subjects cannot share any concepts or beliefs at all unless they are in perfect agreement about everything. He took it for granted that something short of perfect scientific agreement can suffice—the kind that Davidson referred to as "by and large" agreement—and that it is generally in place among scientists who work within the same theoretical paradigm. Yet he argued that such by and large agreement is not in place among scientists who work within different theoretical paradigms, at least not with respect to scientific matters, with the result that these scientists are never really thinking or talking about the same scientific matters. He allowed that they may *seem* to do so, especially when they employ the same lexical items, such as "atom," "space," "time," "mass," "motion," "energy," and so on. But given holism, the meaning of any such term is determined by its position within a set of surrounding beliefs, and when those beliefs are supplied by substantially different theories, they simply cannot mean the same thing. This compounds the difficulty that follows upon the theory-ladenness of observation, because if different scientific theories fail to share meanings, then later ones can neither affirm nor deny the claims of earlier ones. It follows that there is no rational basis whatsoever—empirical or nonempirical—on which an advocate of one theory can rationally persuade advocates of a different one to give theirs up in favor of her own. It also follows that later theories cannot retain and build upon earlier ones in the way that our standard notions of scientific progress would have it, but rather they throw the earlier ones over completely and install themselves in their place—hence the revolutionary character of scientific change that Kuhn announced in the title of his extraordinary book.

As I have said, prima facie it does seem plausible that, on Kuhn's account, incommensurability in science commits him to viewing successive theories as normatively insulated from one another: If successive scientific theories do not share meanings, it would seem to follow that they cannot be inconsistent with one another; if they are rival theories that cannot be embraced together, it would seem to follow that they cannot be consistent with one another either; and if they are neither inconsistent nor consistent, it would seem to follow that they do not stand in any logical relations at all. Furthermore, since he did not reject holism but actually exploited it in his argument for incommensurability, it would seem that his argument would, if it were successful, directly undermine the Argument from Holism Against Normative Insularity.

Clearly, the only way to rescue the latter argument is by showing that holism is uncontained in the way that I described in Section 2, so as to foreclose any possibility that barriers of normative insularity might be erected between any points of view that are mutually intelligible—including even the points of view of scientists who work in different theoretical paradigms. A comprehensive response to Kuhn along these lines would have to show this in detail, by addressing the many specific cases that he drew from the history and sociology of science. But that is beyond the scope of this book, and I shall merely indicate the general lines that such a response would have to follow.

The first task must obviously be to find points of background agreement that Kuhn overlooked, which scientists share even when they work in different theoretical paradigms, and to explore two questions about them: Are these points of agreement sufficiently numerous and interconnected that they would not be dislodged when scientists who work in different paradigms bring their respective theories to bear? Do these points of agreement serve to put their respective theories into logical relation to one another, in spite of the fact that they employ different theoretical terms and concepts?

Here are three obvious places where we might look for such overlooked points of agreement: first, in the many details that we routinely take for granted that are so familiar and so banal as to hardly be worth mentioning—such as that grass is green, the sky is blue, human beings walk on two feet, many other animals crawl on all fours, snakes slither, birds fly, and so on; second, in the most basic metaphysical distinctions that everyone recognizes—such as the distinctions between living and nonliving things, animate and inanimate living things, minded and mindless things, and so on; third, in the obvious forms of order in nature that are evident without the employment of scientific methods—such as the locatedness of all natural phenomena in some sort of spatiotemporal framework, and the predictable patterns of change through which we track days, months, years, the life cycles of living things, and such. When I say that these obvious forms of order in nature are evident without the employment of scientific methods, I do not mean that they can be evident without the use of inductive reasoning. What I mean is that they need not rest on the systematic employment of inductive methods as we find them employed by scientists together with controlled observation and testing. They are the sorts of regularities of which I took note in Section 2 when I observed that even Hume was prepared to acknowledge that they are ubiquitous in our experience (thereby undergirding his eventual argument for determinism, which he offered in connection with his "compatibilist" account of freedom), even as he also pressed a skeptical point about the possibility that any such regularities that we may have discovered in the past could in principle fail to hold in the future.

It is utterly implausible that scientists who work in different paradigms fail to agree about a preponderance of these matters. One reason is the purpose-driven character of interpretation and psychological attribution to which I drew attention in Section 2. We saw there that for some purposes—such as deciding what drink to order at a restaurant—a research chemist and a scientific illiterate can agree that tap water is better than bottled mineral water, not because they have perfectly concordant conceptions of water but because the differences in their conceptions of water are irrelevant to the purpose at hand. Presumably the same holds for scientists who work in different theoretical paradigms—there are a great many purposes for which their theoretical differences are irrelevant and do not prevent them from agreeing about the matters of natural fact that I listed above, concerning banal details, basic distinctions, and obvious forms of natural order.

But what of specifically scientific purposes? Do they undermine our grounds for seeing these matters of fact as points of agreement among scientists who work within different theoretical paradigms? There is certainly one purpose that does *not*, namely, the purpose of explanation—by which I mean, bringing apparently disparate phenomena together, either as having a common cause, or as sharing the same nature, or as being predictable by the same laws (these are not mutually exclusive, because diverse phenomena may be predictable by the same laws precisely because they have common causes or shared natures). In general, scientists who work in different paradigms have different views about what the terms of our more fundamental explanations should be, where these differences reflect underlying differences in ontological commitment. But if I am right that they agree about a great many banal details, basic distinctions, and obvious forms of natural order, then they shall have to take all of these matters as *common explananda* that *any* scientific theory would have to acknowledge, and it follows that their scientific *differences*—both about what there is, and about what the terms of our more fundamental explanations should be—should be viewed in one of two ways: either they provide explanations of different matters of fact about which they are all in agreement, and are themselves consistent and conjoinable (as in the case of a biological explanation of inheritance, which could be conjoined with a physical explanation of the tides), or they provide different explanations of the same matters of fact, which would constitute a theoretical disagreement (as in the Newtonian and Einsteinian explanations of the movements of astronomical bodies).

I claimed above that we can portray incommensurability in science as involving such disagreements without denying any of Kuhn's other claims about the nature of incommensurability and the epistemological difficulties that follow upon it. In particular, we can accept his claim that there is no theory-neutral basis on which scientists who work in different paradigms could ever persuade one another that one of their theories is "better confirmed" than the others. We can also accept a further claim of his that I have not yet mentioned, which is that scientists who work in different paradigms raise different questions and work on different problems in their "normal" investigations, which is to say, their everyday scientific work. These aspects of normal science led Kuhn to describe scientists who work in different paradigms as working in "different worlds," and it is clear that this description was meant to capture a *kind* of insularity, insofar as scientists who work in different paradigms are not investigating the same things and, moreover, cannot reach each other through rational means—which is why he thought that all significant theoretical change in science must be revolutionary. But the insular character of normal science falls short of the sort of full-blown normative insularity that is required by Multimundialism, because it does not suffice to dislodge the many points of agreement, which I mentioned above, in such a way as to deprive scientists who work within different paradigms of their sense that they have genuine disagreements—disagreements about how a great many agreed-upon matters of fact are best explained.

In order to drive home that most of Kuhn's claims about incommensurability can be accepted while seeing it as involving disagreement, I want to return to the example of irresoluble disagreement that I discussed in Part One, between theists and atheists. Although this is not a scientific case, it does exhibit all of the features Kuhn claimed to find in scientific cases, and it helps to make vivid just why his account of science is so disturbing—because according to him we are epistemically no better off when it comes to finding an adequate rational basis on which to resolve our scientific disagreements than theists and atheists are.

Theists and atheists have a basic ontological disagreement over whether God exists, and this ontological disagreement brings in train further disagreements about what the terms of our most fundamental explanations should be. While theists seek to explain each matter of natural fact by appeal to the idea that it is an effect of the divine will and a reflection of the divine nature, atheists seek only to discover various forms of purposeless predictability that might enable us to control natural facts for our own human ends, whether cognitive ends of inquiry or practical ends. There is a sense in which these are perfectly *ordinary* disagreements, as opposed to the sorts *non*ordinary disagreements that advocates of the Disagreement Intuition allege would give rise to relativism—for theists and atheists agree that they cannot both be right. Yet there is a sense in which their disagreements are not altogether ordinary, because they exhibit all of the aspects of incommensurability for which Kuhn argued, which I shall now review.

First, there is no theory-neutral basis on which to settle the matters in dispute among theists and atheists. As a result, any movement from one side to the other in those disputes is bound to involve a revolution in something like Kuhn's sense. In fact, we are quite accustomed to viewing their epistemic situation in exactly this way. There are some minor differences: We tend to conceive revolutionary changes of mind between theism and atheism as taking place within individual lives rather than within institutions, and not everyone regards them as epistemically troubling—in fact, many theists simply accept them as unavoidable, labeling them as "conversions" or "losses of faith," depending on whether their direction is toward or away from God. But these minor differences should not obscure the ways in which this religious case is analogous to the scientific cases that Kuhn discussed, at least as he understood them, and serves as a good model on which to understand the sort of incommensurability for which he argued.

In addition to the revolutionary character of any movement in either direction between theism and atheism, theists and atheists typically engage in very different forms of "normal" investigative activities, in which they raise wholly different questions and focus on wholly different problems—for example, whereas theists might explore the relation of creatures to their creator and attempt to solve the problem of evil, atheists might study the origins of the universe and the phenomenon of life as issues of physical theory.

Finally, there is a strong, albeit mildly misleading, appearance that the theoretical disagreements of theists and atheists prevent them from ever thinking or talking about the same things, just as Kuhn claimed of scientists who work in different theoretical paradigms—and moreover, that this is so even with respect to all of the matters on which I have insisted that scientists by and large agree, concerning banal details, basic distinctions, and the more obvious forms of order in nature. It might fairly be said that when the theist perceives such banal details as that grass is green and the sky is blue, she perceives goods created by God for the benefit of humankind and other creatures, whileatheists (many of them, anyway) would perceive things that have no particular value except insofar as human beings attach value to them; similarly, when the theist recognizes the basic metaphysical distinctions between the living and the nonliving or the minded and the mindless, she sees things that belong to a hierarchy defined in terms of closeness to or distance from the divine nature, while the atheist sees various kinds of organization and complexity; and finally, when the theist apprehends the various forms of order in nature, she sees the effects of intelligent design and divine purpose, while the atheist sees agentless happenings.

This last aspect of Kuhn's account of incommensurability is what invites us to think of it as involving normative insularity—the way in which holism invites us to see the various differences of meaning and belief that owe to our theoretical differences as being reflected throughout our *entire* body of beliefs, thereby putting into doubt whether we share *any* meanings and beliefs at all. However, we need to ask: *What would be the normative point* of supposing that theists and atheists do not share meanings and beliefs with respect to banal details, basic metaphysical distinctions, and the more obvious forms of order in nature? *If the point were to register the presence of normative insularity,* then we should have to suppose that the theist and the atheist are normatively disengaged with respect to all of these matters—that they can neither agree nor disagree about them, and that they have nothing to learn from or teach one another with respect to them. But this would go squarely against their own sense of their normative and epistemic situation. They do *not* view their theoretical disagreements concerning the existence of God and the terms of fundamental explanation as dislodging the many points of agreement between them about whether grass is green and so forth, or as depriving them from occasions on which to occasionally disagree about these matters too—about, for instance, whether a given variety of grass from Kentucky really is green or whether it deserves its name "bluegrass." Accordingly, it makes sense to view them as having disagreements at the more highly theoretical level as well, concerning how best to explain all of the many things about which they really do agree, and occasionally disagree. Given that they can and do disagree in all these ways at all levels, it does not make sense to suppose that they are separated by any barriers of normative insularity—and yet it does make sense to regard their theories as incommensurable, since we have just seen that there is no theory-neutral basis on which they could resolve their disagreements.

My claim, then, is that this is exactly how Kuhn was asking us to view scientists who work in different theoretical paradigms: They have highly theoretical disagreements that they cannot see any way to resolve, and these seemingly irresoluble disagreements generate entirely independent "normal" investigative activities; but these disagreements and disparate investigations run in tandem with a great many other points of agreement, where these agreements allow them to see their respective different theoretical commitments as issuing in genuine disagreements. It follows that incommensurable scientific theories are *not* normatively insulated from one another, and that the scientists who hold them do *not* inhabit "different worlds" in the literal sense that Multimundialism would imply.

My account of how the Argument from Holism Against Normative Insularity may stand, even in the face of Kuhn's arguments for incommensurability in science, requires us to re-understand Quine's metaphor of the web of belief. On Quine's understanding, our system of beliefs is an interconnected whole in which every belief is answerable to experience and potentially revisable in response to it. Yet according to him there is within this whole an important distinction between what lies on the periphery and what lies at the center—though it is not a sharp distinction but a matter of degree. He characterized this distinction in two different ways, which he saw as going together. On one characterization, the beliefs that lie at the periphery are more observational, whereas the beliefs that lie at the center are more theoretical. On the other characterization, the beliefs that lie at the periphery are less holistically embedded, and so they can more easily be revised without disturbing the rest of the web, whereas the beliefs that lie at the center are more holistically embedded, and so they cannot easily be revised without making extensive revisions throughout the rest of the web. But my account of how the thesis of uncontained holism can be reconciled with Kuhnian incommensurability brings out that these two distinctions do not line up in the way that Quine thought. If we suppose that what lies at the center of the web are beliefs that are less easily revised, then the center is not constituted by our most highly theoretical beliefs; it is constituted instead by a weighty and interconnected mass of agreed-upon matters of natural fact that scientists continue to agree upon even as they offer up different theories about what else may exist aside from what is explicitly recognized in this mass. Correlatively, if we suppose that what lies on the periphery of the web are beliefs that are more easily revised, then the periphery is not constituted by beliefs that are somehow closer to the "tribunal of experience" as Quine had said; on the contrary, when the periphery is conceived as constituted by the more easily revised of our beliefs, it will be constituted by our more highly theoretical beliefs. This is not to say that scientists who work within any given scientific paradigm generally find it easy to revise or give up their theories. That may be extremely difficult for all sorts of reasons, including the ones that led Kuhn to suggest that the major changes in science generally require nothing less than revolution. But the point is that such scientific revolutions are *possible* nevertheless, whereas what is not possible is that scientists should overthrow the large mass of detailed and interconnected beliefs that I have argued they all share in common, concerning banal details, basic distinctions, and the more obvious forms of order in nature.

Neurath gave us the image of a boat that must remain afloat as we repair and rebuild it, in order to help us understand why, on a holistic picture, not everything can be revised all at once. There is no ready image for the web of belief as I am proposing to re-understand it. It seems not to float, but to be grounded by a central mass that is large and densely interconnected, though also patterned. Scientists work up from the edges of this mass in order to gain a perch from which they can try to gain a vantage point on the whole, from which they can focus on patterns and relationships that might afford new ways to predict and influence nature, and also new scientific questions and problems for them to tackle in their "normal" scientific investigations, which would be carried out some way up their perch. From the vantage points of their own perches, scientists may find it difficult to see what is visible from other perches, or the value of the normal scientific investigations that others pursue from their perches. Yet they can see that they are all perches overlooking a common ground. Furthermore, insofar as they recognize one another as scientists, they can also see that they all share a broad purpose with respect to their common ground, namely, to provide explanations—that is, to find unity in disparate phenomena by portraying them as exhibiting common natures, or as arising from common causes, or as instantiating the same laws, or as holding a common significance in some other similar way. Yet however successful their respective theoretical efforts might be when considered on their own, and however opposed they might be to one another, they could never be led by their efforts to throw over the mass of shared agreements concerning matters of fact that they all regard as among the things to be explained by any science. This grounded mass is too extensive and too detailed and too interconnected to be disturbed by any given revision of our beliefs; and this is so even though it may take on a different overall significance when viewed from the perspective of one theoretical perch or another. In contrast, our theoretical aspirations tend by their very nature to be revisionist, and this goes together with my point that they are naturally located at the periphery of our web of beliefs, where there is more potential for revisions that leave the whole intact as the whole it is.

I can foresee two objections to my re-understanding of Quine's metaphor, each of which contains a mild misunderstanding that needs clearing up.

One is that I am just wrong about the character of many of our ordinary, everyday beliefs and Quine was right—they are more easily revised because they are more observational, or equivalently, less theoretical. Take, for example, our belief that the sky is blue. It is easy to imagine looking up and finding that the sky *looks* a different color—say, yellow—and to revise our belief that the sky is blue accordingly. Furthermore, insofar as there would be a significant cost in revising that belief, which would make it difficult to revise, that cost would surely include our having to revise those of our current scientific beliefs that aim to explain why the sky looks blue to human perceivers—such as our beliefs about the composition of the atmosphere, the behavior of light, and the nature of human color perception. So why should we not conclude, with Quine, that what makes a belief easier to revise is its being more observational, whereas what makes it harder to revise is its being more holistically embedded among our theoretical beliefs? I give the same answer as before: because he overlooked the way in which our ordinary, everyday beliefs are *already* holistically interrelated in myriad ways, even before we try to offer scientific explanations of why they are true. Consider, for example, how our belief that the sky is blue is related to our beliefs about the following matters: the different colors that the sky shows at different times and places (the night sky, the day sky, the auroral sky, the crepuscular sky, the sunny sky, the stormy sky, the tornado sky, the snowy sky, the Arctic sky, the Mediterranean sky, the desert sky, the English sky); what else is visible in the sky at different times and places aside from its color (the sun, moon, stars, planets, clouds); how what is visible in the sky at different times relates to other conditions (warmth, precipitation, the seasons, geographical location); how many of these differences relate to further, interlocking regularities in nature through which we perceive the passage of time (the phases of the moon, the relative lengths of days and nights at different times of the year); which other things besides the sky looks blue and in what conditions. Scientists are not at liberty to set aside beliefs such as these when they seek to explain why the sky is blue, and yet keeping them in place leaves them free to entertain new, and perhaps (if Kuhn was right) revolutionary, scientific ideas about the nature of light and human perception, whose point must be, in part, to explain why the sky looks blue to us in the conditions that it does.

The second objection that I anticipate to my re-understanding of Quine's metaphor is that it improperly elevates our ordinary, everyday beliefs as having a special epistemic standing, as the first and final court of appeal in any inquiry that aims to go beyond them, whether it be scientific or philosophical inquiry. Not everyone would find this objectionable, especially those who see philosophy as beholden to *common sense*. Nevertheless, it seems to me that too much of the wrong kind of philosophical complacency about common sense *is* objectionable, and so I want to make three quick points in response. First, I want to admit that I am positing a *mass* of shared, detailed agreement that science and philosophy cannot dislodge *en mass*. Second, scientists and philosophers are nevertheless always free to provide new theoretical angles from which to jettison certain *elements* of the mass, and also to alter our overall sense of its larger significance when viewed from the perspective of one or another theoretical paradigm. Third, the presence of this massive agreement does not rule out Kuhn's claim that the justification of theoretical paradigms is always internal to them. These three points help to bring out that theories may go *beyond* our ordinary, everyday beliefs even as they do not call very many of those beliefs directly into question, and insofar as this is so, there is no very special justificatory role for our ordinary, everyday beliefs to play in either scientific or philosophical inquiry. So the effect of my proposed way of re-understanding Quine's metaphor is *not* to elevate the epistemic role of ordinary, everyday beliefs; its effect is to clarify that scientific theories are appropriately viewed as being located on the periphery of a web of beliefs that is otherwise holistic in just the ways for which Quine himself, and Davidson later, argued, and to clarify as well why the natural world is appropriately viewed as *one* even if scientific theories are incommensurable in the ways for which Kuhn argued.

I turn, finally, to my tertiary aim in this section, which is to explore various reasons why, quite apart from the Argument from Holism Against Normative Insularity, Unimundialism seems basic to any outlook that deserves to be labeled as scientific.

I have suggested that it is a common aim of scientists who work in different theoretical paradigms to provide *explanations* of the many matters of natural fact on which they all (mostly and roughly) agree. The point of any explanation is to find unity in diversity—that is, to bring out some way in which apparently disparate phenomena are alike, whether it be by sharing the same nature, having a common cause, falling under the same laws, and so on. Insofar as this is what we value in explanation, then the more comprehensive an explanation is—that is, the broader the range of disparate phenomena that it brings under the same terms of explanation—the more it is to be valued; and the most valuable of all would be a *maximally comprehensive explanation* that subsumes all of the disparate phenomena that are studied in the special sciences within one basic science. (When I referred above to disagreements in science about what the terms of our "fundamental" explanations should be, I was referring to the terms that would figure in such maximally comprehensive explanations offered up by a basic science.) Obviously, if we ever do manage to achieve the goal of maximal comprehensiveness of explanation, we will have at our disposal a powerful account of the *oneness* of nature.

It is a matter of some debate whether the special sciences ought to be constrained by the goal of arriving at maximally comprehensive explanations, or whether they ought to proceed autonomously without regard for how their special explanations might relate to the explanatory terms of a more basic science. On the side of autonomy is the following thought: When the special sciences are primarily concerned with how they relate to more basic sciences, they may overlook interesting theoretical possibilities that would come to light only by focusing more directly on the phenomena with which they are directly concerned. Yet if it does seem sensible to conduct many special scientific investigations without regard for the goal of achieving a unified science, it is also hard to see how any recognizably scientific form of inquiry could be completely indifferent to it if what I said above is true, that what we value in *any* scientific explanation is present in greater degree in more comprehensive explanations—for it would seem to follow that the more comprehensive explanations are, the more value they have.[19] Given this value, even practitioners of the special sciences ought to remain alert to the possibilities—such as they are—of finding ever more unified explanations. But this would be hard, if not impossible, to do, unless they proceeded on the *assumption* that all of the deliverances of the special sciences can be embraced together when true, so that after having embraced them together they might find whatever further connections there are beyond mere consistency.

---

19. Chomsky (2009) made a plea for such methodological autonomy, at the same time conceding the value of unification in science if and when it can be achieved.

To adopt the Unimundial stance in this spirit of open-mindedness about finding unified explanations may seem dangerously like begging the question against Multimundialism. Indeed, we may be reminded here of the point I made in my introductory to this chapter, that it is in any case very easy to beg the question against Multimundialism in the domain of science. All we need to do is adopt the discursivist conception of a scientific theory on which a theory is just a string of sentences, for if that is what the deliverances of the special sciences must always be—a string of sentences—it is hard to see what could ever stand in the way of embracing them together, no matter how resistant they may be to unified explanation. I hope it is clear by now that the specific reason I have just given to prefer Unimundialism over Multimundialism in science goes well beyond this question-begging attitude, insofar as it invokes a fundamental scientific *value* that we could not pursue without adopting the Unimundial stance.

Some self-described "pluralists" among philosophers of science maintain that this value is overestimated.[20] If what they mean is that science can meaningfully proceed by aiming for something less than a fully unified theory of the world, they are certainly right. But if what they mean is that there would be no value in achieving a unified theory of the world, this simply defies credibility. So long as we allow that achieving a unified theory would be something of value, and so long as we do not have absolutely compelling reasons to suppose that it could not ever be achieved, we have reason to embrace the Unimundial stance in science. To be sure, this reason falls short of a direct *metaphysical* argument to show that the world is one—in contrast to the Argument from Holism Against Normative Insularity. But my aim at this point in the dialectic is much less ambitious. At this point, I am merely exploring ways in which the Unimundial stance seems to be fundamental to the scientific outlook, and the value of unity in science seems to be one such way.

Many philosophers, especially self-described "scientific realists," are impressed by the apparent progress that physics has already afforded

---

20. Two important discussions of pluralism and disunity in science are Scheffler 2000 and Dupre 1995.

toward greater comprehensiveness of explanation—first when Newton offered a unified account of the motions of heavenly and terrestrial bodies, and then later when atomic physics afforded a physical account of chemical change. This picture of scientific progress is the very one that Kuhn challenged—it is a picture in which later theories share meanings with earlier theories so as to afford the forms of epistemic engagement that are characteristic of the Unimundial stance, where through such engagement, later theories build on what was correct in earlier theories while jettisoning the rest, and then adding new posits and claims. I said earlier that I would leave it to others to evaluate Kuhn's historical claims; I shall also leave it to others to evaluate the parallel claims of contemporary pluralists about the current disunity of science.

I turn next to another seemingly fundamental commitment of the scientific outlook, namely, the commitment to employing *empirical* methods of justification. Although empiricism has historically had a close association with varieties of idealism (spanning from Berkeleyan idealism through instrumentalism in twentieth-century philosophy of science), the scientific commitment to employing empirical methods generally derives from a realist attitude, because these methods are designed to let *the world itself* tell us which of our scientific beliefs are true and which are false. Yet I have emphasized throughout that there is no direct conceptual connection between realism and Unimundialism, and I will be considering that relationship (or lack thereof) in more detail in Section 4. In the remainder of this one, I want to consider a much more specific matter, which concerns Feyerabend's reevaluation of the scientific commitment to empiricism in the light of Kuhn's challenge to the picture of scientific progress that I just mentioned above. We shall see that Feyerabend's methodological recommendations in response to Kuhn's work are implicitly antirelativist in spirit, because they require scientists to adopt the Unimundial stance even when they come across theories that are incommensurable in Kuhn's sense.

Feyerabend conceded that if there had been a theory-neutral empirical basis for our scientific beliefs, then we would be justified in viewing our earlier theories as well justified, and in using them as a measure of what else is and can be true—so that later theories must accept them and build upon them unless they find a theory-neutral empirical basis for rejecting them. But he also insisted that if we are persuaded by Kuhn that observation is theory-laden and, more generally, that all notions of scientific justification are theory-laden, then to proceed in this way amounts to *dogmatism*. Dogmatism is extremely problematic in his view, for the following reason: If other theories besides our own happened to be true, a dogmatic allegiance to our current theories would prevent us from ever finding that out, and at the same time it would also prevent us from identifying and correcting mistakes within our current theories. This problem appears to have the same form as a skeptical problem, for it raises a possibility of error on grounds that are so general that it is unclear how we could ever lay the possibility to rest, thereby leaving us with two highly unattractive options: either we can dogmatically retain our beliefs while risking error, or we can retreat to a state of doubt from which there may be no rational exit.

Some philosophers and scientists find Feyerabend's suggestion that scientific methods are by nature dogmatic quite unacceptable. One reason is that he extended his point about dogmatism *within* science to dogmatism *about* science itself and, in doing so, he called into question whether the rise of science had been a form of progress to begin with—after all, if there is no theory-neutral notion of justification, then scientific methods have no special epistemic standing in relation to nonscientific ones. But I think the deeper reason many philosophers and scientists find Feyerabend's charge of dogmatism so unacceptable is that he linked it with a difficulty for the scientific aim of devising empirical methods through which the world itself might directly tell us which of our beliefs are true and which false—the difficulty being that scientific confirmation is always internal and theory-laden, as Kuhn had argued.

The most intriguing aspect of Feyerabend's early response to Kuhn is that he did not actually retreat to the sort of skepticism I briefly adverted to above. Instead he earnestly tried to explore whether any scope remains for something like an empiricist aspiration in the wake of Kuhn's arguments—an aspiration to let the world tell us which of our theories is true and which false, so that we might arrive at nondogmatic reasons. Like Quine, he did not completely give up on the idea that theories have empirical content, even though he also accepted Quine's confirmation holism according to which the unit of empirical confirmation must be a *whole theory*. He then proposed a two-part solution to the problem of dogmatism. First, he proposed *methodological pluralism*—a proliferation of theories that he claimed would simultaneously increase empirical content as well as increase the range of methods and standards that we might bring to bear in our inquiries. But such a proliferation of theories cannot help us to identify and correct errors unless we have a decision procedure by which to choose among them. For this purpose, Feyerabend introduced a second innovation, namely, his idea of a *decisive experiment,* which would be expressly designed to pit one whole theoretical outlook against another. If I understand his idea correctly, advocates of incommensurable theories might bring to bear very different descriptions of the same experimental setup, which reflect their disparate ontological and methodological commitments, and yet they might still agree that if the experiment goes one way it will confirm one of their theories and if it goes the other way it will confirm the other.

If we assume for the sake of argument that Kuhn and Feyerabend were right about incommensurability in science, then decisive experiments along these lines seem to present our best, and perhaps our only, hope for finding nondogmatic grounds on which to choose among rival theories. Yet it is unclear how realistic the prospects are for designing such experiments, as it would take a great deal of imagination to transcend our various theoretical viewpoints in the ways that they would require. It might be wondered whether the mass of shared agreements for which I have argued could possibly help on this score. I have argued that it suffices to put incommensurable theories into a minimal sort of logical relation, by supplying a common fund of potential explananda to which they are all answerable in spite of their disparate ontological and methodological commitments, thereby enabling us to see them as being in logical conflict with one another in spite of failing to share any meanings. Perhaps this common fund of explananda would help advocates of incommensurable theories to find a common level of description for a decisive experiment on which they could agree in spite of their theoretical differences. But the real challenge for designing such experiments lies in finding a way to relate that common level of description to both of their theories at once, so as to expose a point of *direct logical conflict* between them *in spite of their failure to share meanings* at the theoretical level, in the form of conflicting predictions about the outcome of the experiment. Inevitably, success along these lines would provide for some common meanings after all, and indeed, this is a good way of seeing the strategy behind Feyerabend's idea of a decisive experiment—it aims to *supply* points of direct logical conflict between incommensurable theories that, on their face, appear not to share any theoretical concepts.

In whatever ways Feyerabend was truly radical, his response to the problem of dogmatism shows that he did not take on the distinctive and controversial metaphysical commitment of the Multimundialist, but was implicitly committed to Unimundialism. Unimundialists hold that the only obstacle that there can be to embracing truth-value-bearers together is that they logically conflict with one another and therefore cannot be equally true, and Feyerabend agreed—indeed, this was already evident in his initial characterization of Kuhnian incommensurability as involving conflict. He did officially endorse Kuhn's claim that incommensurable theories do not share meanings, which prima facie might seem to preclude their standing in any logical relations, including conflict (that is why there is an impression that Kuhnian incommensurability involves normative insularity), and Feyerabend owed us an account of how these two aspects of his view are to be reconciled. To my knowledge, he did not really offer one. He certainly did not appeal to the thesis of uncontained holism as I have done, in order to show that there is a mass of shared agreements that is held in common by advocates of incommensurable theories, in the light of which their theories can be seen to be in indirect conflict even though they do not, strictly speaking, share meanings of their theoretical terms.[21] What he did insist upon is that the project of identifying and

---

21. Feyerabend did come close to recognizing this common fund of agreement, when he considered whether different theories might be viewed as preserving the same inductive regularities even as they describe them with different terms. He pointed out that if we were to view them in this

correcting errors in our own theories requires us to proliferate other theories that might expose such errors,[22] and my point is that this procedure would not make any sense unless we presumed that all of these proliferated theories do stand in logical relations, in spite of their failures to share meanings—so even if these logical relations are not immediately self-evident, his thought seems to have been that they can emerge for us with the help of our ingenuity as we attempt to devise decisive experiments.

We can now see that the Unimundial stance is fundamental to the scientific outlook on at least two counts: First, insofar as it is a fundamental aim of science to offer systematic explanations, and to pursue the possibility of arriving at maximally comprehensive explanations, scientific investigations must proceed on the assumption that logical relations really do run everywhere in the domain of natural facts open to such investigation, even if they are not yet all self-evident in the way that they would be if we already possessed explanatory frameworks that made them perspicuous. Second, if some variety of empiricism is fundamental to the scientific endeavor, which would seek to find ways in which the world itself might correct our errors, and if the unit of empirical confirmation is—as Quine, Kuhn, and Feyerabend all held—a whole theory, then we must find ways to pit whole theories against one another through decisive experiments as Feyerabend recommended, and the very effort to design such experiments presupposes that there are points of direct logical contact among all competing theories waiting to be discovered, even

_____

way, then we would have to view them as preserving the same inductive regularities that are also preserved by nonscientific systems of belief as well. He made this claim, not in order to emphasize the presence of a shared mass of detailed agreement across all theoretical paradigms, but instead to undermine any residual impression that science holds a special epistemic status that myth and other traditional systems of belief do not. All the same, the claim does carry an *implicit* acknowledgment of such agreement—which is to say, an implicit acknowledgment of the grounds that holism provides for regarding the world as one.

22. Here we see a striking similarity between Feyerabend and Mill, on the epistemic value of disagreement.

in cases where they are not yet evident because the theories are in-commensurable and hence fail to share meanings at the theoretical level.

It might be asked, What if these characteristic aims of science—to discover ever more comprehensive explanations, and to devise decisive experiments on the basis of which we might choose among competing theories—were to fail? Would this show that there is room after all for positing normative insularity in the domain of natural facts open to scientific investigation? I think the answer to this question must be *no*, because the Argument from Holism Against Normative Insularity would still stand as a substantive, albeit nonscientific, reason to embrace Unimundialism.

## 4. Does Realism Afford Reasons to Take a Stand on Multimundialism versus Unimundialism?

I will conclude this chapter by turning to realism, defined as the commitment—painting here with a very broad and rudimentary brush—to the mind-independence of reality. How does such a doctrine speak to the logical issue that divides Unimundialists and Multimun-dialists, concerning whether logical relations run everywhere among all truth-value-bearers? I have already said many times that it does not speak with any direct relevance to that issue. So it might be wondered why the topic of realism merits any discussion at all in the context of my project in this chapter, of finding substantive reasons to take a stand on Unimundialism versus Multimundialism specifically in the domain of natural facts open to scientific investigation. There are three reasons why it does.

First, the perspective of realism exposes a limitation on Davidson's anti-conceptual-schemes argument, and on the development of it that I have offered earlier in the chapter. The fact is that these arguments do not establish that alternative conceptual schemes are conceptually impossible, but only that if they existed, they would be unknowable by us. So even if we shall never have occasion to adopt the Multimundial stance in the course of scientific investigation, the question remains open whether there are reasons to allow nonetheless that there might be many worlds rather than one.

Second, realism is often taken to bring skepticism in train, and there is a strong impression that the latter issue is somehow linked to the issue of relativism. This was clearly Davidson's view, who claimed that there is a common philosophical mistake underlying both issues, which is that any effort to articulate them must invoke a version of the so-called "scheme-content" distinction, or to put it differently, they require us to portray the mind-world relation as *mediated* by a conceptual scheme rather than as *unmediated* in the way he affirmed with his closing words of "On the Very Idea of a Conceptual Scheme":

> In giving up the dualism of scheme and world, we do not give up the world, but reestablish unmediated touch with the familiar objects whose antics make our sentences and opinions true or false.

We need to make clear and explicit that when the doctrine of relativism is formulated as Multimundialism, it need *not* embroil us in any version of the scheme–content distinction. We can accept that we have unmediated epistemic touch with reality, and that this undermines skepticism for the reasons Davidson gave, without thereby settling the question whether realism might provide room for the possibility of alternatives—though, as I just admitted on the purely epistemic front, the Argument from Holism Against Normative Insularity entails that they would have to be alternatives-unknowable-by-us.

Third, the mere fact that alternatives-unknowable-by-us are *conceivable* does not count as a good—that is, substantive—reason for taking their possibility seriously, and when we are concerned with the domain of natural facts, there seems to be nowhere else to look for such substantive reasons than science itself. In the light of my claims in Section 3 about the respects in which the Unimundial stance is basic to the scientific outlook, it might seem that the outcome of any investigation into potential scientific grounds for Multimundialism is bound to be negative. However, it is arguable that a commitment to realism is equally basic to that outlook, and insofar as our current best theories are governed by that commitment, they could in principle provide substantive reasons for taking the possibility of alternatives-unknowable-by-us seriously, in the sense of advancing it from one of bare conceptual possibility to the status of genuine *metaphysical* possibility. I shall argue that this is true of some of our best current theories in cognitive science.

Davidson regarded his argument in "On the Very Idea of a Conceptual Scheme" as ruling out the possibility of alternative conceptual schemes altogether, including the bare conceptual possibility of alternative-unknowable-by-us. He made this clear in the leg of the argument that was directed against the possibility of schemes that are *partially* untranslatable, a possibility that he saw as opening the door to a potential argument for the possibility of schemes that are *wholly* untranslatable as well—where these wholly untranslatable schemes would, of course, be unknowable by us. The link between these two possibilities is provided by the following oft-raised thought experiment: Imagine a spectrum of subjects on which all near subjects by and large agree, with only some minor divergences in concepts and beliefs that make their respective languages partially untranslatable; and then imagine that these divergences accumulate as we move along the spectrum, so that subjects who occupy sufficiently distant points do not share any concepts or beliefs at all, with the result that their respective languages are wholly untranslatable.

Davidson responded to this thought experiment by asking why we should suppose that those who would occupy very distant points on this imagined spectrum from ours speak a language, or are minded, at all. The obvious limitation of his response is that it seems to make *us* the measure of *all* minds, thereby forsaking the realist attitude when it applies to minds. Yet this limitation should not distract us from a parallel limitation of the spectrum argument itself. All it manages to do is to raise a conceptual possibility of alternatives-unknowable-by-us, against which Davidson could set another conceptual possibility that goes together with Unimundialism, namely, the possibility of a *View from Everywhere on the spectrum*—that is, a point of view from which every truth that could be known at any point on the spectrum could be recognized and embraced together. Nothing in the spectrum argument itself directly establishes that such a View from Everywhere on the spectrum is impossible. In fact, the argument does not even rule out the possibility that it might actually lie within human capability to attain that larger view, by working our way *through* the spectrum. For consider: By hypothesis, near neighbors on the spectrum by and large agree with us, except for a few concepts that we do not share and cannot translate into our language as it now stands; given the holistic constraints on intelligibility, we cannot find that our near neighbors possess such divergent concepts unless those concepts are supported by surrounding beliefs that we find intelligible; those same holistic constraints invite us to adopt the Unimundial stance toward our near neighbors; from the perspective of that stance we can face only two options with respect to the concepts of theirs that we do not share and cannot translate into our language as it stands—either we can adopt them ourselves and expand our set of beliefs and language accordingly, or we can reject them as false; if these are the only options available at any point on the spectrum, then there are only two ways in which untranslatable differences can accumulate along the spectrum—either they will compound mistakes, or they will add new concepts and beliefs and related forms of linguistic expression; in the first case, a large number of accumulated differences would lead to nonsense (something like insanity), while in the second they would lead to an expanded point of view; in neither case would they issue in wholly untranslatable languages—in alternatives-unknowable-by-us.

Admittedly, the latter way of responding to the thought experiment begs the question in favor of Unimundialism, but so does the original Multimundial interpretation that takes it to illustrate the possibility of alternatives-unknowable-by-us. This is symptomatic of the general methodological predicament that I had identified at the end of Chapter 2: since each position is internally coherent, neither can reasonably expect to refute the other in terms that the other would regard as non-question-begging. The spectrum argument simply provides a fresh angle on this methodological predicament, by bringing out the fact that from the perspective of each position, the spectrum appears to raise a different conceptual possibility. I continue to see no other way to proceed than in the way I have already suggested: we must seek further *substantive* reasons for taking one or the other of these conceptual possibilities more seriously than the other.

However, this is not how Davidson himself viewed the situation. He seemed to think that his account of meaning and belief really did suffice to rule out the conceptual possibility of alternative conceptual schemes, along with the skeptical possibility that our beliefs could be massively mistaken. One of his arguments against skepticism implicitly introduces the idea of a View from Everywhere, through the idea of an omniscient interpreter who by hypothesis knows all of the truths.[23] The contention of the argument is that even such an omniscient interpreter would be bound by holistic constraints, and so she could not identify our concepts and beliefs without finding that we by and large agree with her—in which case, our beliefs are by and large true. Perhaps a determined and resourceful skeptic could find ways to resist this conclusion—possibly by arguing that *we* are obviously *not* omniscient, and so it is not legitimate to assume that an omniscient being would be bound to use the very same methods of interpretation that we use. But what matters more for my purposes is this: suppose that we were prepared to concede for the sake of argument that merely raising the conceptual possibility of an omniscient interpreter, in the way that Davidson did, does provide us with a good reason to dismiss the skeptical possibility that our beliefs might be massively mistaken; this would still leave the debate over Unimundialism versus Multimundialism unresolved because, as I have just said, we would need to establish more before we conclude in favor of Unimundialism than that a View from Everywhere is conceptually possible—we would need to find more substantive reasons for taking that possibility seriously.

The aspect of Davidson's work that speaks most powerfully against skepticism is not holism, but rather his account of the mind–world relation as *unmediated*. So let me now explain why this is so, and then clarify why it does not suffice to rule out Multimundialism.

---

23. See his "The Method of Truth in Metaphysics," reprinted in Davidson 1984.

One good route into this aspect of his work is his "triangulation argument," whose primary aim was to establish that we cannot possess self-knowledge unless we are in communication with others.[24] I have argued elsewhere that this argument affords a transcendental strategy against skepticism, of roughly the same sort that Strawson claimed to find in Kant and that Stroud later criticized as an argument that is bound to fail.[25] Transcendental arguments of this sort begin by noting that the starting point for skepticism is the self-attribution of mental states that purport to put us in epistemic touch with something beyond them, and then they go on to argue that we cannot make sense of this starting point without supposing the very thing that the skeptic denies—which is that such states *do* put us in epistemic touch with something beyond them. Kant argued in particular that the skeptic must take for granted that our mental states are ordered in time, and that we cannot make sense of this without supposing that they put us in touch with objects in space. Davidson argued *en suite* along the following lines: The skeptic must take for granted that we are able to individuate the *contents* of our beliefs (where this involves conceiving what would be the case if they *were* true and therefore conceiving what *did* put us in epistemic touch with something beyond them); but we cannot do this individuating work without "triangulating" with others who share the very same beliefs that we do; in this process of triangulation we and they must conceive one another as being in direct epistemic touch with the very same things. The middle step is of course the controversial one, and here is the best I can do to try to make it plausible: when we self-ascribe beliefs with definite contents, we must take it for granted that they have some cause or other; if our beliefs *did* put us in epistemic touch with something beyond them, there would be a coincidence between their contents and their causes (this is something that not even Descartes denied in his most extreme states of hyperbolical doubt); but beliefs are always preceded by very long causal chains, and the question arises why a given element, as opposed to any other, is somehow tied to the belief's

---

24. See "The Second Person," reprinted in Davidson 2001.
25. See Rovane 2010; Strawson 1959; Stroud 1968.

content—so that we are able to think, if *that* is what caused my belief, then it is *true;* Davidson claimed that the only basis on which we can answer this question (about which element in the causal chain is the right one) is by appealing to a social condition in which two (or more) subjects possess beliefs whose antecedent causal chains intersect, and they are able to see that this is so—thereby enabling them to view one another as responding to a *common* cause, and therefore as having the *same* belief (that is, beliefs with the same content). The most graphic and compelling illustrations of such triangulation involve perception. Take, for example, my current vision-based perceptual belief that there is now a puppy sleeping at my feet. This belief has many causes, including not only the sleeping puppy itself, but the causal origins of the puppy, the light waves traveling from the puppy to my eyes, the retinal image that those light waves produce, and so on. If I am in a position to self-ascribe the belief that a puppy is sleeping at my feet, it is because I can see that I and the other members of my family are all responsive to this common cause, in such a way that it makes sense to suppose that we all believe there is a sleeping puppy at my feet. However, the point is not supposed to be confined to situations of joint attention in which I and others arrive at the same perceptual beliefs. It is supposed to apply generally to all beliefs.[26]

---

26. If the triangulation argument is sound, then Davidson managed to complete a line of thought about the social conditions of self-consciousness that began with Rousseau, and that continued with Hegel, Freud, Mead, and Wittgenstein (among others). The first four on this list did not aim to establish an antiskeptical result, but took for granted that we are in epistemic touch with an external world and then offered an account of what would turn our cognitive focus inward onto ourselves rather than outward onto that world. Their common thought was that self-consciousness is a social achievement to which we are driven by a need to cope with strategic social relations in which others exploit their knowledge of our thoughts for ends of their own that we do not share—so if we want to effectively pursue our ends, or at least resist being exploited for theirs, then we must come to know what others know about us. Wittgenstein's anti-private-language argument was more directly antiskeptical in its ambition. He raised a problem about how we can ever identify what rule we are applying in

If Davidson's triangulation argument were to succeed, that would clarify and vindicate his closing remark in "On the Very Idea of a Conceptual Scheme" about the directness of our epistemic touch with objects, for when we individuate our thoughts via triangulation with others, we must conceive them as they do, as arising with shared responses to intersubjectively available objects, and so there is no question of failing to be in direct epistemic touch with them. Furthermore, he would have offered a much more satisfying form of resistance to skepticism than the one to be found in Kant, because the triangulation argument does not require us to forsake the realist's conception of reality as mind-independent, in the way that Kant expressly did when he introduced the doctrine of transcendental idealism. That doctrine really does make *us* the measure of *things,* insofar as the latter are to be defined in terms of their knowability by us, given the particular forms of our sensibility and understanding. Although I complained above that Davidson appeared to be making a similar move in his response to the spectrum argument—by making intelligibility to us the measure of all mindedness—he did not make any such move in the triangulation argument. If this latter argument succeeds in closing a threatened gap between our beliefs and what makes them true, it does not do so by portraying reality as in any way mind-dependent, but does so rather by portraying minds as reality-dependent, for the argument's central claim is that in order to be minded, one must occupy a common world with others, in which one's own and others' points of view exhibit mutually intelligible responses to that world. One final note about this antiskeptical result: If the argument for it

---

thought, which he proposed to solve by situating our efforts to apply rules in social practices against which it can become clear what rule we are applying, and also what counts as a mistaken application of a rule. Davidson's account of triangulation can be viewed as supplying a companion solution to this problem. Rather than invoke the idea of a social practice, he argued that the very idea of intentionality involves the idea of a subjective relation to an objective order, which we cannot conceive except by appealing to the idea of another subject's relation to that order, from which our own relation to it can be apprehended.

goes through, it supplies an additional support for a charitable approach to interpretation, over and above the holistic considerations that I have discussed at length throughout this chapter, because its overall thrust is that the route to *self*-knowledge—which requires self-attribution of thoughts—runs via social knowledge of what others know about oneself, and just as this precludes any substantial misalignment between beliefs and the causes that fix their contents, it also precludes any substantial misalignment between our beliefs and those of others.

How are these interesting proceedings and results to be related to the overarching topic of this chapter? Even if the triangulation argument fully succeeds on its own terms, by establishing that there are social conditions on thought that secure our unmediated epistemic touch with objects, thereby ruling out skepticism without giving up on realism, it does not on its face provide a substantive reason to embrace Unimundialism. What it establishes is that any given subject must be in communication with other subjects who inhabit a common world; whereas what it would need to establish is that there is only one such world—or equivalently, that all of the truths that can be known by any subject can in principle be embraced together. Davidson certainly believed this. He made it explicit in his response to the spectrum argument, when he refused to allow the possibility of alternatives-unknowable-by-us on the ground that nothing should count as minded unless it is intelligible to (and therefore, in turn, largely agrees with) us; and he made it explicit again when he exploited the idea of an omniscient interpreter, who by hypothesis knows all of the truths, against skepticism. But I have already shown that these moves can justly be viewed as question-begging.

I have also urged that the right response is not to beg the question the other way, but to continue to explore what substantive reasons there might be to take a stand on whether there is one world or many—bearing in mind that, at this point in the investigation, we are confining our attention to the domain of natural facts open to scientific investigation, and we are accepting that the Argument from Holism Against Normative Insularity rules out the possibility of our ever coming to encounter a multiplicity of worlds within that domain. So if we can find substantive reasons to affirm Multimundialism, they will be reasons for thinking there are (or at least can be) alternatives-unknowable-by-us. I see no other place to turn at this point in this investigation but to science.

In physics, there is a "many-worlds" interpretation of quantum mechanics, and there is some talk of a "multiverse" as well. As far as I can see, neither of these physical hypotheses is necessarily committed to the idea of normative insularity—to the idea that some truth-value-bearers fail to stand in logical relations, with the Multimundial implication that there are many bodies of truths that in principle cannot be embraced together. But I shall leave it to the physicists to pronounce on this matter.

Recent developments in cognitive science provide somewhat more definite, substantive reasons to affirm Multimundialism. They are reasons that speak in favor of the possibility of alternatives-unknowable-by-us, and against the possibility of a View from Everywhere, and they are drawn from Chomsky's account of cognitive abilities.[27]

Chomsky conceives cognitive abilities on a par with other biologically based abilities, and in his view, all such abilities are bound to be *limiting* as well as *enabling.* This is relatively easy to see in connection with motor abilities: If one is *able* to walk, run, and jump, then one will also be *unable* to do other things, such as slither like a snake. But this means that these diverse motor abilities—walking, running, and jumping, on the one hand, and slithering, on the other—cannot be jointly possessed and exercised within a single organism. So if we view cognitive abilities on a par with other biologically based abilities like motor abilities, then we shall have to conclude that they are also limited, and cannot therefore always be possessed and exercised together. Thus, Chomsky's vision of cognitive abilities speaks in a very general way against the possibility of a View from Everywhere. Such a view would require that everything that could be known via every cognitive ability could be known together, and this would require in turn that all of these cognitive abilities could be possessed and exercised together by a

---

27. Chomsky 2000.

single organism—and in Chomsky's view this is no more plausible than that all motor abilities could be possessed and exercised together.

There is an aspect of Chomsky's view that I have not mentioned so far, but which is crucial for generating this anti-Unimundial conclusion. He views the mind as *modular*—as composed of lots of highly specialized cognitive abilities that can function quite independently of one another, even as they contribute to a cognitive life that is, overall, highly integrated. So, for example, there are different perceptual abilities, mnemonic abilities, mathematical abilities, linguistic abilities, musical abilities, social abilities, and so forth. This raises two related questions whose answers might suggest ways in which a View from Everywhere might be possible after all: First, perhaps the ways in which cognitive abilities are specialized does not preclude their being used to know *the same things,* albeit in different ways; second, perhaps there are certain, more *generic* cognitive abilities through which we can represent the deliverances of other, more *specialized* cognitive abilities. On the first question, we are quite accustomed to think of sensory modalities as providing us with very different ways of knowing the same things: I can feel the spherical shape of an orange through touch when I hold it in my hand, and also apprehend its shape in through vision. Moreover, our sensory modalities can provide us with knowledge of the very same things that other species know through sensory modalities that we do not even possess: a bat may come to know through "echolocation" certain spatial facts that we know on the basis of our sight and touch. (This turns Nagel's point about bats on its head; while he emphasized that we can never know what it is like to *be* a bat, I am emphasizing that we can nevertheless know the same things about the world that bats know.)[28] Yet this feature of cognitive abilities cannot help us make sense of the possibility of a View from Everywhere unless it holds more generally—unless, that is, different cognitive abilities can *in general* afford knowledge of the very same facts. But this seems quite implausible. It is implausible, for example, that we can know through hearing all of the things that we know through

---

28. Nagel 1974.

sight and touch, let alone that we can know through hearing all that a bat knows through echolocation; and the generalization seems even less plausible when we consider how limited our perceptual abilities are as compared, say, with our mathematical abilities. This is why the second question I raised above is so important: Might it be the case that some cognitive abilities are more generic than others, so that they can be used to represent the deliverances of other cognitive abilities? There has been a marked tendency in the history of philosophy to regard the human capacity for *language* in this way. That is, the tendency has been to suppose that *all* of human knowledge can be expressed in human language, and moreover, that human language is a sort of *universal instrument* through which *any other* variety of knowledge can in principle be expressed, even the knowledge of *non*human species. I think this view of human language has led some philosophers to be implicitly optimistic about the possibility of a View from Everywhere, because in their view, anything that can be known at all can in principle be articulated in a human language and therefore known together from a single point of view—if not an actual human point of view, then a suitably extended version of one, as Davidson seemed to imagine would be possessed by an omniscient interpreter.

This vision of human language puts in mind the discursivist conception of scientific theories, on which the whole of our scientific knowledge can be expressed in a long conjunction of *sentences*. I complained earlier that this discursivist conception comes close to begging the question in favor of Unimundialism, because it employs a merely syntactic conception of what would be involved in embracing truths together, and noted as well that there are other, much more substantive reasons in favor of adopting the Unimundial stance in science—such as the Argument from Holism Against Normative Insularity, and the value of unified scientific explanations, and the value of avoiding dogmatism. But Chomsky's account of cognitive abilities, as both limited and also diverse, provides an even deeper criticism of this discursivist conception of scientific theories. In Chomsky's view, human linguistic abilities enable human beings to recognize and produce items with a highly specific syntactic structure that has no essential connection with the structures at work in their other cognitive abilities, and as a result, there is no reason to suppose that human language is suited to representing all of the deliverances of those other cognitive abilities, which is to say, all of what human beings can know. To put the same point in terms that philosophers would use, Chomsky holds that a great deal of human knowledge is not *propositional* in form—it is not knowledge that we can express by *stating* what is the case and what is not the case. In Gilbert Ryle's terms, much of our knowledge is knowledge *how* rather than knowledge *that*.[29] But if we agree with Chomsky that not even all of *human* knowledge can be expressed in human language, then we cannot coherently regard human language as a universal instrument through which the knowledge of all *other* species can in principle be expressed. Furthermore, if we agree with him that the reason human language is not a universal instrument is that it is specialized and limited in just that way that all cognitive abilities are both specialized and limited, then we have very powerful reasons to reject the possibility of a View from Everywhere. That would require that all of the cognitive abilities that are possessed by different species could in principle be possessed and exercised together in an integrated way within one mind—and that is no more possible than that all of the motor abilities that are possessed by different species could in principle be possessed and exercised together by a single organism.

This scientific argument against Unimundialism is also an argument for Multimundialism. To sum it up: We cannot know other minds without knowing what they know; but if Chomsky is right, what we know about our own minds gives us reason to accept the possibility of other kinds of minds that can know things we cannot know, because their cognitive abilities are different from ours; when we take this possibility seriously, we must accept that there may be alternatives-unknowable-by-us—and hence many worlds rather than just one.

In one respect, this cognitive-scientific route to a Multimundial conclusion resembles the Kantian route: if we have reason to suppose

---

29. One influential account of this distinction was offered by Gilbert Ryle (1945).

that there may be many worlds rather than one, it is because we have reason to suppose that there may be different kinds of minds that know different worlds. Yet this route to Multimundialism goes via *realism* and not transcendental idealism, for there is no suggestion that the different worlds that different kinds of minds would know are in any way mind-dependent.

It might be protested that the contrast with Kant cannot be so great as I have claimed. On my account, if there are many worlds rather than one, it is because there is no single perspective from which everything can be known together, but rather many different perspectives from which different worlds are known, and this "perspectivalist" approach to conceiving worlds makes essential reference to their knowability by *someone*. So it may seem a fair question: Is this approach really so very different from the Kantian one that defines objects in terms of their knowability by *us*? The answer to this question is, *yes, it is very different*. I have taken it for granted that all of the natural facts are mind-independent, and that minded things are equipped by their cognitive abilities to learn some of those facts—not as they *appear* but as they really are, via just the sort of unmediated epistemic touch that Davidson described at the end of "On the Very Idea of a Conceptual Scheme." So there are no transcendental idealist commitments here—no assertion of a subjective condition on objects themselves.

Still, it might be protested that my perspectivalist approach to individuating worlds is not truly realist in spirit, because it does not offer us an account of what it is about *things themselves* that would locate them in different worlds, but locates them in the same or different worlds depending upon their epistemic accessibility to the same or different kinds of knowers. In response to this protest, all I can say is that if we take the Alternatives Intuition seriously as a starting point for formulating the doctrine of relativism, then the metaphysical issue that divides relativists from their opponents has to do with whether or not all of the truths can in principle be embraced together, and this issue makes essential reference to the concept of a point of view from which (at least some) truths can be embraced together. So any attempt to make sense of what is at stake in debates about relativism without bringing in the concept of a point of view would be misguided, even if it incorporates a commitment to realism. Once we appreciate how and why the idea of a point of view should be brought in, scientific explorations into the nature of mind that are carried out *within* a realist framework provide significant support for relativism—because they bring to light substantive reasons for taking the possibility of alternatives-unknowable-by-us seriously, at least within the domain of natural facts open to scientific investigation.

But the more important conclusion of this chapter is not that we have reason to take this possibility seriously, but that when we do take it seriously, we are not thereby presented with any occasion for adopting the Multimundial stance in the actual course of scientific investigation, or in our actual dealings with anyone whose beliefs about natural facts we can understand. This follows from the Argument from Holism Against Normative Insularity.

Some philosophers might argue against the possibility of alternatives-unknowable-by-us by giving up on the strong metaphysical realism that I have been assuming in this section, and arguing instead that the metaphysical possibilities are epistemically constrained in one way or another. Pragmatists might argue, for example, that the idea of alternatives-unknowable-by-us does not satisfy their pragmatist conception of meaningfulness. Neo-Kantians might try to bring a transcendental strategy to bear, which would proceed along roughly the same lines I described above in connection with antiskeptical arguments, as follows: Unimundialism is defined as the view that all of the truths can in principle be embraced together; Multimundialism is defined as the view that some truths are alternatives that cannot be embraced together, because they fail to stand in logical relations; but these notions of *truth* and *logical relation* are drawn from specifically *human* thought and language, and they can have clear application only in connection with the propositional forms of knowledge that arise in the human context—with knowledge *that* and not knowledge *how*; but the alleged reasons that are supposed to speak in favor of the possibility of alternatives-unknowable-by-us, and against the possibility of the Unimundialist's View from Everywhere, are drawn from a conception of *non*propositional knowledge to which our notions of truth and logical relations cannot apply; those reasons can therefore be dismissed.

In the light of the considerations drawn from Chomsky's work that I presented above, it would appear that the discursivist stance of this argument reflects an unduly narrow view of the nature of our own human cognitive abilities, as well as an unduly narrow view of the possibilities for cognition in general. But I will not try to press the case for alternatives-unknowable-by-us further than I already have. I will simply note that realists are generally willing to apply our concepts beyond their ordinary scope in order to conceive possibilities that lie beyond the limits of human knowledge. In order to conceive the possibility of alternatives-unknowable-by-us, we would need to apply our concepts of "truth" and "logical relation" in this expansive realist spirit. We would have to suppose that the varieties of knowledge *how* that might be possessed by nonhuman minds can in a sense be true—in the sense of enabling their possessors to track and get "right" some features of their environment with which they must cope (or to get them "wrong" and cope less well, or perhaps not at all); and we would have to suppose as well that there is a broad notion of logical relation that applies to cases of knowledge *how,* and that can sometimes be absent as well, in cases of "normatively insulated" knowledge *how*—these would be cases where varieties of knowledge *how* cannot be possessed together even though they are equally "true." Of course, the transcendental strategy for ruling out the possibility of alternatives-unknowable-by-us would reject these ways of extending our concepts of truth and logical relation beyond their ordinary application. In contrast, realists would argue that our concept of truth is bound up with a conception of objectivity that invites us do precisely that—to conceive "reality" as *not* defined in terms of human ways of knowing it. I will leave this familiar philosophical conflict to be sorted out as it will (or will not).

The more important point remains, that there is no scope or occasion for *living* as Multimundialists in the domain of natural facts open to scientific investigation. The idea of *living* as Multimundialists in the domain of natural facts open to scientific investigation would presumably be found in the *practice* of scientific inquiry. That practice, as I have been arguing in the course of this entire chapter, invites the Unimundial stance for various reasons. The most important such reason is given by the Argument from Holism Against Normative Insularity, and we have seen that that argument is not undermined by any of the considerations that might seem to be speak against it, such as those I have addressed here having to do with nature of meaning, mind, and scientific method.

# 4

## Relativism concerning Moral Values

What reasons are there to embrace or reject Multimundialism—or equivalently, to reject or embrace Unimundialism—in the domain of morals?

I observed at the outset of Chapter 3 that there is some controversy among philosophers about how inclusive the domain of natural facts (viewed as facts that are susceptible to natural scientific inquiry) might prove to be—whether it includes all matters where truth might be at issue, including matters of value. If that domain were all-inclusive in this way, then there were would be nothing further for me to consider in this chapter, because the arguments of the last would already have settled the issue of *moral* relativism as I have formulated it. But I shall take it for granted that matters of value are not susceptible to any naturalistic reduction because values are *irreducibly* normative. This is something for which G. E. Moore directly argued in these very terms, and for which Hume had at least left space, when he claimed that we cannot derive an "ought" from an "is"—though he himself did not eventually occupy that space because he treated values as grounded in psychologistic states such as desires and moral sentiments.[1] An important variant of such irreducibility has surfaced in contemporary arguments to show that a science of the mind is impossible owing to the *normative* dimensions of rationality.[2] It seems unlikely that the division among philosophers who accept the irreducible normativity of value and those who do not will be overcome by any effort on my part here to rehearse these or other similar arguments. So let me just baldly state the position from which I will proceed: We are capable of reflecting on whether the things we *actually* think and do are in accord with our various conceptions of what we *ought* to think and do, or what it would be *good* (or *better* or *best*) for us to think and do; these forms of reflection provide the deliberative basis from which we arrive at our own choices—though, of course, not all choices are based on deliberation—as well as the critical basis on which we assess our own and others' choices once made; and all of this presupposes that there is an irreducibly normative dimension to thought, choice, and action that cannot be captured in the descriptive language of science. Relativism regarding values, if such a thing is formulable, will therefore have to be discussed in terms and with arguments that are distinct from those I discussed in the last chapter, which were restricted to relativism regarding facts of nature, conceived as susceptible to natural scientific inquiry.

The particular domain of my concern in this chapter is not all values, but specifically *moral* values. We, then, first need to specify that domain. I will try to specify it broadly enough to accommodate a vari-

---

1. Moore (1903) 1993; Hume (1740) 1978.

2. This idea drives Davidson's argument against the possibility of psychological laws in "Mental Events" (reprinted in Davidson 2001), and it is fundamental to Isaac Levi's distinction between mental attitudes conceived as *normative commitments* and as causal dispositions (see Levi 1990). A version of that distinction drives Bilgrami's agency-based account of the special features of self-knowledge in Bilgrami 2006, where he offers an account of the first-person point of view of agency that entails that the entire domain of value is normatively insulated from the domain of natural facts construed as objects of scientific investigation.

ety of philosophical views about the metaphysics of morals, the foundations of morals, and the nature of the demands that morals place on us. A good path in to such a specification can begin with a distinction made by Bernard Williams. He reserved the term "moral" for the domain with which philosophers are concerned when they engage in the project of moral *theorizing*—a project that he regarded as a failure, and even more or less welcomed as such; and, by contrast, he used the term "ethics" to cover the domain that is circumscribed by Socrates's question, *How should one live?*[3] The domain of morals, as I specify it and discuss it below, will emerge as broader than his domain of moral theorizing and narrower than his domain of ethics.

Although Williams raised Socrates's question in an impersonal form, it is really a *first-person* question, in the sense that it seeks practical guidance that each of us must apply in her own life. When I ask about how *one* should live, what I really want to know is how *I* should live, and the impersonal form of my question merely brings out that it is a general question with general answers that apply to anyone who is relevantly like me. Yet we may agree with Williams that this does not suffice to make it a moral question, because it is really a question of what might be called *personal* ethics. No specifically *moral* issue can arise for me until I explicitly recognize, and take into account, that there are others besides myself. So as a first pass at specifying the moral domain, we might revise the Socratic question as follows: *How should one live, given that there are others besides oneself?* But we might also ask, does it suffice to put one in the domain of morals that one recognizes others, and so is not a solipsist, or does it require as well some sort of *responsiveness* to others and, if so, what sort? I am going to answer this latter question in the most liberal way that I can, so that I do not build into my very specification of the domain of morals a particular moral view, but leave scope for diverse and opposed moral views. My strategy, then, is to raise a question that, though it places the psychopath *outside* the domain of morals, it leaves a certain kind of egoist *within*—not every kind, since nonrational animals and small children (as well as psychopaths) qualify as egoists and they do not function

---

3. See Williams 1985.

within the domain of morals. Of course, animals and children are all appropriate *objects* of moral concern. But what I want to capture is that they are not moral *subjects* who *have* such concerns, because they are *amoral*. So my aim is to specify the domain of morals by reference to the sort of being who is capable of moral reflection, as well as by reference to what the topic of such reflection is.

When reflective beings who are capable of moral response raise the revised Socratic question above, what they recognize is that *others* are relevantly *like themselves*. Like them in what respect? In respect of not being mere things, but in having first-person points of view of their own from which to raise the original Socratic question (that Williams posed) for themselves. Anyone who raises this question gains reflective distance, a vantage point from which to evaluate whether she should allow her instincts and desires free rein, or whether she should cultivate other motives that might function alongside her more immediate inclinations (and sometimes even subvert those inclinations); and in the course of such reflection she comes to recognize a special way in which things *matter* from her own point of view.[4] When we move from purely personal ethical reflection to specifically moral reflection, we generalize this insight about how things matter from our own points of view to other points of view besides our own. I am not sure which step in moral reflection the psychopath omits—whether it is the move that generalizes from the personal case to the case of others, or whether it occurs further back because the psychopath lacks the self-critical perspective to address Socrates's original question to begin with.[5] But in any case, it seems to me that we are definitely concerned with the moral domain when we fully acknowledge that things do matter from our own points of view and from any other points of view that are like ours (or perhaps I should say, *sufficiently* like ours, in order to broaden the scope of moral regard to include nonhuman animals). My pro-

---

4. Parfit has rightly emphasized the language of *mattering* both in his early work on personal identity (Parfit 1984) and in his recent moral tract, whose very title incorporates it (Parfit 2011).

5. Robert Hare's psychopathology checklist indicates that the omission is indeed at the beginning. See Hare 2003.

posal, then, is that we should specify the domain of morals with a suitably revised version of Socrates's question that takes all of this duly into account, as follows: *How should one live, given that there are other points of view besides one's own from which things matter?*

In principle, this proposal leaves room for egoism as a considered *moral* position, *if* the following is possible: One can acknowledge that the way in which things matter from other points of view is exactly like the way in which things matter from one's own, and then respond to this insight by resolving always to rank what matters from one's own point of view ahead of what matters from anyone else's, with the consequence that what matters from others' points of view can ultimately be set aside as irrelevant to one's deliberations about what to do, *except* insofar as it bears on the pursuit of one's own interests. But the proposal can stand even if there is no interesting distinction to be drawn between the seemingly unreflective amorality of the psychopath and any more reflective way of being egoistic. The most important point about it is that it incorporates within Williams's original Socratic question a social consciousness and, in doing so, prompts truly moral reflection.

The proposal does not commit itself to Williams's view that the philosophical project of moral theorizing is doomed to fail. It also does not commit us to any particular view about the logical dimensions of moral thought and talk, or even whether there is such a thing as moral truth. As a result, for all I have said so far, it does not ensure that it is possible to raise the issue of Unimundialism versus Multimundialism in the moral domain. That is, it does not ensure that it makes sense to ask whether logical relations run everywhere in the domain of morals, so that all of the moral *truths* can be embraced together, thereby achieving a View from Everywhere with respect to morals.

I will clear the way for raising the issue in Section 1, by laying down some basic assumptions about moral (and indeed all evaluative) thought and talk, which have to do with its contested status as truth-value-bearing, and with what logical relatedness amounts to in the moral domain (and other evaluative domains). Once I have cleared the way for raising the issue, I will consider what substantive reasons there are to take one side or the other on it. As always, I shall be seeking substantive reasons, and in this case I shall be seeking them in a variety of different views about morality, including some of the major moral theories, some varieties of conventionalism about morals, and Davidsonian considerations.

## 1. Some Preliminaries: Logic and Truth in the Domain of Morals

When advocates of the prevailing consensus view of relativism—those who take the Disagreement Intuition seriously, and their supplementing fellow travelers who propose that truth is relative—turn their attention to the issue of moral relativism, they generally begin by observing that moral discourse appears, in its surface grammar, to be truth-value-bearing, and go on to declare that they take this surface grammatical appearance at face value. Although it is tempting to follow their example, I want to begin by conceding much more to the philosophers who hold that moral discourse is not truth-value-bearing, in order to show that, even if they are right, we should not immediately conclude that the dividing issue between Unimundialists and Multimundialists cannot be raised in the domain of morals. Instead, we should consider whether the issue can be reformulated accordingly.

There are two main views that regard the surface grammatical appearance of moral discourse as misleading.

First, is the so-called "error" theory explicitly articulated with that term by J. L. Mackie.[6] He argued that moral discourse is not truth-value-bearing even though it appears to be, because no discourse is genuinely truth-value-bearing unless there are mind-independent facts to which it must answer in order to be true, and there are no such facts in the moral domain. Mackie proposed to explain away the appearance that there are such facts in Humean fashion, by suggesting that matters of value are constituted by our subjective responses to objective matters of fact (matters that are not to be described in evaluative terms), and that when we take evaluative matters to be objective, we in effect merely project our own subjective responses onto the facts

---

6. Mackie 1977.

themselves.[7] Prima facie, it would seem that we could accept this pro-jectivist account of value and then reformulate the issue that divides Unimundialists and Multimundialists in terms of *apparent* truth—the reformulated issue then being whether all of the apparent moral truths can or cannot be embraced together.[8] Whether this would be a mean-ingful exercise depends upon the extent to which a projectivist ac-count of value would provide for significant logical relations among apparent truth-value-bearers in the domain of value, so that we could make sense of the possibility of their absence—normative insularity—by way of contrast.

The second view that denies that moral discourse is truth-value-bearing is a form of noncognitivism that, instead of stressing projec-tion on the subject's part, stresses that the function and content of evaluative attitudes are quite different from the function and content of factual beliefs. While the function of factual beliefs is to accord with the facts so as to represent them as they are, the function of evaluative attitudes is to guide deliberation and action with a view to bringing the facts into line with our sense of how we wish them to be, or think they ought to be.[9] Hume located this action-guiding force of our evaluative attitudes in sentiment and desire, and he is the central historical model for the first noncognitivist interpretations of the con-tent of evaluative discourse along these lines that were put forward in the twentieth century, which portrayed such discourse as *expressive* rather than descriptive. On the emotivist interpretation that was put

---

7. In making this suggestion, Mackie self-consciously followed Hume's account of why we mistakenly think that there are necessary causal connec-tions among events—because we mistakenly project the effects of our own psychological processes, in the light of which various events are subjectively associated in our own minds, onto events themselves.

8. We might do this by drawing on the framework of *quasi realism* that Simon Blackburn (1993) developed in the wake of Mackie's and other challenges to our notions of moral objectivity.

9. These two functions are often distinguished in terms of their "direc-tion of fit"—from mind to world or from world to mind. Elizabeth Ans-combe is credited by John Searle as having given a particularly clear account of this distinction in Anscombe 1957.

forward by some of the logical positivists, our evaluative claims express our emotive responses of liking and not liking.[10] On R. M. Hare's prescriptivist interpretation, our evaluative claims do not merely express our emotive responses but *prescribe* or commend our responses to others.

Although all noncognitivist interpretations of moral discourse reject the idea that moral claims are truth-value-bearing, they do not all reject the idea that there are logical constraints in the moral domain. Prescriptivists especially tend to emphasize the *general* character of our evaluative concepts, and the resulting normative pressure on us to value like cases alike. To recognize this normative pressure is to recognize a minimal requirement of *consistency* in our evaluative responses across a range of relevantly similar cases. I say it is a *minimal* requirement for two related reasons: First, it is a condition on our possessing evaluative concepts to begin with that they demand such consistency of evaluative response; second, it seems possible that we might be committed to this form of consistency that is involved in the very possession of evaluative concepts without recognizing any further logical relations of consistency that might hold (or fail to hold) *among* moral attitudes that employ different moral concepts. These latter, less minimal, logical relations are the ones we must find in the moral domain in order to raise the issue of Unimundialism versus Multimundialism there, and in the remainder of this section I shall be making a specific proposal about how we *can* raise the issue—a proposal that does not require us to settle the dispute between cognitivists and noncognitivists. But first I want to conclude my preliminary discussion of noncognitivism.

It might be suggested that noncognitivism need not be committed to even the minimal requirement of consistency, to treat like cases alike in the way we characteristically do whenever we employ recognizably evaluative concepts. This suggestion would require us to conceive our evaluative responses in something like the way that Hume conceived events when he argued for skepticism about causation and induction.

---

10. By far the most thorough elaboration and defense of emotivism is to be found in Stevenson 1944.

He claimed that all events are "loose" and "separate," in the sense that they could in principle come in any order or combination—so even if our experience up until now has revealed very regular and predictable relations among events, reason does not entitle us to suppose that these relations are necessary, in the sense of being guaranteed to hold in the future as well. Now consider a parallel claim about evaluation construed as an emotional response of, say, liking (or not liking). The claim would have to be that these responses are similarly "loose" and "separate," in the sense that they too can in principle come in any order and combination—so if human beings happened to exhibit patterned emotional responses that appear to be minimally consistent— responses in which liking (or not liking) one thing went together with liking (or not liking) all relevantly similar things—reason would not entitle us to suppose that our emotive responses *ought* to be consistent in this way. To accept this claim is to accept what might properly be indicted as an "anything goes" account of evaluation on which we cannot be said to possess evaluative concepts at all—we simply like (or do not like) things on a strictly occasional basis, without normative constraints of any kind.

This cavalierly unconstrained account should not be confused with Hume's claim that we cannot derive an "ought" from an "is." When we deny that an "ought" can be derived from an "is," we are not necessarily denying that we possess evaluative *concepts* that lead us to be minimally consistent in our evaluative responses; what we are denying is that the *facts* can ever dictate *which* evaluative concepts we should employ. Thus, on the Humean view, you and I might agree about all of the relevant matters of fact about swimming, such as that it works all of the muscle groups, that it works the cardiovascular system, and so on, and yet hold different and opposed evaluative attitudes toward swimming, each of which is minimally consistent—thus, while I consistently *like* having my muscles and cardiovascular system worked by swimming, you consistently *do not*. The "anything goes" view is much more radical, insofar as it denies that either of us need be minimally consistent in our own evaluative responses to swimming.

It must be evident from how I have been describing things that I think that it is hard to take the "anything goes" view seriously, and the fact is, not even Hume took it seriously.[11] But setting aside whether he or any of the twentieth-century emotivists actually endorsed such a crude account of our evaluative responses, it should be clear such an account would carry nihilistic moral implications. It is especially clear when we specify the domain of morals as I have done via the revised Socratic question, *How should one live, given that there are other points of view besides one's own from which things matter?* On an "anything goes" account of our evaluative responses, there is no answer to any question about how one *should* live.

I have raised this possibility, of an emotivism that is so unconstrained that it amounts to nihilism, in order to bring out by way of contrast that the more familiar noncognitivist positions are not nihilistic. They generally take it for granted that we are committed to the minimal form of consistency that goes together with possessing evaluative concepts. Many of them also leave room for rich accounts of further normative demands to which morally reflective subjects are

---

11. Hume tended to argue in two modes, one of which was skeptical and one of which was not, and there is certainly scope to mount a Humean argument in skeptical mode for the "anything goes" claim in the moral domain that apes his skeptical argument about causation. Just as the latter argument claims that the course of events is not metaphysically constrained by any necessary connections, but can *in principle* come in any order and combination, likewise, he might also have claimed that the same holds for our own evaluative responses—that they too can *in principle* come in any order and combination. But when he was in nonskeptical mode he did allow that our experience has *in fact* exhibited many interesting regularities and patterns, and that this is so in the domain of human action as well as in the rest of nature. Indeed, the entirety of his account of morals rests on the empirically grounded expectation that human emotional responses are extremely regular and predictable, which is to say, they exhibit a significant form of consistency. Of course, if we conceive logical requirements as irreducibly normative requirements, then we cannot count this sort of de facto consistency as a full-blown logical relation. But all the same, it is what passes for a logical relation within a naturalistic framework like Hume's that aims to blur the distinction between logic and psychology by portraying the normative requirements of logic as laws that govern the operations of the mind.

answerable. Hume situated these normative demands in an account of our moral sentiments, which Strawson later developed in his account of our "reactive attitudes" of praise, blame, and the like.[12] Some Kantians try to derive these normative demands from conditions of rationality, in such a way as to preserve a kind of objectivity within noncognitivism—construing the categorical imperative as a prescription that is universally binding on all rational agents. What matters for my project is that *some* varieties of noncognitivism do recognize some basis on which to count our moral attitudes as *correct* and *incorrect,* even if they do not strictly speaking portray them as *truth-value-bearing.* In these cases, it will be relatively easy to move back and forth between cognitivist portrayals of our moral attitudes on which they are true and false, and counterpart noncognitivist portrayals of them on which they are correct and incorrect. This seems especially plausible in connection with some versions of prescriptivism: If there are true and false propositions about what we morally ought to do, then there are corresponding correct and incorrect moral prescriptions that tell us to do those things (and vice versa). So, at the risk of being unduly dismissive of a debate that has been with us for some time within moral philosophy, I will be bold and take it for granted that my project in this chapter does not require me to defend cognitivism over noncognitivism. And although I will usually formulate issues in the terms that cognitivists prefer, by speaking of truth-value-bearers in the moral domain, I shall take it for granted that we can comfortably reformulate them in the terms that noncognitivists prefer, provided that their overall account of morals provides for some dimension of correctness and incorrectness of moral attitudes.[13]

---

12. Hume 1751; Strawson 1962.

13. The usual terms in which the non-cognitivist's position are cast are *linguistic* in their orientation, that is, they aim to capture the meaning of evaluative *discourse* in which our evaluative attitudes are *expressed*—where what is expressed is either our emotional responses of liking or not liking certain things, or a more social response in which we commend our responses to others. But these usual terms in which the non-cognitivist's

The more important task before me is thus not to settle the debate about cognitivism versus noncognitivism, but to explore what logical relations amount to in the domain of morals, so that we may enquire whether or not they run everywhere, among all truth-value-bears *or* their noncognitivist counterparts—so that we may enquire, in other words, whether there is one moral world or many. For the purposes of this task, I will not try to offer a fully worked out proposal about the "logic of value," but will only lay down the central planks of a working position. Its driving assumption is that the proper role of moral attitudes is to provide a moral guide for moral deliberation and action. This is in keeping with the "action-guiding" character of values that has led so many philosophers to prefer noncognitivism over cognitivism; at the same time, I shall also try to accommodate the dimension of corrigibility in moral thought and talk that has led so many philosophers to the opposite preference.

_____

position is cast are not wholly apt to capture the primary role that moral attitudes play in practical life, which is to guide moral deliberation and action. What I think needs developing for the purposes of capturing that role within the framework of noncognitivism is the idea of an *evaluation* of something, in which that thing is *recognized as worth pursuing or doing*—and concomitantly, as *more or less* worth pursuing or doing than other things—where such evaluations play a different role in deliberation from that of beliefs about how things are. If this idea were adequately developed, then the point I made above in the text could easily be extended to it. What I said above is that there is a way to go back and forth between cognitivist construals of evaluative discourse as asserting *that* something is good or worthy of pursuit, and non-cognitivist construals of evalutive discourse as expressing our evaluative responses—because what we say in such discourse can be regarded as having a similar normative dimension on both construals, through which it counts either as true or false, or as correct or incorrect. The same holds for construals of our evaluative attitudes themselves. We can go back and forth between a cognitivist construal of them as *beliefs that* something is good or worthy of pursuit, and a non-cognitivist construal of them as *evaluations of* something *as* good or worthy of pursuit—where on both construals our evaluative attitudes emerge as *corrigible* in a sense that presupposes that there is a normative dimension along which they count either as true or false or as correct or incorrect.

These are the central planks of my working position: (1) Insofar as moral agents have anything to deliberate about it is because they face *multiple options* among which they must *choose*. (2) To be faced with multiple options is to be faced with the deliberative question: Which of one's options would it be *best* to choose and implement? (3) This deliberative question puts in view a certain *rational ideal*, which is to arrive at and act upon *all-things-considered judgments* that determine what it would be best to do in the light of all that one thinks. (4) We cannot strive to meet this rational ideal without also striving to arrive at a *transitive ordering* of all of the things-to-be-valued on a single scale from worst to best. (5) Such transitive orderings provide for logical relations of *consistency* in domains of value, insofar as they remove what would otherwise be conflicts among one's various evaluative commitments by settling priorities among them—that is, by determining which of the things-to-be-valued are better than which, thereby affording deliberative conclusions about which of the options one faces it would be best to choose, all things considered.[14]

In one way or another, all of these planks of my working position are controversial, and although I cannot mount a full-scale defense of them here, I do want to clarify why they nevertheless seem well motivated to me, and why I think some of the most familiar reservations that have been raised about them can safely be set aside. By the end of the section, we will see that part of the attraction of my overall working position lies in the help that it gives in framing the dividing issue between Unimundialists and Multimundialists in the domain of morals; and over the course of the chapter we will see that it also helps us to discern how various considerations speak for or against one side of

---

14. My choice of the term "evaluative commitment" is deliberately neutral between the cognitivist conception of our evaluative attitudes as *beliefs that* various things are good, and better and worse than one another, and the noncognitivist conception of our evaluative attitudes as *evaluations of* things as good, and as better and worse than one another. I shall not always be so careful to speak in such neutral terms as I proceed, but will often allow myself to lapse into cognitivist terms—assuming, as I have said, that we can always reformulate things in noncognitivist terms.

the issue or the other. But before bringing out these advantages, I want to briefly address some objections to my governing assumptions, or planks as I have called them.

It might be objected that the rational ideal of arriving at and acting upon all-things-considered judgments is too normatively demanding and, therefore, psychologically unrealistic. In response, I want to emphasize first of all that the ideal does not impose a normative demand to literally consider *all things* when we deliberate—that would require omniscience—but only to take due account of *all that we actually think.* More specifically, the ideal asks us to determine what our beliefs about matters of fact entail about the practical possibilities before us: what it lies within our power to do given our general abilities and particular circumstances; what means are available for achieving various ends; what the consequences would be of achieving various ends by various means. Once we are armed with these preliminary deliberative conclusions about the options we face, the ideal asks us to determine which of them it would be best to choose and implement in the light of our beliefs about matters of value—our beliefs about which of the things-to-be-valued is better than which. This description that I have just given of the deliberative process should not be misconstrued as an attempt to describe how we normally proceed when we are deciding what to do. It is a description of how we *would* proceed *if* we were *fully rational*—that is why I have invoked the notion of a rational *ideal.* It is important to see that we may be committed to this rational ideal even when we fail to live up to it—that is, even when we deliberate poorly, and indeed, even when we act without deliberating at all—because after we have acted, we can always ask whether what we *actually* did was what we *ought* to have done in the sense implied by the ideal, of being the thing that would have emerged as best by our own lights if we had deliberated and taken due account of all that we thought at the time of action. If it matters to us what the answer to this question is, that suffices to show that we implicitly embrace the rational ideal and recognize its normative force, along with its concomitant normative demand that things-to-be-valued must be transitively ordered from worst to best.

Even granting that I am right, that the rational ideal is something to which we may remain committed even as we find ourselves not living up to it, it might still be objected that it is *inessential* to agency. I take this objection to be raising one of the following two possibilities: either that agents could adopt different, presumably less demanding, normative standards, or that agents need not recognize any such normative standards at all.

The second possibility recalls the "anything goes" view that I discussed above in connection with emotivism. If we were to accept such a view, we would be *wantons* in something like the sense that Frankfurt discussed in his account of freedom of the will.[15] We would not care what moves us to act, and so our current impulse would always prevail, and no matter what that impulse happened to be, we would have no basis for thinking that we *ought* to have done otherwise. I think there is good reason to doubt whether we would qualify as *agents* at all in this wanton condition.[16] But leaving aside that doubt, I want to emphasize that the possibility of such wantonness is quite beside the point for my present task, which is to explore what logical relations might hold in domains of value. We should not expect to discover what these logical relations are by conceiving a point of view from which their normative force would be invisible and inoperative. Let me try to put this point a little more forcefully. Precisely because the normative force of logical relations would be entirely invisible from a wanton's point of view, a wanton could never have any basis for normative engagement with others, and so there would be no occasion for adopting either the Unimundial or the Multimundial stance. As a result, there would be nothing further for me to investigate regarding relativism in the domain of morals, unless I could reasonably suppose that there are *non*wanton agents, who recognize normative demands in the light of which they can regard their own moral attitudes as true or false (correct or incorrect) and, also, as standing in logical relations to

---

15. Frankfurt 1971.

16. See Bilgrami 2006 for an account of agency as irreducibly normative in a sense that supports this doubt.

one another. I think we can and must suppose this if we occupy the domain of morals at all, for only *non*wanton agents can raise the revised Socratic question for themselves, concerning how they *should* live, given that there are other points of view besides their own from which things matter.

What, then, about the first possibility I raised above—not that agents might proceed without any normative standards at all, but that they might operate with a less-demanding normative standard than the rational ideal of arriving at and acting upon all-things-considered judgments? Again, I want to emphasize that the ideal is not so demanding as it may seem. It does not require that we always deliberate and act in accord with it, by actually arriving at all-things-considered judgments and acting upon them. All it requires is that we accept that the sum total of our own thoughts about what is true (or correct), with respect to matters of both fact and value, set a normative standard against which to judge whether our choices and actions are for the best. I frankly do not see how it could make sense to adopt a normative picture according to which it would be appropriate to *dis*regard the normative force of our own thoughts taken together in this way. This is not to say that it can never be rational to act in the moment, without taking the time that it would require to work out the all-things-considered significance of everything that one thinks. But the point is, even in such cases one must still recognize that there is a possibility of falling short of what would have been best by one's own lights, precisely because one did not deliberate fully—and this signals the persisting critical hold that the rational ideal exerts on us in such cases.

This last point in favor of the rational ideal is not undermined, or even compromised, by accounts of morality that attach importance to *spontaneous* moral response that is not filtered by deliberation. Aristotle argued for the importance of such spontaneity when he argued for the importance of character—that we need *habits* of virtuous response, in which it is automatically clear to us in various situations what we ought to do.[17] John McDowell endorses this Aristotelian view, and highlights the role of surrounding social practices in which habits of

17. Aristotle 2009.

virtuous moral response are acquired.[18] Arguing in a somewhat different mode, Niko Kolodny holds that we should respond directly to objective moral reasons as they present themselves in particular situations, without recourse to any form of reasoning.[19] We can acknowledge the moral importance of these more spontaneous forms of moral response while also, at the same time, acknowledging that they can never foreclose the further normative issue that is raised by the rational ideal, which is always a live issue for us—concerning whether what we have done when we have acted spontaneously is really what was best, all things considered.

I suspect that some philosophers who advocate moral spontaneity, and who wish to downplay the role of deliberation and reasoning in moral life, will think I have missed *their* point. They may wish to emphasize that a given reason can speak to us *all on its* own—thereby suggesting not only that we *may* appropriately act without deliberating first, but also that the wider considerations that would be brought to bear by taking up a deliberative perspective are not morally relevant, even in hindsight. But my goal, remember, is not to insist on the importance of deliberation *per se*. My goal is to investigate what logical relations amount to in the moral domain. My approach to that investigation has centered on deliberation because it is a process that attends to the normative force that different considerations contribute to deliberative conclusions, and wherever such normative force is present, so are logical relations. I find it hard to take seriously the proposition that our capacity for *immediate* response to certain moral demands somehow shows that they lack this sort of normative force—so that when we apprehend them, we apprehend them as completely lacking in any logical relation to the rest of what we think, and that, as a result, there is nothing that it would consist in to try to consider them together with the rest of what we think. Even McDowell's suggestion that some reasons *silence* all others leaves room for the thought that the silenced reasons are still *there* to be considered as well, even though they cannot

---

18. See his essays on ethics in McDowell 1998.
19. Kolodny 2005.

quite be heard at the time of action, and even though due consideration of them would reveal them to be quite insignificant, because they are somehow made irrelevant by the reason that had silenced them.

A far more important source of reservations about the rational ideal of arriving at and acting upon all-things-considered judgments lies in worries about whether the logical relations to which we attend when we deliberate (which I have admitted we often do not and need not do) are really there—specifically, the logical relations that we register when we arrive at a transitive ordering of things-to-be-valued on a single scale from worst to best. In one way or another, these reservations all have to do with the possibility of *incommensurability*. Now, for my part, I do *not* dismiss the possibility of incommensurability of values, but on the contrary I shall be arguing for a direct connection between the incommensurability of values and normative insularity in domains of value—in particular, I shall be arguing that encounters with incommensurability in the domain of moral value are occasions for adopting the normatively disengaged stance of the Multimundialist. But the reservations regarding the pervasive ideal of all-things-considered judgments that I am now addressing are not directly concerned with the issue of relativism, because they concern the possibility of incommensurability *within* the point of view of a single deliberator. Obviously, this possibility is hard to reconcile with the rational ideal of arriving at and acting upon all-things-considered judgments. So let me briefly explain why I think it makes sense to retain the ideal, along with its presumption of commensurability of values *within* points of view, in spite of various reasons philosophers have offered in favor of incommensurability of this rather specific sort.[20]

First, it does not suffice to establish incommensurability within a point of view to argue against the assumption of many utilitarians, that there must be a common measure for comparing the values of disparate things, in the form of a single and ubiquitous value to which

---

20. See Chang 1998 for a sampling of philosophical work on the topic of incommensurability.

all other values are related, such as pleasure or monetary value. Some critics of utilitarianism have argued that there is no such common measure because values are ineliminably *plural,* and they have referred to this as "incommensurability."[21] But *surely,* we can allow that values are ineliminably plural—because the things-to-be-valued are valuable in different ways and for different reasons—and still ask meaningful questions about which of the many different things-to-be-valued are better than which. We can meaningfully ask, for example, whether it would be better to own a pet or to be free to travel, without supposing that we can translate this question into one about how much pleasure each would yield, or how much money each would cost.[22] Thus, the way to argue against the sort of commensurability that my working position requires cannot be by pointing to the plurality and diversity of things-to-be-valued.

Just as it will not suffice for such an argument to show that there is no one value to which all others are related, it also will not suffice to show that matters of comparative value are exceedingly complex owing to the ways in which the comparative values of things may *vary with context.* For example, the same thing may be more or less good depending upon the quantities of it that are at issue—a bit of ice cream may have a very high value, while a huge quantity of it may have much less value or even negative value. This does not mean that there are no objective truths about how the value of ice cream compares to the values of other things that we have options to pursue; it simply means that our comparative evaluations must take due account of how the goodness of ice cream varies with quantity. Similarly, some things may be more or less good depending upon whether and how they are combined with other things-to-be-valued. So, for example, if we possess a home by the seashore, then the value of access to flood insurance will be relatively high in comparison with many other things, but this will not be so if our home is in the desert. Again, this does not mean that there are no objective truths about the comparative value of flood

---

21. The theme of value pluralism runs through the work of Isaiah Berlin—see his collected essays, Hardy 2002.

22. See Griffin 1977 for a more extended defense of this point.

insurance, but only that such truths are conditional truths that depend upon what other things-to-be-valued are at stake.[23]

Finally, it will not suffice for an argument against commensurability within a point of view to point out that it is often difficult to *know* what is better than what. It is indeed often difficult to know this—partly because things are valuable in so many different respects in the way that pluralist critics of utilitarianism contend, and partly because the task of ranking the plurality of things-to-be-valued is complex and contextual in the ways I just noted. As a result, we may sometimes find ourselves at a loss when we try to determine which of the things-to-be-valued that we have an opportunity to pursue is better than which. I see no reason to conclude that there are no truths to learn concerning these matters of comparative value, rather than concluding that these truths are hard to know.[24] Insofar as these truths are hard to know, we may sometimes have to choose among things without knowing which of them is really better than which. But of course, this is not a special problem about values, since it also arises in connection with natural facts. When we come to a fork in the road, we may not know which way to go, not because we are in doubt about the value of getting to our destination but because we are in doubt about which of the roads before us will in fact take us there; similarly, when we come to a momentous choice between two careers, we may not know which to pursue, not because we take ourselves to be ignorant of relevant matters of fact concerning what each career would involve but because we take ourselves to be ignorant about a matter of value—that is, *given* the facts about what each career would involve, we still do not know which of them would be better. It might be tempting to suppose that if we really

---

23. The case of means to ends is a special case of this general point about how things are conditionally valuable depending upon what other things-to-be-valued are at stake. Going back to the case of ice cream, although a small quantity of ice cream may have greater value than a large quantity in contexts where we want to eat it, the opposite will be so in contexts where we want to sell ice cream as a means to earning a living.

24. See Levi 1990 for an account of the role of doubt and ignorance in value inquiry.

do not know which career would be better, then there must be matters of fact about them that we do not know. But to suppose this is to reject outright the possibility that as life unfolds it might *teach* us something that we do not already know about the values of things—in this particular case, that life might eventually show us new ways to evaluate the facts that we can now anticipate would follow upon adopting one career or another, where to concede this possibility is to have grounds for self-ascribing ignorance now with respect to what their comparative value might eventually emerge to be.

Joseph Raz has argued at some length that the very sort of case I just raised is plausibly construed as a case of incommensurability within a single point of view.[25] I want to take some time to address the specific considerations he adduces in favor of this construal, because doing so will allow me to make an even stronger case for the presumption of commensurability within a point of view than I have so far managed. Although I did begin with one positive consideration in favor of the presumption—that it is invited by the rational ideal of arriving at and acting upon all-things-considered judgments—the rest of my case for it has been largely defensive, concentrating on why we are not forced to give it up by such considerations as the plurality of values, or the contextual character of comparative evaluation, or the difficulty of knowing what is truly better than what. But as I confront the positive considerations that Raz invokes in favor of positing incommensurability within a point of view, I shall uncover a decisive consideration *against* positing it, which is that *it makes no normative difference* to posit incommensurability *within* a point of view. In other words, if an individual agent ever did suppose that some of the options she faces are incommensurable, then she would find that her individual deliberations should proceed in exactly the same way as they should if she had retained the presumption that the options are commensurable.

When we presume that all of our options are commensurable, we presume that for any pair of them, either one of them is better than (or worse than) the other or they are of equal value. Whereas, if we were to

---

25. See Raz 1986.

allow that some of our options are incommensurable, we would have to allow that for some pair(s) of them, neither is better than (or worse than) the other and, yet, they are not of equal value either. In Raz's example, a person is faced with a choice between a legal career and a career as a clarinetist. He first *stipulates* that she explicitly believes that neither career would be better than the other, and then he goes on to impose further conditions on the example through which he aims to establish that she could not believe that the two careers are of equal value either, as the presumption of commensurability would have us suppose, given her belief that neither is better than the other. The first condition is that adding a small improvement to one of the careers does not lead her to prefer it over the other. Raz takes this to show that she does not—could not—regard the two careers as being otherwise equal in value. But this overlooks the complex and contextual character of comparative evaluation as I discussed above. Although it is often true that a small improvement should tip the balance between things that are otherwise equal in value, it is not always so—it depends upon the case. If I must choose which of two equally good station wagons to buy, then if the dealer is willing to add a "small improvement" to one—say, floor mats—perhaps that should tip the balance in its favor; but if I must choose which of two equally good multi-million-dollar apartments to buy, then if the realtor is willing to add a "small improvement" to one—say, a door mat—that probably should not tip the balance in its favor. So unlike Raz, I do not assume that if a person regards two career options as equally good, then she should allow a relatively "small improvement" to one to tip the balance in its favor. Indeed, it seems to me that such a "small improvement" would be the wrong kind of consideration to appeal to in order to break such a tie in his particular example, given how momentous a career choice generally is—given that such a choice, once made, will have an organizing role in the rest of one's deliberative life. This point leads straight to the second condition that Raz imposes on the example in order to show that the careers are not regarded by the person as equal in value, which is precisely that she regards the choice between them as momentous. Raz's thought here is that if she really did regard the careers as having equal value, then she ought to be *indifferent* between them, and he does not see how she could be indifferent between them while regarding the choice between them as momentous. He may be right that it is indeed difficult to reconcile these two attitudes. But what he does not see is that this is just as grave a problem for his own construal of his example, on which the options are incommensurable—and this is related to the main point that I want to make about incommensurability, which is that it makes no normative difference to posit incommensurability of values within a point of view rather than retain the presumption of commensurability, as I shall now explain.

Let us consider, what sort of indifference between two options should follow upon regarding them, not as incommensurable, but as having equal value? The answer is, a *normative* indifference, in which the person believes that if she were forced to choose between the options, then no matter which she chose she would not be making a mistake—for the only condition in which it is possible to make a mistake in choosing one option over another is by choosing the worse over the better, and this is not possible when options are of equal value. But now consider, what attitude should a person take toward two options if she regards them as incommensurable rather than as having equal value? She should have the very same normative indifference, and for the very same reason. For in this case, too, she must suppose that neither option is better or worse than the other, and that, as a result, it is impossible for her to make a mistake in choosing one over the other.

However, it might be wondered: If there is normative parity here, why privilege the presumption of commensurability rather than posit incommensurability? My answer all along has been that the business of deliberation requires it. A related answer is that the person in Raz's example is already in that business anyway, and unavoidably so. If we consider the scenario that he asks us to envisage with any sense of realism at all, we shall want to know how the person *arrived* at the point of having to choose between a legal career and a career as a clarinetist. Anyone who confronts this choice presumably has it within her capabilities to pursue many other careers, such as bus driver, bank teller, insurance agent, school teacher, and so on. So if she has narrowed her options down to just the two careers, she must already have ranked both of them ahead of all of these other options, and this implicitly puts them on the same scale after all, and moreover, on the same place on that scale, because by assumption, she believes that neither is better than the other. I do not see how this sort of comparative evaluation is to be avoided *unless* she becomes a wanton who ceases to be in the business of deliberation.

Let me return to the problem Raz raises for the presumption of commensurability, that a person who is faced with this career choice cannot be indifferent between her options while at the same time regarding the choice between them as momentous. My discussion above established that this is just as grave a problem for Raz's understanding of the example as involving incommensurability as it is for the understanding of it on which the options have equal value—since on both understandings it is impossible to make a mistake in choosing either option, the appropriate attitude on both understandings is normative indifference. But it will prove instructive to consider more directly, what *would* make a choice between a legal career and a career as a clarinetist momentous? Intuitively, it seems to me that what would make such a choice momentous is the very aspect of it that I drew on when I explained how the careers could be of equal value even though adding a "small improvement" to one might not tip the balance in its favor—namely, that the choice once made will determine so many other choices to come in a person's life. When we are faced with such a *large* and *life-determining* choice, it is hard to be sanguine that we can *know enough* to know that we would *definitely not* be making a mistake to choose one over the other—that would require us to foresee how two whole lives would play out, with all of their consequent choices. But of course, we cannot be in suspense about this without presuming that our options are commensurable after all, even if we are not yet in a position to know what their comparative value is. For this reason, I do not see Raz's example as forcing us to give up that presumption; on the contrary, I see it as bringing to light further support for it.

To sum up this somewhat overextended, and yet admittedly incomplete, defense of the two most controversial planks of my working position on the logic of value, concerning the *rational ideal* of arriving at and acting upon all-things-considered judgments, and its attendant requirement of a *transitive ordering* of things-to-be-valued: As individual deliberators who face multiple options, we cannot but be interested in the joint significance of all that we think for the deliberative question, which of our options would it be best to choose; this reflects an implicit commitment to the rational ideal of arriving at and acting upon all-things-considered judgments; we cannot strive to meet that ideal without also striving to arrive at a transitive ordering of all the things-we-value on a single scale from worst to best—though we shall confront many complexities in the task of comparative evaluation, and we may often have to choose while remaining ignorant about relevant matters of comparative value (as well as matters of fact), and we may often have to choose without deliberating at all.

What does my working position imply for the issue of Unimundialism versus Multimundialism in the domain of morals? Very roughly, it implies that the co-tenability of moral truths will rest on whether they can be jointly embraced and ranked together for the purposes of moral deliberation, and that the possibilities for normative engagement with others concerning moral matters will rest on whether we and they can embrace the same bases for our respective moral deliberations.

More specifically, according to the Unimundial view of morals, there is a complete set of things-to-be-morally-valued, all of which stand in a single transitive ordering from worst to best, where the presence of this transitive order ensures that moral truths can be a guide to moral deliberation and action. If there is just one moral world in this sense, then with respect to all moral matters, we will always find either that we agree with others about them or that we disagree about them; and these will be occasions on which we can learn from and teach one another concerning what are the things-to-be-morally-valued, and which of them is better than which.

Multimundialists hold that there is more than one moral world, in the sense that there is more than one set of things-to-be-morally-valued, each of which can be transitively ordered on its own but not together with the others. This means that there are separate and incomplete bodies of moral truths that cannot be embraced together, and so moral truths are not truths for everyone, but are truths-for-some. The recognition of moral-truths-for-others—of moral alternatives—will arise insofar as we recognize that others may correctly embrace and deliberate from moral values that we cannot ourselves embrace as a basis for our own moral deliberations. This will amount to a recognition of relations of incommensurability among moral values, which impose barriers of normative insularity that place us in different moral worlds. When we encounter others who live in different moral worlds, we can neither agree nor disagree with them about moral matters. We must allow that our answers to the revised Socratic question, *how should one live given that there are other points of view besides one's own from which things matter,* have only local significance and so cannot provide moral guidance to others who do not live in our moral world; they will not have anything to learn from us, nor we from them, concerning how to conduct moral life, and so the appropriate response to one another will be normative disengagement on moral matters.

Both views, the Unimundial and the Multimundial, may seem to be emerging as breathtakingly *extreme* positions: If there is just one moral world, then all moral agents should be deliberating from the very same moral values, and ranking them in the very same way; and if there are many moral worlds, then moral agents who inhabit different moral worlds will have no shared moral values at all. But the views are not quite so extreme as they may seem. If there is just *one* moral world, this does not mean that we must all *agree* on all of the moral truths, but only that we must recognize our moral differences as occasions for normative engagement, on which we have something to teach or learn from one another. Furthermore, the oneness of the moral world would not rule out that moral values might be ineliminably plural, or that we might be subject to a great deal of uncertainty about which of the many disparate things-to-be-morally-valued really are better than which. What the Unimundial stance requires is that we should regard it as a morally relevant, and often a morally urgent, matter to learn about this and to engage with one another about it. In contrast, if we were adopt the disengaged stance of Multimundialist, this would not mean that we could not regard ourselves as having a great deal in common with those who inhabit different worlds from ours. If the arguments of Chapter 3 are correct, we would still agree with them by and large about matters of fact, and furthermore, we would recognize them as moral agents who are capable of moral reflection. It may seem difficult to imagine how moral agents who have this much in common could fail to have grounds for normative engagement about moral matters; and insofar as this is difficult to imagine, it serves to show how hard it is to imagine being in a position to take Multimundialism about morals seriously. Nevertheless, in Sections 4, 5, and 6, I will consider some potential reasons for doing so.

What we ultimately conclude about the issue of Unimundialism versus Multimundialism in the domain of morals may well be a function of our moral commitments themselves, or our metaphysics of morals, or our understanding of the normative foundations of morals. It is entirely fitting that we turn to these areas of philosophical study in order to find substantive reasons for taking a stand on the issue. So let me turn to that task, paying special attention to some of the reasons that other philosophers have offered in the course of arguing for and against moral relativism, as they have understood that doctrine.

## 2. Moral Theory and Unimundialism

In this section I will focus on two major moral theories that provide unequivocal support for Unimundialism, namely Kantianism and utilitarianism. Egoism is a third major moral theory whose significance for the debate over Unimundialism versus Multimundialism is far less straightforward, and I'll reserve it for separate discussion in the next section, except for a few passing remarks along the way.

Kantianism and utilitarianism both provide unequivocal support for Unimundialism, because each recognizes just one central moral truth from which all others flow as special instances or applications, where this one moral truth articulates the moral importance of just one moral good. Thus, on one formulation, Kant's categorical imperative commands us to show respect for persons by acting only on reasons that are universalizable; and the most familiar formulation of the principle of utility instructs us to act for the greatest happiness of the greatest number.

I said at the end of the last section that Unimundialism in the moral domain requires that there be just one set of things-to-be-morally-valued, all of which can be ranked together in a single transitive ordering from worst to best. There is a sense in which Kant's moral theory obviates the need for such a ranking at all. The domain of morals is a domain in which rational agents recognize the universally binding and unconditional force of the categorical imperative, and when they act in accord with it they are right and when they act out of accord with it they are wrong—and no issues about what is morally better and worse arise. In contrast, the principle of utility does provide a criterion by which to rank various actions as morally better and worse depending on whether they contribute to greater or less overall happiness. But because this ranking is generated by a single criterion, it is most definitely *one* ranking, and so there is no doubt about the *oneness* of the moral world that utilitarians envisage.

I indicated in the introduction to this chapter that Williams regarded the entire project of moral theorizing as a failure.[26] Rather than review his detailed arguments against each of the major moral theories, I will merely register and endorse their common thrust—that there is a *plurality* of moral values. It should be clear in the wake of my arguments in the last section that the existence of such a plurality of moral values would not suffice by itself to rule out Unimundialism, since that would depend upon whether all of the disparate things-to-be-morally-valued can be transitively ordered as better and worse on a

---

26. This aspect of his view comes through in virtually all of his moral writings, but the most concentrated presentation of it can be found in Williams 1985. I should mention that he included, among the moral theories, eudaimonistic moral theories as well as Kantian and utilitarian moral theories. I should also mention that if there were a single, positive account of what human flourishing consists in, conceived apart from varying social conditions, then eudaimonism would be another moral theory that promises to provide unqualified support for Unimundialism. Williams himself regarded eudaimonism as the most promising of all of the failed approaches to moral theorizing. But it failed nonetheless, according to him, for the very reason that it fails to support Unimundialism—namely, that there is no *single* positive account of what human flourishing consists in.

single scale. But nevertheless, what I want to emphasize in this chapter is that Williams's pluralism would undermine the *automatic* support for Unimundialism that would have been forthcoming from moral theories that recognize only one moral good.

Williams noted that moral theories tend to deal in *thin* moral values, such as rights and duties, happiness, and self-interest, which he contrasted with the *thick* moral values that guide so many of our moral decisions and actions. In the present time and in our broad social vicinity, some of the thick moral values that are exemplified in people's lives include self-reliance, privacy, relatively high levels of industriousness, a sense of professional duty, certain meritocratic ideals, and the complementary duties of parents and children that arise within the nuclear family; in other times and places, people have lived by such values as piety, honor, and the various duties that arise within extended families and small, intimate communities. In various places, mostly in periods of transition, some people have attempted to live, and have to some extent succeeded in living, according to values that have *dissented* from these sets of values, repudiating the values of the nuclear family and of the routines of the workplace as well as the competitive values of meritocracies, or the confining values of intimate communities, for more freely and creatively individual conceptions of the good life with more loosely understood values of solidarity and affection.

According to Williams, one common mistake of the major moral theories is to overlook the ways in which moral life is dominated by thick moral values such as these rather than the thin ones that have been the primary objects of theoretical attention. I think he was right, for two related reasons. One reason he particularly emphasized in his sustained attacks on utilitarianism over the years concerns the importance of "fundamental life projects," which are the long-term personal projects around which we tend to organize so many of our activities and personal relationships, and which set the actual contexts in which our moral concerns for ourselves and for others arise. In his view there is no coherent point in a moral theory like utilitarianism that proposes to organize our moral priorities around conceptions of happiness and well-being that abstract from the much more specific moral concerns that attend these "life projects." The other reason moral life is bound to be dominated by thick moral values over thin ones is that moral life is always situated in historically specific social conditions in which only the thick moral values can serve as a useful guide. I will have much more to say about why this is so in Sections 4, 5, and 6, when I consider the strongest case for Multimundialism in the moral domain, and some sources of resistance to it. At this point I will just rest with the unexplored *assertion* that Williams was right to complain that any moral theory that abstracts from the importance of life projects, and their situatedness in historically particular social conditions, is bound to have a distorted and distorting view of the moral terrain that we must traverse, and it will not provide us with the sort of moral guidance that we need in order to navigate that terrain.

As a supplement to Williams's main qualm about the major moral theories, I will add another, related complaint: Insofar as the thin moral values that moral theorists focus on ever could or should hold our moral interest on their own, in abstraction from thick moral values and our various life projects, it would not make sense to give primacy to just one of them in the way that each of the major moral theories tries to do; rather, we should acknowledge that they all lay legitimate claim to our moral attention, and moreover, they do so in ways that make competing moral demands on us. Here I am referring not only to utility and to the Kantian ideal of respect for persons, but also to the value of self-interest that drives egoism. The plurality of these three *thin* moral values, over and above the plurality of thick moral values, is *another* reason that stands in the way of regarding any of the major moral theories as an adequate basis for Unimundialism.

Matters would be different if it could be shown that just *one* of the thin moral values actually subsumes all of the others, and this is a common strategy by which some moral theorists have attempted to square their own preferred theory with the various moral intuitions that seem to support the other, seemingly opposed theories. Through this strategy they aspire not only to overcome important objections to their preferred theory, but also to achieve a unified account of morals.

These efforts have included consequentialist derivations of rights that would reconcile a utilitarian approach to morals with some Kantian intuitions, and some contractualist accounts of morality that aim to show how morals can ultimately be grounded in self-interest.

Although these unifying efforts are clearly well intentioned, what they gain in apparent moral consistency comes at the cost of a full appreciation of the moral insights that originally drove each of the major moral theories—because a full appreciation of those insights require us to acknowledge the ways in which the various thin moral values really do make competing demands on us. Thus, on my reading of Kant, if there is a categorical imperative not to lie, then it would be wrong to lie *even* in a circumstance where, according to the utilitarian point of view, it would be right to lie, such as a circumstance where nothing short of an out-and-out lie would prevent a terrorist from locating and detonating a bomb that would kill a great many people. Although it is understandable that promoters of Kantian moral theory wish to rescue it from this morally problematic implication, what is most moving and powerful about Kant's account of universal respect for the autonomy persons is precisely that it identifies a moral cost in lying to a terrorist, which is due to the fact that such a lie would *not* embody respect for the autonomy of the terrorist—and we can feel the normative pull of this Kantian conception of respect even as we decide that lying to a terrorist is morally right.[27] Of course, the very

___

27. Some Kantians contend that we would not be wrong to lie to a terrorist if we did so in order to prevent a wrong. Although this attitude would make good moral sense, I simply do not see how it would reflect the sort of universal respect for persons that is recommended by Kant's categorical imperative, especially when we conceive such respect as safeguarding individual autonomy. It is a clear and foreseeable consequence of a determination to promote the autonomy of all that we would be leaving others free to make their own decisions, even if those decisions are wrong. I do not mean to suggest that a committed Kantian should not attempt to influence prospective wrongdoers by trying to dissuade them from their immoral decisions. But what I do mean to suggest is that attempts to influence other persons do not embody respect for their autonomy if such attempts are manipulative in the way that lies are.

same case reveals the moral cost that we would incur if we did show respect for the autonomy of the terrorist, which is noted by utilitarian moral theory. In general, the conflicts among the major moral theories are too blatant to require any further discussion, and I shall leave it to the reader to think up cases in which acting for the sake of either Kantian or utilitarian values would incur a cost to self-interest and vice versa.

I do not want to exaggerate the significance of these last remarks. I do not claim to have shown that it is impossible to arrive at a moral theory that incorporates all of the thin moral values in a consistent way, so that they can all be embraced together.[28] Nor, for that matter, am I claiming that Williams, or positions sympathetic to Williams, have shown that it is impossible to arrive at a systematic account of how all of the thick moral values by which we live can be embraced together, by ranking all of the things-to-be-morally-valued in a single, transitive preference ranking as Unimundialism would require. But on the other hand, it is surely not a foregone conclusion that this *is* possible. My starting point in this section was to acknowledge that such a transitive ordering would be guaranteed by either a Kantian or a utilitarian moral theory, and my larger aim has been to bring out some important reasons that stand in the way of embracing these theories, including most especially the important role that thick moral values play in moral life.

So I want to concede that my discussion in this section leaves us with an open question concerning whether it is—or is not—reasonable to suppose that the plurality of things-to-be-morally-valued can all be ranked in a single transitive ordering from morally worst to morally best, in such a way that all of the moral truths can be embraced together, and can figure as a joint basis for practical deliberations. In Section 3 I want to approach matters from the other side, by considering whether egoism provides us with clear reasons for regarding this question as closed, on the ground that we definitely *cannot* rank all of the things-to-be-morally-valued on a single scale.

---

28. As Parfit proposes in Parfit 2011.

### 3. Hobbesian Conventionalism Does Not Support Multimundialism

I have noted that it might seem misguided to count egoism as a moral position at all, given that it does not incorporate any positive *regard* for others' points of view. All the same, I have deliberately specified the domain of morals in a broad way so that some varieties of egoism might qualify as moral positions, insofar as they are undertaken in the light of genuine moral reflection, as a considered response to the revised Socratic question, *How should one live, given that there are other points of view besides one's own from which things matter?* My motive for doing so was to leave scope for exploring the question whether egoism might provide us with reasons to affirm Multimundialism in the domain of morals.

I take egoism to be the view that one ought to systematically rank what matters from one's own point of view ahead of what matters from all other points of view, with the result that one can always set aside what matters from others' points of view as irrelevant to one's deliberations about what to do *except* insofar as it bears on the pursuit of one's own interests. Egoism so conceived does seem to entail a Multimundial conclusion—that is, it does seem to entail that there are as many moral worlds as there are points of view from which self-interest can be pursued, each providing a different set of things-to-be-morally-valued, and therewith, a different body of moral truths corresponding to each egoistic point of view. So it might be thought that there is nothing more, or at any rate nothing very interesting, to say about the connection between egoism and Multimundialism, because we are consigned either to argue against egoism as a mistaken account of morals or to accept its Multimundial implication—or perhaps we might argue that it is not a view *within* the moral domain at all, but really a form of psychopathology.

But this conclusion would ignore an important line of argument for moral relativism that draws on the Hobbesian conception of morals as arising when self-interested agents convene to enter into, or have reason to enter into, *agreements to abide by common rules*. These would be conventional agreements in which each party has self-interested reasons to abide by certain rules conditionally on others abiding by them too. Hobbes described our condition outside such agreements as a war in which there is no morality at all: "To this war of every man against every man, this also is consequent; that nothing can be just or unjust. The notions of right and wrong and justice and injustice have there no place."[29] But we need not agree with him that our condition outside of such agreements is war in order to suppose that self-interested agents might have reason to enter into them, or that their relations take on a certain kind of moral significance only when they do enter into them, or have reason to enter into them. My aim in this section is to explore whether such a conventionalist vision of morals would give us reasons to affirm Multimundialism in the domain of morals.

Prima facie, it seems that Hobbesian conventionalism does invite the sort of neo-Kantian metaphysical argument that was standardly employed in twentieth-century arguments for relativism. The argument starts with an antirealist premise, observing that, because they are generated by Hobbesian agreements, moral "facts" are not mind-independent; it goes on to observe that there is a plurality of such agreements; and it concludes that the moral "facts" are in some sense "relative" to such agreements. As I have repeatedly explained, this neo-Kantian line of argument does not directly address the logical issue that divides Unimundialists and Multimundialists, which concerns whether logical relations run everywhere among all truth-value-bearers, or whether some of them are normatively insulated from one another. So if we wish to determine whether Hobbesian conventionalism provides support for relativism when it is formulated as Multimundialism, we need to address this dividing issue. We need to deter-

---

29. Hobbes (1660) 1996, p. 85. In this passage Hobbes was actually more focused on the state of nature as being one without a sovereign power to enforce the rules of justice and right—but nevertheless, it was his clear view that these rules arise with agreements, and the reason he thought a sovereign power would be necessary as well is that such agreements would be null and void if they could not be enforced, which it is the function of the sovereign to do.

mine whether Hobbesian agreements are separated by barriers of normative insularity; and we need to consider this question bearing in mind that the most distinctive and important logical relations in the domain of morals have to do with the transitive ordering of things-to-be-morally-valued on the same scale.

Before proceeding, I want to make a brief aside to consider whether *all* of the rules that arise with Hobbesian conventional agreements should be counted as specifically *moral* rules. This may seem counterintuitive—rules of the road come to mind, for example, as conventional rules that we do not ordinarily think of as moral rules. Yet on my way of specifying the domain of morals, a rule is a *moral* rule if questions about whether to adopt it and abide by it involve, or are special applications of, the revised Socratic question—*How should I live, given that there are other points of view besides my own from which things matter?* And it would appear that they *are*—for if one has entered into an agreement to abide by rules of the road, then *part* of one's answer to the revised Socratic question must be that one should abide by those rules. The fact that this may seem counterintuitive does not compromise my proposal to specify the domain of morals in the way I have, for it was my express aim to specify that domain in the broadest terms possible. It also does not compromise my more specific aim in this section, for what matters to my aim here is not that all conventional rules might qualify as moral rules, but rather, that the converse can coherently be assumed to hold for the sake of argument—namely, that all moral rules are conventional rules. My aim, to repeat, is to determine whether Multimundialism follows from this Hobbesian assumption.

To this end, it will be helpful to consider Gilbert Harman's elaboration of the Hobbesian view, which he has argued does entail a significant form of relativism.[30] In that defense of relativism, he agrees with Hobbes that the ultimate foundation of all moral rules is rational self-interest, and that we do not bear any moral obligations toward others unless, as self-interested agents and with our self-interest in mind, we have entered into moral agreements with them to abide by

---

30. Harman 1975.

common moral rules.[31] He claims that moral relativism immediately follows, because when moral judgments express the strong "ought" of moral obligation, they make sense only *in relation to* particular moral agreements—by which he means that the normative force of this strong moral "ought" is always confined within particular moral agreements and does not extend to those who stand outside them.

Harman does not deny that we often make evaluative judgments about those who stand outside our own moral agreements. His point is that these "outer" judgments do not express the strong "ought" of moral obligation—only "inner" judgments do. He illustrates this point with the case of Hitler, declaring that it makes no sense to judge that Hitler *ought not* to have done what he did, or that he was *morally wrong* to do it, because these are inner judgments that presuppose that he had entered into a moral agreement to abide by our moral rules—which Hitler manifestly never did. On the other hand, Harman allows that it does make sense to judge that Hitler was *evil,* because this negative evaluation does not falsely presuppose that Hitler had ever agreed to abide by our moral rules. This is not a completely convincing example, because to many ears, including my own, the "outer" judgment that Hitler is evil rings with a distinctly moral tone. Nevertheless, one can see Harman's point: *If* we accepted his Hobbesian assumption that one is never obliged to abide by moral rules unless one has entered into an agreement to do so, then it would indeed be inappropriate to claim

---

31. Harman's account of why we should take this egoistic account of the foundations of morals seriously is far more compelling than Hobbes's own account. Rather than draw a dark picture of what we are like in a state of nature, Harman simply asks how we might explain certain features of commonsense morality that seem perplexing. For example, why do we find it more important not to transgress against others than to positively help them—in particular, why are there rules against stealing, but not in favor of sharing wealth? He claims we can explain this if we consider what common rules self-interested agents might have reason to abide by even if their interests are different—because some are stronger and richer than others. Rich and poor alike wish to keep what they have, but only the poor wish to redistribute the wealth.

that Hitler ought not to have done what he did, in the strong sense of "ought" that implies the presence of a moral obligation.

The form of moral relativism that Harman defends is, in his words, "a soberly logical thesis": Given that inner moral judgments make sense only in relation to particular moral agreements, any adequate account of their logical form should make this explicit. This logical thesis may seem reminiscent of the semantic relativists' proposal that I discussed in Chapter 1, to portray moral truth as relative to moral context. But their view is very different from Harman's. They endorse the prevailing consensus view of relativism as arising with irresoluble disagreements in which both parties are right, and they propose to portray moral truth as relative to context in order to avoid the resulting threat of contradiction. When I discussed their proposal, I had not yet put in place any assumptions about the specific forms that logical relations take in domains of value. I confined my attention to two aspects of their proposal: First, it is designed to make it formally possible to embrace all of the moral truths together, and insofar as it succeeds, it may make formal room for Unimundialism; but second, the sorts of cases for which it is designed can also be understood, in line with the Multimundial view, as ones in which the parties involved do not disagree because they are not employing the same moral concepts and values, and yet their moral attitudes cannot be embraced together because they are normatively insulated from one another. I concluded that we cannot reasonably formulate the doctrine of relativism as the sort of "soberly logical thesis" in the way that Harman offers. Accordingly, the interest of his defense of moral relativism for my project does not lie in the fact that it incorporates a formal maneuver that makes explicit the relativity of moral judgments to context. Its interest lies in the fact that he portrays the normative force of certain moral judgments as *confined* to the moral agreements in which they are made. What I want to explore is whether his reasons for positing this form of normative confinement amount to, or perhaps bring to light, reasons for positing normative insularity as well—reasons for thinking that, within the framework of Hobbesian conventionalism about morals, logical relations hold within different moral agreements but not across them.

At first glance it may seem plausible that Harman's account of moral agreements does provide such reasons. I have emphasized all along in this chapter that to *embrace* moral truth is to take it as a basis for deliberating about what the morally best thing to do is, and so it may seem plausible that if these truths arise through moral agreements, then there will be as many bodies of such truths as there are moral agreements, and none of them will be embraceable together with the others—*unless* it is possible to be a party to more than one moral agreement at a time, but that is certainly not the picture Harman has in mind, and not the issue of primary concern here. The issue is whether logical relations may reach across moral agreements, as well as hold within them, in cases where agents are not party to more than one such agreement. Harman does make one allowance that seems to bear on this issue, for he expressly states that his account of moral relativism does not rule out the possibility that some moral agreements may be *objectively better* than others, and also that some may be *more just* than others. It is not immediately clear why he makes this concession, since it looks like giving up on the central claim of Hobbesian conventionalism, which is that the only moral facts there are—aside from those that concern self-interest—are the various emergent facts that are generated when self-interested agents actually enter into moral agreements. When we accept that claim, we must also accept that the only basis on which it makes sense to try to compare the relative merits of different moral agreements is self-interest—other bases of comparison, that would employ more idealized or impersonal moral and political concepts, are simply not available. For the sake of argument, I shall accept that this is indeed so, in order to explore what follows about the presence or absence of logical relations that reach across different moral agreements.

On closer inspection, it is not hard to see that self-interest *does* provide a basis on which to compare the relative merits of different moral agreements, and moreover that such comparative evaluation is intrinsic to the process of arriving at such agreements, because otherwise moral bargainers would not have *reasons* to enter into the agreements they do. As part of their deliberations they must consider all of the following: which moral agreements are *conceptually* possible, in the sense of being moral agreements that *some* group of moral bargainers might have reason to enter into; which of the conceivable agreements are *practically* possible for *them,* in the sense of being feasible for the particular group of agents they find themselves among; which of these feasible agreements would be the most stable, in the sense of serving the various interests of all of the bargainers sufficiently well to give them all reason to enter into them and abide by them; how different specific aspects of different agreements would affect this last consideration concerning prospective stability—we can easily see, for example, that different agreements might provide for different kinds and degrees and distributions of power, wealth, and liberty and that this might affect their prospective stability; and of course, the ultimate goal is to determine which of these moral agreements would *best* serve one's own interests, taking all of this (and no doubt more) into account.

Obviously, the more specific considerations I just mentioned above—concerning the different kinds and degrees and distributions of power, wealth, and personal liberty that would be provided for by different moral agreements—could serve as direct bases for comparing the relative merits of those agreements, without regard for how well they would serve one's own interests. This has been of enormous importance in the contractarian tradition of moral and political theorizing that Hobbes pioneered, which led to much more idealized accounts of what sorts of agreements rational agents have reason to enter into.[32] But my present point is that even on the strictest Hobbesian assumptions about how self-interest must always be our overriding concern when we contemplate entering into moral agreements with others, we still have reason to compare the ways in which different possible agreements would provide for different kinds and degrees and distributions of power, wealth, and liberty, because these considerations bear on the question how feasible and stable different moral agreements promise to be, and this is not a question that self-interested moral bargainers can reasonably ignore.

---

32. These include Rousseau's account of the social contract as well as Kant's conception of legislating for a Kingdom of Ends, and more recently, Rawls's theory of justice and Scanlon's account of what we owe one another.

Insofar as the comparative evaluation of different possible moral agreements is intrinsic to the process of moral bargaining, we must grant that logical relations can and do reach across different moral agreements as well as hold within them. It would appear to follow that parties to different *actual* moral agreements are not consigned to adopt the Multimundial stance toward one another, even though they are determinedly self-interested in their moral concerns. There is plenty of scope for instead adopting the Unimundial stance, from which they might learn from one another about which sorts of moral agreements have served the interests of their parties in more and less stable ways, depending upon the kinds and degrees and distributions of power, wealth, and liberty that they provide for. Should this be called *moral* learning? Certainly, on my broad way of specifying the domain of morals. When we are devising and entering into moral agreements, we are just as much concerned with answering the revised Socratic question as we are when we are asking what we should do once we have entered into such agreements. So even if Harman is right that the normative force of the strong "ought" of moral obligation is always confined within moral agreements, it does not follow that these agreements are necessarily separated by barriers of normative insularity, and that parties to different agreements therefore occupy different moral worlds from which there is no prospect of agreeing or disagreeing about any moral matters at all, or teaching or learning from one another about them.

Hobbes himself did not think there is much point in trying to compare the merits of different possible moral agreements. He assumed that the situation we face when we stand outside of moral agreements is so dire that we have reason to prefer *any* moral agreement to none and, moreover, that no such agreement can be stable without a sufficiently strong sovereign in place who is empowered to enforce it. But the form of conventionalism about morals for which he argued, and which Harman defends, does not depend on these assumptions about what life would be like outside of moral agreements and the necessity of a strong sovereign to keep them in place. What it depends upon is his egoistic assumption that it is always rational to pursue one's own interests, and on his further claims about how and why rational agents may pursue their own interests by entering into moral agreements with one another. I have been arguing that such agents *can,* and also *have reason to,* compare the relative merits of different possible and actual moral agreements, and that this presupposes that logical relations reach across moral agreements in addition to holding within them.

However, my argument so far falls short of establishing that Hobbesian conventionalism actually entails or even supports Unimundialism, for it does not go so far as to establish that logical relations are guaranteed to reach across *all* Hobbesian agreements, but only that the process of arriving at such agreements involves comparing *some* of them. The only ones that moral bargainers *need* to compare are the ones that promise to afford feasible and stable solutions to the particular problems that they face, concerning how to pursue their own interests given the presence of particular others around them who are doing the same. This may seem to point to a line of thought that would lead us back to a Multimundial conclusion after all. All we need to do, it would appear, is to suppose that different groups of moral bargainers find themselves in very different social conditions, and that these different social conditions present them with very different problems to be solved through moral agreements, and furthermore, that even when these different social conditions present the same problems, they require very different solutions. Given these suppositions, it seems that when moral bargainers are situated in different social conditions, they will not be concerned to evaluate the same possible moral agreements, but rather, each differently situated group will be concerned to evaluate the moral agreements that are relevant to their concerns—the ones that would provide solutions to the particular problems they face and that it would be feasible for them to implement. There would be nothing for them to learn from comparing the agreements that would be possible *for them* and the agreements that would be possible *for others* who occupy different social conditions. If such comparisons would be useless and pointless, this does seem to suggest that perhaps logical relations would not reach across moral agreements that were arrived at in very different social conditions, and that the moral bargainers who occupy those conditions cannot engage one another about moral matters, but occupy different moral worlds.

The crucial premise of this argument in favor of a Multimundial conclusion seems true enough—different human beings may indeed find themselves in very different social conditions that present them with very different problems to be solved in order to live together. But it would be quite misguided to think that it can serve as a premise in an argument to show that Multimundialism follows from Hobbesian conventionalism about morals. This is because Hobbesian conventionalism is governed by *two* commitments, each of which helps to secure its Unimundial orientation. The first commitment is a commitment to a kind of *rationalism* about morals—to the idea that human beings are rational agents, and that it is rational for them to pursue their own interests, and that rational self-interest is therefore the ultimate foundation of morals. The second is a commitment to a kind of *voluntarism*—to the idea that it is *up to* human beings to devise and implement moral agreements through which they can effectively pursue their own individual interests. This second commitment presupposes that it lies within the power of human beings to *shape* their social conditions through moral agreements, and to *reshape* them as the occasion and need arise. The first commitment gives human beings the common project of shaping and reshaping their social conditions for the purpose of arriving at moral agreements that serve their own self-interest. Taken together, these two commitments of the Hobbesian project ensure that there would always be a point in comparing the relative merits of the different moral agreements that are feasible in different social conditions, and so there would be no threat of normative insularity that might close different social conditions off from one another, and no occasion to adopt the Multimundial stance that refuses to compare the moral values that others live by against one's own. But when we imagine that different social conditions might throw up barriers of normative insularity, we are giving up on these two Hobbesian commitments, most especially the second. That is, we are imagining a case in which it is not possible for us to shape and reshape at will the social conditions in which find ourselves, for the purpose of implementing moral agreements that suit our self-interest—for if we could, then we would be back in the business of finding it appropriate to compare our moral agreements with others.

I do not think the two Hobbesian commitments I just identified can be maintained in the face of the history of human efforts to shape and reshape their social conditions. So I see the arguments of this section as leaving room for Multimundialism after all, even though I have been at pains to show that Hobbesian conventionalism provides support for Unimundialism. It should be stressed that my reservations about the Hobbesian view are quite different from other objections that have standardly been made against accounts of morals by agreement—for example, that there are no explicit moral agreements to be found anywhere, or that merely implicit agreements are not really agreements.[33] My worry is that when we suppose that the specific social conditions in which human beings find themselves severely constrain what it is feasible for them to do together, then it is highly misleading to describe them as *making* moral rules at all, as opposed to learning about the form of moral life that is embodied in, and also dictated by, their social conditions. With this point in place, it should now be clear why the suppositions on which Hobbesian conventionalism might be thought to yield Multimundialism would require us to give up *both* of the commitments that characterize it—not only the voluntarism but also the egoistic account of the foundations of morals. Even if all human beings generally do pursue their own interests in the various and specific social conditions in which they find themselves, when we suppose that those social conditions dictate the terms on which they must live together, then it is *those social conditions that are providing the foundation of their moral outlook* and not rational self-interest *per se.*

Sometimes the word "conventional" is used very broadly, to mark a contrast with "what is given by biological nature." On this usage, everything having to do with history and culture is a matter of convention,

---

33. Harman sensibly does not insist that moral agreements must be explicit. He claims that it suffices to have what he calls an "agreement in intentions"—which are constituted by intentions to follow rules conditionally on others' intentions to follow the same rules.

and all it takes to be a conventionalist about morals is to deny that moral facts are biologically determined. This leaves out the distinctive features of Hobbesian conventionalism that I have been discussing in this section—that morals have a rational ground in self-interest, and that they are literally *made* by us. At the outset it may have seemed plausible that if morals are literally made by us, then some form of relativism must follow. But I have shown that *Multimundialism* does *not* plausibly follow. Insofar as morals are made by rational agents capable of pursuing their own self-interest via voluntary agreements to abide by common moral rules, they have a common nature and a common project that plausibly places them in the same moral world even as they devise and implement different moral agreements.

## 4. The Strongest Case for Multimundialism

The picture on which morals are products of history and culture, which I just contrasted with Hobbesian conventionalism, is often regarded as bringing relativism in train. On this picture, moral values are not timeless and universal, because their proper function is to enable human beings to assess the morally significant choices that arise for them given the specific social conditions in which they find themselves, and these conditions vary from place to place and time to time. I have already indicated that this view is not well described as "conventionalism." The temptation to call it that arises in part because the historical and cultural forces that create different social conditions exist only *through* human intentional activity—which is just to say, if human beings never consciously acted for reasons at all, then there would not be any history or culture. But this does not mean that history and culture are subject to our direct intentional control in the way that true conventions are. In the main, history and culture are the unintended by-products of what we intentionally do, and these unintended by-products *give* us various practical possibilities around which to organize our lives—possibilities for carrying out personal projects, or for entering into certain kinds of relationships, or for taking on roles in institutions, or for various modes of participation in community, and so forth. So, for example, if it is in some sense *up to us* to become philosophy professors or psychiatrists, the *options* to become such things must already be in place; and it is not up to us whether these options are available or not, for they are put in place by forces that are beyond our control. Of course we sometimes do alter the space of our practical possibilities by creating things that have not been seen before, such as the automobile or the Internet. But insofar as we cannot foresee what their ultimate historical and cultural effects will be, we cannot possibly *intend* those effects. That is why it does not really make sense to call these and other effects of history and culture "conventions" in the strict sense of the word.

Yet much more is required to establish Multimundialism than pointing out that history and culture are not generally within our intentional control. It must also be shown that history and culture have delivered a multiplicity of highly specific social conditions in which people live by completely different bodies of moral truths, where these different bodies of moral truths cannot be embraced together but are normatively insulated from one another. This would be so if different social conditions presented us with quite different practical possibilities and if, in order to navigate those different possibilities, we needed quite different thick moral values that speak specifically to them, much as I described in my example in Chapter 1 about Anjali and me. In that example, it became clear that what I need in order to navigate my situation as a self-made financialist on Wall Street are liberal values like self-reliance, whereas my Indian counterpart in a rural village has no use for such values but needs quite other values having to do with *katarvya*—the duties that follow upon one's location in an extended family and community. Earlier I used this example to *illustrate* the Multimundial stance, making clear that the example cannot by itself justify us in taking up that stance—for that we would need to find *substantive reasons*. In this section, I want to explain why the picture of morals as products of history and culture supplies such reasons.

As I have said, this picture is often taken to have relativistic implications, and as a preliminary I want to take note of some common ways of understanding why it might be so. This will help to clarify which features of the picture provide specific support for Multimundialism, and it will have the added benefit of further clarifying why it makes sense to formulate relativism as Multimundialism to begin with. A common thread in all of these various ways of understanding the relativistic implications of the picture—including mine—is that we ought to refrain from certain responses to others who face different social conditions from the ones we face. But the question is, which responses ought we to refrain from and why?

Here, first, are three answers that do *not* involve adopting the Multimundial stance.

Tolerance. When we are tolerant, we refrain from trying to stop the practices of others that reflect beliefs that we do not share. But we do not refrain from adopting a critical perspective from which the beliefs of others that we do not share qualify as *mistaken,* and this shows that a tolerant attitude typically arises from *within* the engaged stance of the Unimundialist. Historically, the direct target of our tolerant attitudes has not been the *moral* beliefs of others but rather their religious beliefs, and the best reason to be tolerant is the one that Luther identified in his criticisms of Catholic intolerance, which is that religious belief is not something we can coerce, and so when our efforts to persuade others to share our beliefs fail, we have no other sensible choice but to tolerate their mistakes—though of course there may be limits to what we should tolerate, depending upon what others are likely to *do* when they act on the basis of their mistaken beliefs. (It may seem much less attractive to tolerate others' *moral* mistakes than their *religious* mistakes, because we tend to place a moral premium on preventing moral wrongdoing. But the idea of moral tolerance should seem less unattractive if we keep in view how, on the picture of morals as historically and culturally situated, our own moral beliefs incorporate *thick* moral values. As a committed atheist, I might adopt the Unimundial stance and regard others as mistaken when they believe that chastity is a moral virtue demanded by God, and yet at the same time I may adopt a tolerant attitude toward their commitment to chastity insofar as I see no pressing moral reason to correct that moral mistake.)

Nihilism. The relativist's attitude differs from a tolerant attitude I just described, in the respect that the relativist refuses to embrace certain attitudes of others even though she does not reject them as false. When philosophers try to make sense of why we might thus refrain from rejecting as false the moral beliefs of others that we do not share, they sometimes infer that it must be due to the fact that there are no objective facts to which their beliefs must answer in order to be true. And sometimes the very sort of diversity of moral practices and outlooks that I am now exploring as a possible basis for Multimundialism is offered as *evidence* that this is so—the thought apparently being that if there were objective moral facts to inquire into, and we came to learn about them, that would put an end to this diversity.[34] This looks like the usual conflation of the realist's conception of reality as *mind-independent* and the Unimundialist's conception of reality as *one*. But my present point is that if there were no mistakes in the moral domain—because there was nothing to get right—then what we would have is nihilism, and although nihilism is often described as "relativism," it does not deserve to be called that. Relativism arises *not* when there are no truths but when there are *alternatives*—that is, when not all truths can be embraced together.

All the same, if we bracket the question whether nihilism amounts to relativism, there is still a persistent impression that the picture of morals I am now exploring, on which moral values arise and evolve with various historical and cultural developments, does have nihilistic implications. If it did, then it could not support Multimundialism, which presupposes that there *are* truths even though they cannot all be embraced together.[35] But I simply do not see why we should grant that the picture does have nihilistic implications. If moral life is always

---

34. Mackie (1977) argues along these lines.

35. Here it is perhaps worth reiterating that the Multimundialist need not insist on a cognitivist as opposed to a noncognitivist account of morals, so long as noncognitivism provides for some notion of moral correctness and incorrectness, and for significant logical relations among moral attitudes and claims.

*situated* in highly specific social conditions, it does not follow that there are no moral truths about what is morally right and wrong, or better and worse, in those social conditions.[36]

When-in-Rome-Morality. (This is an expansion of some points I already made in Chapter 1.) My last remark in the paragraph above immediately brings to mind the possibility that moral truths are generally conditional in form—that they specify what it would be morally right or wrong, or good or bad, to do in certain specific social conditions, by bringing to bear the thick moral values that apply in those conditions. This does help us understand how we could consistently regard others' moral beliefs as true (*really* true), without living by them ourselves: all we would need to do is to recognize that their beliefs are effectively and appropriately action-guiding in their social condition but not in ours. We might then reason that if we happened to go to their social condition, we ought ourselves to act by those moral beliefs too. But if we did reason in this way, then there would be no bar to embracing all of the moral truths together. To put it another way, there would be no difficulty in supposing, with the Unimundialist, that there could in principle be a View from Everywhere in the moral domain—a point of view from which all of the conditional truths about what it is morally right or wrong or good or bad to do in each different social condition could be embraced together. So the form of "relativism" that follows upon the "When in Rome . . ." view is definitely not Multimundialism.

However, the "When in Rome . . ." view does not follow directly from the picture on which morals are products of history and culture. What follows is that all moral choice and action must be made and taken in one social condition or another, and that in different social conditions, different thick moral values are appropriate guides to moral choice and action; it does not follow that it is possible for anyone to *move out* of their particular social condition into another. It might be asked why this would not be possible. The only answer I can give is that on the picture I am now exploring, it is not only social conditions

---

36. This is an issue that was rightly in dispute when John McDowell (1986) reviewed Williams's *Ethics and the Limits of Philosophy*.

themselves that are the products of historical and cultural forces, along with the thick moral values that are required for navigating them, but also the very *identities* of their inhabitants. This is very much part of what is being illustrated in the example about Anjali and me. The example brings out well that it would not really be possible for either of us to try to move to the other's social conditions in order to live by the moral values that prevail there. Although I could of course go to Anajli's physical location in rural India, it is not open to me to move to her social condition, for I cannot become someone who occupies a particular place and role in an extended family in her village. So when I recognize the sense in which it is correct for her to live by the thick moral values that are an appropriate guide in her moral context, I am recognizing something that would not be an appropriate basis for my own moral deliberations. As a result, when I learn *about* her moral beliefs, I am not myself acquiring any new moral beliefs of my own—contrary to what the "When in Rome . . ." view suggests.

With this last reflection, it should now be starting to come into focus how the picture of morals as products of history and culture might provide substantive reasons to affirm Multimundialism. It does so insofar as moral life and moral choices are always deeply situated in specific social conditions and, as a result, there is no prospect of moral learning, and correlatively for moral teaching, across certain of social conditions.

But if a Multimundial conclusion is to follow from this, it must be the case that different moral contexts are separated by barriers of normative insularity across which *no* logical relations reach among truth-value-bearers concerning morals. I have been saying all along in this chapter that the most important logical relations in the domain of morals are relations of comparative value through which we can arrive at transitive orderings of things-to-be-morally-valued from worst to best. In spite of all that I have said so far in this section about how different thick moral values are appropriate moral guides in different social conditions, it might be insisted that it is always possible to comparatively evaluate different social conditions as better and worse, and therewith the things-that-are-thickly-morally-valued within them. In turn, I want to insist that the mere conceivability of such rankings cannot establish that logical relations run everywhere in the *moral* domain unless the rankings themselves are *morally* significant, and in order to be morally significant they must potentially be able to serve as guides in moral deliberation and action.

Suppose, then, that I came to believe that a life governed by traditional Indian values would *in some sense* be better than a life governed by the values of American individualism that now govern mine. More specifically, suppose that I came to believe that the ideal of self-determination has given rise to a great deal of unhappiness and loneliness in American culture, and I also came to believe that Anjali is not unhappy because she is free of the strains of trying to live up the ideal of self-determination, and furthermore, that she is not lonely because her life is organized around the many duties that come with her place in her extended family. The question is, should these beliefs count as a form of moral learning in which I give up or demote the values of American individualism and put the values of Indian tradition in their place? We can answer *yes* if the beliefs can serve as a basis for my own moral deliberations and actions, and I think there are conditions in which this might conceivably be so. For example: it may be open to me to live by traditional Indian values in my American context just as it is; or it may be that I cannot live by traditional Indian values in the American context as it is, but I can realistically work and fight for social changes in that context that would make it possible for me to live by them; finally, it may be that I cannot import traditional Indian values into the American context as it is, or change that context in order to accommodate them, and yet I nevertheless can move to a different social context in which it would be possible for me to live by them there.

It should already be evident from my earlier discussions of this example that it presents a situation in which *none* of these conditions holds. I cannot live by traditional Indian values in my American context just as it is, because I have no traditional Indian family into which to insert myself. If I were to try to change my context in order to accommodate living by traditional Indian values, there are definite limits on what I could do. I might set about to *create* a cohesive social network of some kind in which I have duties that mimic the duties around which Anjali's life is organized—her *katarvya*. But these duties would not have been *given* to me in the way that hers are given to her—instead, *I* would have given them to *myself*. So insofar as my aim in doing so was to escape the strains of having to live up to the liberal ideal of self-determination, there would be something oddly self-defeating in the effort to *create* a little space within the American context in which I could mimic a more traditional form of life—doing so would hardly suffice to alter the fact that I live in an individualist culture where the ideal of self-determination prevails. Finally, as I have already made plain, it is not open to me to simply take residence in the requisite sort of traditional society—one would have to be born into it or to have been long acculturated in it.

But let me return to the main point: Unless *some* condition can be identified, in which my comparative evaluation of traditional Indian values as *in some sense* better than my individualist values could be brought to bear in guiding my moral deliberations and actions, there is no reason to regard the comparison as a specifically *moral* evaluation. It does not hold any instruction for me about how I might respond to the revised Socratic question, *How should I live, given that there are other points of view besides my own from which things matter?* This question is to be answered by considering the practical possibilities that are actually open to me, and not by learning about various forms of life that are closed to me. Although such learning might be enriching in all sorts of ways, its insights would properly be viewed as sociological (a detached study of that form of life), not moral (a form of engagement with elements of that form of life).

Let me now put the same points about Unimundialism versus Multimundialism in the domain of morals a bit more abstractly. On the Unimundial view, there is one set of things-to-be-morally-valued, all of which are transitively ordered on a single scale from worst to best, so that they can be an effective guide in our deliberations about what it would be morally best to do. These would constitute a single, consistent, and complete body of moral truths that can be embraced together and are truths for everyone. The picture of morals as products of history and culture does not automatically undermine the Unimundial stance, because even if history and culture have produced a very diverse set of things-to-be-thickly-morally-valued, this does not necessarily mean that there is not just a single set of them that can be transitively ordered from worst to best, thereby providing for a single body of moral truths. Likewise, even if people who occupy very different social conditions find it difficult to agree on what belongs to this set and how they should be ordered, this does not necessarily mean that there is not a single set of them, and a correct ordering of them. To try to discover these things would be to adopt the Unimundial stance for the purposes of moral inquiry. But if such an inquiry is to have a real moral point, then there must be significant scope for morally significant action across different social conditions—such as importing and exporting thick moral values across them, or working and fighting to change them so that such importation and exportation becomes feasible, or moving ourselves to different ones. The less scope there is for such action, the less scope there is for maintaining the Unimundial ideal together with the picture on which morals are products of history and culture.

I take the example about Anjali and me to suggest that sometimes there is no scope for these things, and when this is so we should adopt the Multimundial stance. This should not lead us to give up on the very idea of moral inquiry—that is, we should not conclude that there is nothing to inquire into in the moral domain. We should conclude rather that moral inquiry may have to be carried out within the boundaries set by particular social conditions—its appropriate topic would be: What are the things-to-be-morally-valued *there,* and how are they to be ordered with respect to one another? This gives the sense in which there might really and literally be different moral worlds. If there are many moral worlds, we might be able to envisage the possibility of a *kind* of View from Everywhere, that looks *upon* everything in the moral domain and *takes note* of what is morally known in this and that and every social condition. But it would not be a *moral* point of view, from which moral decisions were arrived at and acted upon, because moral knowledge must bear on moral life, which must always be situated within one social condition or another.

It seems to me that the most important sources of resistance to this strongest case for Multimundialism lie in the contention that it underestimates what scope there is for *directed* social change, and that it therefore underestimates the pointfulness of certain forms of moral and political inquiry whose goal it would be to identify the *best* courses for such directed efforts. It should be clear that this contention does not amount to an objection to my main argument in this section, which is that Multimundialism *follows* from the picture on which morals are products of history and culture—for it is really an objection to the picture itself, on the ground that the forces of history and culture do not lie beyond our intentional control, and that it is therefore up to us to shape our social conditions to accord with our moral views rather than vice versa.

I will briefly touch on these matters and related matters in Section 6. But first I want to consider another conceivable source of resistance that would have been of supreme importance if only it were effective, but I do not believe it is. This would be the Davidsonian strategy against relativism carried over to the domain of morals.

## 5. Why the Davidsonian Strategy Does Not Carry Over to Morals

Davidson held that there is no significant diversity of moral opinion, because we all by and large agree about moral matters. Although he did not offer a detailed argument for this conclusion, he did make clear that he thought such an argument should follow roughly the same lines as his general argument against the very idea of a conceptual scheme.[37]

We saw in Chapter 3 that there is a quick charity-based argument against Multimundialism that is not very impressive, which exploits Quine's principle of charity in a particularly direct way, so that the only criterion of whether we have understood someone correctly is

---

37. That Davidson took it for granted that his argument in "On the Very Idea of a Conceptual Scheme" (Davidson 1973) can be carried over to the domain of morals, and values more generally, is something that I know well from many conversations with him. The place to look in his published work for the general direction of his thought on this matter is his Lindley Lecture, "Expressing Evaluations" (reprinted in Davidson 2004).

that they emerge as agreeing with us. I urged there that we should not accept this argument unless we can satisfy ourselves that a charitable approach would not involve an unwarranted projection of our own beliefs onto others. I also observed that the principle of charity is silent on the issue whether logical relations run everywhere, among all truth-value-bearers. But I went on to suggest that if we can find a supporting justification for the principle, then we can reconsider whether it might speak to that issue after all, and thereby render Davidson's general strategy against the relativist effective, even when we construe her position specifically as Multimundialism. After pursuing that suggestion, I argued that the most powerful consideration that Davidson brought to bear in favor of charity, and against the idea of a conceptual scheme, turns on holism, and that holism *can* speak against Multimundialism in a particularly direct way, because there may not be any room for normative insularity if concepts and beliefs owe their very identities to their systematic logical relations with one another in a whole web of belief. (I will emphasize again that, in the domain of natural facts studied by science, it is appropriate to conceive logical relations broadly, to include many "material" relations over and above ordinary deductive relations, such as inductive, evidentiary, conceptual, and subsumption relations.) This Argument from Holism Against Normative Insularity depends upon holism being *uncontained,* so that the web of beliefs is *all-inclusive,* thereby ensuring that there is just *one, comprehensive* body of truths, all of which can be embraced together.

In support of this Davidsonian argument, I marshaled evidence for the thesis of uncontained holism in the domain of natural facts, though I conceded that the evidence is limited to the parts of that domain that are accessible to human ways of knowing. What we find there is large-scale agreement on a vast number of interconnected details that are too banal to deserve mention in most philosophical discussions, but that nevertheless serve as points of agreement to which different scientific theories are all answerable, including the ones that Kuhn and Feyerabend characterized as incommensurable. As a result, even if Kuhn and Feyerabend were right that there is no rational or empirical basis on which to choose among scientific theories that operate with different theoretical paradigms, it does not follow that such theories are separated by barriers of normative insularity. What follows is that they occasion irresoluble disagreements—irresoluble and yet *ordinary* in the sense that the parties cannot all be right (unlike the "disagreements" that are alleged to be relativism-inducing, which, as we saw in Chapter 1, are not convincingly portrayed as disagreements at all). For this reason, scientists who work in different theoretical paradigms do not work in different "worlds" in the literal sense that defines Multimundialism, but rather carry out their work from very distant vantage points on a common world. That was the dark, undermining shadow that holism, if intelligently cultivated and developed in a Davidson-style argument, could cast upon all efforts to establish Multimundialism in the domain of natural facts, as they are studied by science.

In the course of elaborating the Argument from Holism Against Normative Insularity, I allowed that holism, as it applies in the domain of natural facts, is an empirical thesis whose truth can be established only by observing lots of cases. I also followed Davidson's own preferred strategy for establishing the presence of holistic interconnections, which is to focus on cases that involve some form of *difference,* in order to bring out that these differences are intelligible only against a background of agreement.

It would make sense, then, to proceed in the same empirical way in the domain of morals by investigating how and why moral differences are intelligible, and what sort of agreement they might—or might not—presuppose.

To give a preview in a nutshell, this is what such an empirical investigation will turn up: There does seem to be some prima facie evidence of universal agreement in the moral domain, but it takes a very different form there. As opposed to the masses of banal and interrelated details upon which we all agree in the domain of natural facts, what we seem to agree on in the moral domain is a very short list of highly general moral platitudes. This suggests that holism is *not* uncontained in the moral domain, and precisely because this is so, the platitudes on which we seem to agree are not really points of agreement at all, because their meanings *shift* from one social context to another in something like the way that Kuhn and Feyerabend held that the meanings of theoretical terms shift when they are embedded in one theoretical paradigm or another. Because these platitudes do not constitute points of universal moral agreement whose meaning remains invariant across different moral contexts, a conceptual and metaphysical space is cleared for the possibility of normative insularity in the moral domain—that is, for the possibility that there might be many, incomplete bodies of moral truths that cannot be embraced together, and that constitute distinct moral worlds, and for this reason, the general Davidsonian strategy against relativism fails when it is applied against Multimundialism in the domain of morals.

Let me now work up to this conclusion without trying to force it, by considering various cases of moral difference and exploring what forms of background agreement they might be claimed to presuppose.

*Many* (though not all) moral differences can be traced back to background disagreements with respect to natural facts. Take, for example, practices like human sacrifice and head-hunting. We find these practices so appalling and bizarre that we automatically assume that they must spring from moral values that are genuinely different from ours. Yet when we look for an explanation of these practices, we find that we can often get a complete explanation by pointing to underlying factual disagreements. Those who have practiced human sacrifice have done so because they believed that the gods would inflict horrible suffering on their communities unless the sacrifices were made. And head-hunters have believed that the only way to contain the destructive spirits of their enemies is by hunting their heads. It should occur to us that if we ourselves actually held the same beliefs, then we too would have reasons to engage in the practices that we find so appalling and bizarre, and moreover we would have such reasons *given the actual values we now hold*—such as the values we place on the well-being of our communities and on protecting ourselves from destructive forces. So, somewhat surprisingly, *these* moral differences are not, strictly speaking, *moral* differences at all—they merely reflect what our actual moral commitments would imply if we believed the natural facts to be different from what we actually believe them to be.

However, some of our disagreements about natural facts do point to genuinely moral differences. For example, disagreements about whether the Christian God exists are in part disagreements about matters of natural fact, concerning the correct framework through which to explain the origins of the natural world and the mass of interconnected details we find in it. But when Christians adopt a theological approach to explanation, in preference to what we now regard as a more properly scientific approach, they also come to embrace whole ranges of thick moral values that atheists and those of other faiths do not, such as those having to do with piety, original sin, repentance, and grace. Although non-Christians can recognize that coming to believe that the Christian God exists would involve coming to embrace these thick moral values, they cannot make sense of these values just by working out what their actual moral commitments would imply if their beliefs about the natural facts happened to include the belief that the Christian God exists. They need to work out that acquiring that belief would have to go hand in hand with acquiring some thick moral concepts as well, whose content cannot be known without coming to see how they operate in a specifically Christian form of life—for example, what it would mean to regard the purpose of one's life as bound up with following God's will, to take Jesus Christ as one's moral model, to accept that one is born into a condition of original sin without yet having acted at all, to anticipate the possibility of an afterlife with God that cannot be deserved and that cannot be earned through good works, . . .

If *all* moral differences could be traced back to underlying disagreements about natural facts, then insofar as we find it appropriate to adopt the Unimundial stance toward one another regarding the latter, we should extend our stance to the former as well. But not all moral differences can be traced back to factual disagreements in this way, as the example about Anjali and me makes clear. In the example, she and I live by different thick moral values—she by traditional values that have to do with duties and roles in an extended family and I by liberal values that have to do with self-reliance, meritocracy, privacy, and such—and the reason we live by such different values does not have to do with any profound disagreements about natural facts (though we presumably have some), but it has rather to do with the very different social conditions in which we find ourselves. Similar cases that have attracted attention in the Western media in recent years involve moral codes in which the concepts of personal and family honor figure centrally—as we seem to find in Sicilian mafia culture and in certain pockets of Muslim culture. Those who live by these codes regard many violent acts, including revenge killings, as justified when they are undertaken in order to maintain honor. Insofar as those of us who do not live by honor codes regard these violent acts with disapproval, this appears to be a case where a divergence in moral concepts leads to moral disagreements well. But as we have seen from the beginning of this book when I first introduced the example about Anjali and me, it is not always clear whether a given situation ought to be interpreted as involving a disagreement or as a divergence in concepts—and this interpretive point will come up yet again in Section 6. What I want to emphasize now is that whichever way we describe the moral difference presently under discussion, between living by an honor code and living by a moral code that leaves no particular room for honor, it is not a difference that can be traced back to any underlying disagreements about natural facts. If we do not ourselves live by an honor code, then in order to make sense of such a life, we must come to understand the specific social conditions in which the concept of honor plays its characteristic evaluative role, and how they differ from ours.

Let me turn now to the task that the Davidsonian strategy against relativism sets, of trying to identify a background of moral agreement in these cases, where others embrace thick moral concepts different from ours. Can we find such a background of moral agreement? Prima facie, it does seem so. When I see that others are prepared to kill or harm for the sake of their honor, I do not infer that they think killing and harming are in general good, but on the contrary I take it for granted that they think that killing and harming are in general bad, and that these things are bad because they undermine the positive good that generally attaches to life and well-being. It seems that the difference between us concerns the extent to which these goods can sometimes be justifiably sacrificed for the sake of maintaining one's honor. Similarly, when I find that traditional Indian values require a great deal of deference, in which women and younger members of a family must subordinate their wishes to the wishes of their (usually male) elders, I do not infer that traditional Indians think that it is generally good to hinder the agency of others, and that they do not attach any positive value to exercising agency as one sees fit from one's own point of view. It seems rather that the difference between us concerns whether the good that there is in the exercise of agency can be realized within the confines of extended family life; and if I cannot set aside the impression that the (usually male) elders of an Indian family really are prepared to deliberately hinder the agency of some of their subordinate family members, then it still seems appropriate to view our difference as a difference concerning whether and why it is ever fitting to hinder agency, but not as evidence that they think hindering agency is in general good.

This seems to suggest that there are some very general moral *platitudes*—about the moral wrongness or badness of killing and harming and hindering agency—that remain in place alongside the detailed moral differences that I have been discussing. Furthermore, it seems reasonable to expect that these platitudes are *bound* to be in place, because they are bound to be recognized by anyone who is capable of moral reflection at all. For when we raise the revised Socratic question that circumscribes the domain of morals—*How should one live, given that there are other points of view besides one's own from which things matter?*—the *mattering* in question is due precisely to the fact that we are *living, sentient,* and *active* beings, and so we cannot help but value our life, well-being, and agency; and it does seem that to recognize the positive value of these things is to be in a position to recognize three corresponding moral platitudes—*that, in general, killing, harming, and hindering agency are bad.*

In addition to being living, sentient, and active beings, the agents who can raise the revised Socratic question must also be *rational* beings, and this puts in view a fourth moral platitude as well. As rational beings, we cannot affirm the value of anything without affirming that it is valuable in a general way, so that we must value like things alike. This, of course, is just the minimal form of consistency that I claimed in Section 1 is essential for possessing evaluative concepts at all. The interest that rational beings must take in this minimal form of consistency immediately suggests that they should *disvalue arbitrariness in moral responses to situations and people, which fail to treat like cases alike,* and so the fourth moral platitude would be that arbitariness of moral response is in general wrong. Arguably, this platitude underlies much of our current thinking about the moral goodness of fairness and the moral badness of discrimination. Yet it would be a mistake to construe the platitude in such a way that it concerns exactly and only these moral values, for they are thick moral values that historically arose in the following highly specific social contexts: Western democratic institutions, as well as a history of oppression within those institutions, which then gave rise to movements to constrain the oppression, such as, for instance, the civil rights movements and other forms of social and political activism, not to mention influential political theories, such as Rawls's theory of justice. But it seems to me that this fourth platitude might in some way be acknowledged even in social conditions where there is very little equality, but rather a great many ranks and stations and roles in the light of which people treat one another very differently, because there would still be room in such conditions for people to morally object to what they see as arbitrary departures from what is customary and expected. Indeed, I think this platitude could be recognized even in social conditions where it is granted that a sovereign may rightly exercise arbitrary power, insofar as such conditions would still provide for customary expectations among most people about how they ought to treat one another, given their places and roles; and so long as they have such expectations they will naturally object to what they see as arbitrariness of moral response.

If the other three platitudes seem easier to capture, it is because the concepts of killing and harming and hindering agency seem to have some moral content and significance that we can identify without relating them to thick moral concepts—and this seems to contrast with the seemingly much vaguer idea of arbitrary moral response. However, I shall be arguing that all of these platitudes are vague in the same way. More specifically, I shall be arguing that they are all too generic to be action-guiding except in conjunction with thick moral values, and this prevents them from being significant points of moral *agreement* at all, thereby closing off all realistic prospects for running the Davidsonian strategy against relativism, now identified in terms of Multimundialism, in the domain of morals.

As an aside, let me clarify that the argument to come will not be negatively affected if I have not identified all of the moral platitudes on which everyone seems to agree in the face of our moral differences. All the argument requires is that there is some such list of platitudes, and that they all have the same basis, function, and character as the four I have identified: Their basis will lie in the very idea of what *matters* from a point of view, as we reflect upon that idea in response to the revised Socratic question concerning *how one should live, given that there are other points of view besides one's own from which things matter;* their function will be to signal that specifically moral issues are at stake, insofar as the domain of morals is to be specified via the revised Socratic question; their character will be completely *generic,* because they abstract from the very different social conditions in which differently situated people must pose and answer the revised Socratic question for themselves.

Another aside: We should not confuse the *generic* character of the values that figure in the moral platitudes that I have identified with the *thin* character of the values that are the focus of the two major moral theories that I discussed in Section 2, namely Kantian respect and utility. Both sorts of values are conceived in abstraction from the varied social conditions in which people live their moral lives. In the case of these two moral theories, the purpose of such abstraction is to establish universal moral truths that can be appropriate moral guides to all people in all situations. Williams regarded this universalist ambition as misguided precisely because it leads us to underestimate the importance of our moral differences, and how our notions of moral rectitude are tied to our different moral contexts. In contrast with the characteristically universalist ambition of moral theory, my goal has not been to deny our moral differences but rather to underscore them, because what the Davidsonian strategy directs us to do is to examine our moral differences to see if they presuppose any points of moral agreement, and then to explore whether and why those points of agreement might somehow ensure the oneness of the moral world.

The specific question I am now exploring in connection with the Davidsonian strategy is this: Do the moral platitudes that I have identified qualify as such points of moral agreement, which are universally shared even when people employ different thick moral concepts, and if so, do these platitudes suffice to ensure that it is always appropriate for us to embrace the engaged stance of the Unimundialist toward one another, no matter what our thick moral differences might happen to be? If the answer to this question were *yes*, that would undermine what I claimed in the last section is the strongest case for Multimundialism about morals.

Here is one thing that seems relevant to answering this question: Virtually *anything* we value as an instance of a thick moral concept can be seen as an instance of one or another of the generic goods recognized in the platitudes, namely, life, well-being, unhindered agency, and nonarbitrary moral response. Well-being stands out in particular as an all-purpose generic good that we would be pursuing, no matter what other morally significant goods we might also be pursuing (unless we are pathological). Moreover, insofar as our thick moral values ever seem to lead us to act against one of the platitudes, it seems that we would still be acting for the sake of the values that these platitudes register. Thus, earlier I had claimed that when some people inflict harm on others in order to maintain their own honor, we ought not to infer that they reject the platitudinous idea that harming is in general morally bad; rather, we should view them as acting in accord with their thick sense of what is required for their own well being, in the light of their sense of what counts as a harm done to them, and what counts as an appropriately non-arbitrary moral response to that harm done to them. Similarly, when the samurai commit hara-kiri, we ought not to see them as rejecting the platitude against killing, but as displaying their thick moral sense of what the value of life requires, which is that their own life be free of shame. Reflection on cases such as these does seem to invite the conclusion that, whenever people act on their thick moral values and this seems to put them out of accord with one or another of the moral platitudes I have identified, they can neverthe-less be seen as acting in accord with the platitudes.

But does this conclusion really speak against what I have claimed is the strongest case for a Multimundial conclusion? According to that argument, thick moral values are specific to certain social conditions, and they may therefore be *completely irrelevant* in the moral lives of people who are not born to the social conditions to which they are specific—and moreover, it may be that they cannot *become* relevant ei-ther, insofar as it is not always possible for us to import thick moral values from other social conditions and live by them in our own, or to change our social conditions so as to accommodate living by them, or to move to the conditions in which others live by them. What should strike us about this argument is that it does not depend on *denying* that others who occupy different social conditions from ours recog-nize the general moral platitudes against killing, harming, hindering agency, and arbitrary moral response. Everything that I have been say-ing in this section confirms rather that we should allow that they do recognize these platitudes. The difficulty for the Davidsonian argu-ment I am now trying to construct is that these points of agreement do not guarantee that others' thick moral concepts are potentially relevant to our own moral deliberations and inquiries, because of the way in which those thick moral concepts are geared to social condi-tions that are not ours; and in turn, we can see that our thick moral concepts may not be potentially relevant to the moral lives of others either, when others occupy social conditions that are sufficiently dif-ferent from ours. This means that we may have nothing to learn from one another concerning *many* moral matters, and no basis on which to correct one another either. So even if we do accept various moral plati-tudes in common, we must allow that there are other moral matters about which we neither agree nor disagree, because we live by divergent thick moral concepts that are appropriate guides to moral life in our different moral worlds. When we allow this, it seems that we are recog-nizing a boundary of normative insularity in response to which the only appropriate response is to adopt the Multimundial stance.

However, recall that in Section 1 I portrayed the Multimundial view of morals as a very extreme view, on which people who occupy distinct moral worlds do not embrace *any* of the same moral truths. This would not have been established by the strongest case for Multimundialism, if that case left the moral platitudes in place as points of universal moral agreement. Should we conclude, then, that the strongest case for Multimundialism really would be undermined by the pervasiveness of these platitudes in moral life? Or should we conclude, perhaps, that I must have been wrong to portray Multimundialism as such an extreme view that precludes any points of moral agreement at all? I do not think we should draw either of these conclusions. Instead, we should reconsider whether the moral platitudes that I have identified really *are* points of universal moral agreement, or whether they just *appear* to be that.

This is precisely where the issue of holism enters. Only rather than helping to ensure that we are all by and large agree about all moral matters, considerations of holism suggest instead that we do not necessarily agree even on the most basic moral platitudes. We have already seen the reason why: We can never apply these platitudes on their own, without bringing our *thick* moral concepts to bear along with them; and when different people apply them in conjunction with *different* thick moral concepts, this transforms their very meaning. Take, for example, the general value that we place on agency. What we can reasonably regard as the *full* exercise of our agency, and correlatively, what we can reasonably protest against as a hindering of our agency, is largely a function of what we can reasonably expect to *do* in the first place; and the options we face are largely dictated by the social conditions in which we find ourselves—options, as I have said before, for personal projects, relationships, institutional roles, community participation, and such. We must appeal to many thick moral values to guide us in all of these socially situated pursuits, and they in turn help to determine what counts as fully exercised versus hindered agency. The same holds for our conceptions of well-being and correlative harms, because there are obviously many different kinds of social actions that differently situated people might regard as depriving them of their basic well-being, and therefore as harming them—wounds to their honor, pride, work, station, property, relationships, body, or reputation. We saw from the start that what counts as arbitrary and nonarbitrary moral response is highly variable across different social conditions, and must always be fleshed out with the help of thick moral values. It might seem that the value we attach to life itself is different—that the value we place on it when we subscribe to the platitude that killing is wrong can apply in a straightforward way without the help of thick moral values, because unlike our concepts of well-being and fully exercised agency and non-arbitrary moral response, the concept of life has a determinate content that does not need to be fleshed out via thick moral concepts. Yet as I observed above, most everyone allows that we may have occasion to consider sacrificing life for the sake of other goods—to name just a few: honor, shame, punishment, and war—and these allowances reflect different ways in which the value we place on life itself is determined by our sense of our specific practical possibilities, and the thick moral values to which we appeal as we pursue them. These reflections serve to show that we never really do deliberate or act directly from the moral platitudes that I have somewhat misleadingly portrayed as universal points of moral agreement, but always from *versions* of them that are determined by our thick moral values.

As I anticipated at the start of this discussion, this is the very same implication of holism that Kuhn and Feyerabend exploited when they argued that theoretical terms do not retain the same meanings across different theoretical paradigms. In Chapter 3 I tried to show, not that they were wrong about this, but rather that incommensurable scientific theories that arise in different paradigms stand in logical relations nonetheless. I identified *two* conditions that jointly provide for such logical relatedness across paradigms.

First, there is the presence of a very large-scale agreement concerning many interrelated, albeit banal, details. Viewed from the perspective of holism, the presence of these interrelations helps to nail down the *content* of this large-scale agreement sufficiently well that we are within our rights to suppose that it can truly be shared across different theoretical paradigms, even when viewed through the lens of divergent theoretical concepts. Second, proponents of different paradigms have a common explanatory purpose, which is to make systematic sense of those agreed-upon details. Thus, it is their common purpose with respect to the same mass of interconnected details that ensures that their theoretical divergences do not erect barriers of normative insularity but instead put them into scientific disagreement (in those cases where their theories cannot be embraced together).

Let me speak to each of these conditions in turn, in the light of my discussion above of the moral platitudes and their relation to thick moral values.

What my discussion has shown is that the *first* of these conditions that jointly provide for logical relations across incommensurable scientific theories may be missing in the domain of morals. That is, there may be no analogous, holistically pinned-down fund of *detailed* agreement in the domain of morals. The reason is that moral life is lived in particular, historically situated social conditions that can throw up very different practical possibilities, for various life projects, personal relationships, social positions, institutional roles, and the like. What we need from our moral concepts are effective guides to help us evaluate these different practical possibilities in the light of their *thick* moral significance—that is, in the light of the ways in which pursuing them might matter from the points of view of particular others among whom we live in our actual social context. So insofar as we occupy different social contexts that present different practical possibilities, which call for guidance from different thick moral concepts, the *details* of moral life are precisely *not* shared. Furthermore, what I have conceded we *do* share, namely, a common recognition of some highly general moral platitudes, cannot serve as moral guides unless they are suitably qualified to take due account of these details of moral life, which may vary significantly from context to context. It follows that differently situated moral agents are bound to arrive at different understandings of the *contents* of the platitudes, and this calls into question whether they really are points of agreement after all. Yet they are not properly viewed as points of disagreement either—unlike the divergent theoretical claims of incommensurable scientific theories, which *do* conflict because they all relate to a common mass of detailed shared agreements, which provides a common fund of explananda for them all. What we have instead are cases of *alternativeness*, because each divergent construal of the platitudes functions in a different set of social conditions as an effective moral guide *there*, with no bearing on the moral deliberations and inquiries that others might carry out in *other* social conditions. This is all a way of saying that holism is *not* uncontained in the domain of morals, and as a result, there is no scope for an Argument from Holism Against Normative Insularity there.

However, coming now to the second condition, it does seem that differently situated moral agents *do* all share a common purpose, which seems to be analogous to the common explanatory purpose that is shared by all scientists—namely, to address the revised Socratic question, *How should one live, given that there are other points of view besides one's own from which things matter?* This provides a perspective from which they can all see themselves and one another as commonly engaged in specifically *moral* reflection. It also exposes why it seems plausible to say that they *agree* on the moral platitudes in their underspecified, generic form—*in spite* of all I have said about how the platitudes cannot serve as guides to moral life until their contents have been pinned down through connections with thick moral concepts, which may vary from one moral context to another. But the important point is that the platitudes cannot be points of *moral* agreement unless they have a specifically moral content, through which they can be guides to moral life; and insofar as this moral, action-guiding content is supplied through connections with different thick moral concepts, the platitudes emerge as points of moral *difference* rather than as points of moral agreement. The only way to avoid this implication would be by showing that the Argument from Holism Against Normative Insularity does go through in the domain of morals—for then there would be a vast, common fund of content-determining *moral details* to determine common contents for the moral platitudes. But according to the picture of morals that I've said provides the best case for Multimundialism, the moral details of life are precisely *not* the same across different historical and social contexts, and as a result, the meanings of the platitudes vary across such contexts in much the way that Kuhn and Feyerabend had claimed the meanings of scientific terms vary across theoretical paradigms—because they overlooked the presence of a vast, common fund of details in relation to which different scientific theories emerge as logically related, as either consistent and co-tenable or as conflicting. Whereas in morals, if we find that we cannot share others' ways of understanding certain moral platitudes and living by them, we may take ourselves to have encountered a boundary of normative insularity that separates us from another moral world.

I conclude that it simply isn't feasible to apply the Davidsonian strategy, which seeks to show that we all by and large agree about morals, in order to rebut the strongest case for Multiumundialism in the domain of morals.

## 6. Which Stance to Adopt, All Things Considered?

Having come this far in the argument of the entire book, which has sought to provide the correct formulation, if there is one, of relativism, we are left only with the book's final question: If relativism is to be formulated in terms of the notion of alternativeness—itself characterized in terms of the idea of normative insularity—and if, when so formulated, it involves a Multimundial stance rather than a Unimundial stance toward both inquiry and interpersonal relations, which stance do we have *most* reason to adopt in the moral domain?

In this chapter I have specifically argued: that Kantian or utilitarian moral theory would invite Unimundialism if either could claim to capture all of the moral truths, but neither takes due account of the plurality of thick moral values by which we actually live; that although Hobbesian conventionalism about morals might seem to invite Multimundialism, it does not, because the project of morals by agreement gives people a common moral project that invites them to comparatively evaluate different moral agreements, thereby placing them in a single moral world even when they are parties to different moral agreements; that the strongest case for Multimundialism derives from a picture of morals as products of history and culture, on which thick moral values must dominate in moral life, and are tied to specific social conditions; that the Davidsonian strategy of argument against Multimundialism is not successful in the domain of morals, because the background of moral "agreement" that is presupposed by intelligible moral difference amounts to a short list of moral platitudes that are so generic that they cannot serve as guides to moral life except in conjunction with thick moral concepts, and both the thick concepts and the very meanings of the platitudes vary from one moral context to another—from which it follows that the platitudes are not strictly speaking points of moral agreement, and their real function is to establish when we are concerned with the domain of morals, rather than to ensure that we all inhabit the same moral world.

At this point I must declare that the strongest case for Multimundialism in the domain of morals seems to me compelling. But we ought to consider whether there are reasons for caution here, which might deter us from being determined to take up the Multimundial stance for the purposes of moral inquiry, and more generally in our interpersonal dealings with others concerning moral matters. In closing the book, I want to mention just three—and then to say why I think that only the third should give us pause.

(1) The first is one that I have already discussed along the way, but it is important enough that it deserves to be highlighted one last time. It concerns whether, if we decided to adopt moral relativism, we would have to give up on the idea that our moral beliefs can ever put us in touch with *objective truths* about how we should live our moral lives. Many philosophers and nonphilosophers take it for granted that, almost by definition, relativism must incorporate a direct and explicit challenge to the very idea of objectivity. But I want to reiterate that no such challenge is incorporated within the idea of an *alternative* that I have taken as my starting point. What that idea challenges is the *universality* of truth, and it would be a mistake to conflate that with a challenge to its *objectivity*. Thus, when the Multimundialist claims that there is something *local* (that is, not universal) about moral truth, her point is that what we need from our moral beliefs is guidance as we try to navigate the specific moral choices that are thrown up by the specific social conditions in which we find ourselves; she is not claiming that there is nothing to get *right* or *wrong* concerning what it would be morally best for her to do.

(2) Clearly, then, the loss of universality that would come with Multimundialism is not the *metaphysical* cost of having to give up on the very idea of moral objectivity. But it might be wondered whether it would nevertheless bring an unacceptable *moral* cost. In raising this worry, I am not referring to the cost that proponents of the major

moral theories would see in it, which is that we would be giving up on their aspiration to establish universal moral truths. I am taking it as a given that the major theories, dealing as they do in thin moral values, cannot be effective guides to moral life except in conjunction with thick moral values, in much the way I argued in connection with the various moral platitudes I identified in the last section; and this is not properly regarded as a *cost* of moral relativism so much as a *reason* we ought to take it seriously. All the same, it might still seem that if we ever do adopt the Multimundial stance toward others, we will be in danger of overlooking important moral dimensions of our relations to them insofar as they are *persons* in a universal sense that extends across moral contexts and across moral worlds. So let me now try to elaborate how, even as moral relativists, we can, and ought to, acknowledge that the concept of a person really is a universal concept and really does hold a distinctive moral significance.

Such an acknowledgment is an unavoidable consequence of raising the revised Socratic question through which I have proposed to circumscribe the entire domain of morals—to wit, *How shall I live, given that there are other points of view besides my own from which things matter?* Only a person can raise this question; furthermore, any person who does raise it will thereby be led to reflect on the fact that everyone who can and does raise it is a person in exactly the same sense they are, namely, a reflective rational being capable of entering into distinctively interpersonal forms of engagement; and finally, any such person can see that it generally *matters* to persons whether and why and how other persons choose to engage them. It follows that persons together constitute a distinct *moral kind,* the members of which mutually recognize one another as both occasioning and facing the same morally significant choices with respect to one another, concerning whether and why and how to engage one another specifically *as persons.* It also follows that one way in which a person can *morally wrong* another person is by failing to duly acknowledge their personhood, along with the distinctive moral significance that follows upon it. Historically, this has happened when certain polities have failed to extend certain political rights to members of certain groups (such as when the United States did not grant suffrage, and other rights laid down by the U.S. Consti-

tution, to women and African American slaves). One particularly gall-
ing feature of such discrimination was that it did not rest on the claim
that we can sometimes be justified in withholding rights from some
persons (as Locke argued with respect to conquered enemies of war),
but rather, it proceeded from a denial that the persons in question really were persons, or at any rate, *fully* persons. There is good reason to
think that these denials must have been hypocritical, since it was obviously possible to enter into many forms of distinctively interpersonal
engagement with the persons in question. The aim of such hypocrisy
would have been to pretend that no moral wrong was being done in
depriving them of their rights, whereas it actually just compounded
the wrong of that pretense with another wrong—that of failing to accord to some persons within the polity the rights that were supposed
to be accorded to all persons within it, while in the course of life manifestly engaging with them in all sorts of interpersonal ways.[38] If moral
relativism were to embroil us in a related sort of moral wrong, that
would obviously be an unacceptable moral cost. What related moral
wrong might we worry about being embroiled in? Perhaps this: If we
ever were to adopt the Multimundial stance toward others in the moral
domain, then we could not be duly acknowledging their personhood,
precisely because we would be withdrawing from certain forms of interpersonal engagement with them on moral matters. Note that this
would not amount to the hypocrisy of engaging with someone in
distinctively interpersonal ways while explicitly denying their personhood. The situation would rather be the opposite one, of explicitly acknowledging another's personhood while not entering into certain
forms of interpersonal engagement with them—so the worry would be
that this, too, would amount to a failure to *duly* acknowledge their
personhood.

I see no real worry here. When we find grounds for adopting the
Multimundial stance toward others, as I have described in the example

---

38. See Rovane 1998 for further discussion of this hypocritical form of
prejudice against persons, along with an extended defense of the idea that
persons constitute a distinct moral kind that includes all and only those
things that can engage with one another specifically as persons.

about Anjali and me, it is not as though we come to regard them as mere *things* that cannot be engaged in distinctively interpersonal ways. In fact, we cannot so much as raise the issue for ourselves, concerning *which* stance to adopt toward others—the Multimundial or the Unimundial—without thereby acknowledging that others *are* persons who *can* be engaged in distinctively interpersonal ways. Clearly, then, there is no danger that if we ever do adopt the Multimundial stance, we will fall into the kind of hypocritical denial of personhood that has been so appalling in the history of interpersonal relations, or that we would in any other way be led to deny that there is a universal concept of a person that is available across moral contexts and worlds. Nor is there any danger that we would fail to take due account of the ways in which it *matters* to other persons whether and why and how we enter into various forms of interpersonal engagement with them. After all, if we ever do encounter barriers of normative insularity that stand in the way of such engagements, they will be detectable from both sides, just as we saw in the example about Anjali and me. This ensures that none of the parties involved could have a coherent wish for the specific forms of interpersonal engagement that they would already have concluded are not available; correlatively, they could not coherently regard themselves as somehow wronged, or not properly recognized as persons, merely because others have adopted the Multimundial stance toward them. So there is no unacceptable moral cost associated with the concept of a person that would be incurred by adopting the Multimundial stance in the moral domain. We would be denying that moral truths are universal. But we would not be denying that there is a universal concept of a person. On the contrary, we would be acknowledging that anyone toward whom we could adopt the Multimundial Stance is an instance of that universal concept—though at the same time, we would also be acknowledging that persons live their moral lives in particular places and times, and that this may require them to employ *other* moral concepts, besides the concept of a person, *thick* moral concepts that do not have universal application.[39]

---

39. It might be wondered whether the argument I just gave coheres with the argument I gave in the last section. There I argued that the moral

(3) In Chapter 3 I allowed that no case for Multimundialism can ever be so strong as to *refute* Unimundialism on purely logical grounds, because we can always coherently retain a commitment to the Unimundial ideal by *assuming* that logical relations must run everywhere among all truth-value-bearers. If we were to assume this, then whenever we encountered an alleged case of alternativeness in which others' views seem to be normatively insulated from our own, we would have to reinterpret the case to accord with our Unimundial assumption— either by taking it to be a case in which both views really are consistent and co-tenable, or by construing it as a case of disagreement in which one or both of us is mistaken in some way. The point then is, this is always possible, and this requires us to admit that what I have called the "strongest" case for Multimundialism in the moral domain does not suffice to rule out Unimundialism as untenable. Moreover, we must also admit that if we were determined to cleave to the Unimundial stance, we could always view others as moral interlocutors whom we might teach, and from whom we might learn.

Now, if there is *any* possibility for moral learning, then it would seem sensible from both a moral and an epistemic point of view to try to remain *open* to it; and prima facie, this may seem to supply us with an important reason *not* to take up the disengaged stance of the

---

platitudes against harming, killing, hindering agency, and arbitrary moral response may vary in their meanings from one moral context to another, whereas here I have just argued that there is a universal concept of a person that applies in all moral contexts. But here is what accounts for the difference: The concept of a person, though it has moral significance, is not a purely moral concept. It is also a metaphysical and psychological concept that applies in nonmoral contexts as well, and indeed in all contexts where it is possible to give intentional explanations of someone's thoughts and intentional actions. Thus when I regard certain *persons* as inhabiting different moral worlds, I also regard them as inhabiting the same world of natural facts available for scientific inquiry, and as sharing the same vast web of belief that I discussed in the last chapter—indeed it is only then that I can be sure I have encountered someone for whom the moral question arises, and go on to ask whether or not she inhabits the same moral world, in which the very same moral truths are an appropriate guide to moral life.

Multimundialist in the moral domain, precisely because doing so would seem to close us off from these possibilities of moral learning that are afforded by the Unimundial stance.

This, I think, is the strongest source of reservation about the strongest case for Multimundialism with respect to morals. When I first considered it, I concluded all too swiftly that we ought, *in general,* to make Unimundialism our default position.[40] My thought was that if we generally proceed on the assumption that logical relations *do* run everywhere, among all truth-value-bearers, then we shall be far less likely to overlook what opportunities there are for learning from one another, because our assumption will always be prompting us to attempt engagement with others in inquiry and interpersonal relations. I also thought that there would be no harm in proceeding on this assumption, because if we tried to engage others and failed, we could always retreat to the Multimundial stance, in just the way I described in the example about Anjali and me in Chapter 1. As I presented the example there, she and I begin by adopting the Unimundial stance toward one another, and initially take ourselves to have a moral disagreement about whether one is morally obliged to defer to one's parents, and then we retreat to the Multimundial stance only after we have determined that we live in very different moral contexts, and that neither of us has anything to teach or learn from the other about how to live in her own moral context.

However, I should have been more sensitive to the fact that there are real dangers that would attend making the Unimundial stance our default position in the domain of morals. In a way these are *obvious* dangers, since they are due to the very feature of the case that make it possible to cleave to the Unimundial stance come what may—namely, that we cannot refute it on purely logical grounds, because there is always an internally coherent way to maintain it so long as we are prepared to make the appropriate interpretive adjustments, so that we can put our own moral attitudes and claims in logical relation to those of others. To see these dangers, consider again the fact that a Unimundial stance, adopted in this way, would have us approach all of our dealings with others in the following manner: whenever we find

---

40. See Rovane 2002.

that their moral beliefs differ from ours, and we also find that we wish to retain ours without adopting theirs, we should infer that they are mistaken. As is well known, this approach to moral difference has prompted misplaced missionary zeal, misguided efforts at social planning and control, imperial adventures justified as pedagogical projects, and so on. One traditional way of avoiding such harms is through the embrace of tolerance toward the others in question. But when we are tolerant, we are still presuming that when we are not prepared to embrace the moral attitudes of others for ourselves, they must be mistaken—in other words, we are still presuming that all unresolved moral *difference* is to be understood on the model of *disagreement.* And that in itself may be a mistake of another kind with harms of its own—it may be an *interpretive* mistake that puts us on the *wrong moral footing* with others.

Of course, unresolved moral differences may *look* to us like moral disagreements, because we cannot help but focus on the fact that *we* would not act as others do. But we are not really faced with a disagreement with others unless there is some moral proposition to which they assent and from which we dissent (or vice versa), and the question arises, Why should we portray the situation in this particular way? To return to a Davidsonian interpretive theme, we may ask, more specifically, which portrayal would be the most *charitable,* in the sense of making others *fully intelligible*? The situations we are envisaging are not ones that invite the simpleminded application of charity that sees only agreement everywhere, because by hypothesis they are situations of difference. But it would hardly be charitable to *leap* to the conclusion that if we do not face a situation of agreement, then it must be a situation of disagreement. What charity demands is that we ask a series of questions *in advance* of moving to that conclusion: *Why* are others acting in a way that I would not? What moral problem are they trying to solve, with what things-to-be-morally-valued in view as their aims? What thick moral concepts are they bringing to bear in their understanding of that problem, and in their judgment about what solutions to it are available to them, given their particular situation? Then, only *after* determining whether there is a coincidence in the moral problems we face, and in the solutions that are available for solving such problems, can we reasonably draw any conclusions about whether we are faced with a *common* moral matter about which we disagree, and about which we might engage in order to try to resolve that disagreement. When we approach others in this way, we leave open the possibility of discovering that we are *not* faced with a common moral matter about which we disagree, because the moral problems they face are not ones that we ourselves face, and their problems call for the application of thick moral concepts and values that are not appropriate guides for solving our own moral problems— and of course, if this is what we discover, then the appropriate response on our part will be to adopt the Multimundial stance.

The process I just described is one in which we approach others from a state of *suspense* about whether the Unimundial or the Multi-mundial stance is the more appropriate stance to take toward them in the moral domain. It seems to me that this is the *only* approach that can remain truly *open* to moral learning from others without falling into the mistakes we might incur if we were to adopt either the Uni-mundial or the Multimundial stance as our default position. When we withhold default status from both stances and adopt instead a position of suspense between them, we generate just the right combination of attitudes to, and method in, moral inquiry.

This, then, is what the procedure of such moral inquiry would look like: When we encounter moral attitudes and claims different from our own, we ought not to presume either that they do or that they do not stand in direct logical relations to our own. We ought to approach the task of interpreting others' moral attitudes and claims with more *curiosity* about the specific conditions they face than the Unimundial stance embodies, so that we are open to learning that it is appropriate for them to live by thick moral values that we do not share. At the same time, we ought to remain alive to possibilities for engagement that the Multimundial stance forsakes, so that *if* the thick moral truths that others know can be truths for us too, we will not fail to discover them. Yet this is an openness to learning that is quite unlike the open-ness implied by the Unimundial stance, because the openness may re-veal that, in some cases, the world of our moral concerns is, in a quite literal and metaphysical sense, distinct from that of others. It is an open-minded stance of moral curiosity, then, that acknowledges the potential limits of moral engagement.

References

Acknowledgments

Index

# References

Anscombe, G. E. M. (1957) 1963. *Intention*. Oxford: Basil Blackwell.

Aristotle. 2009. *Nicomachean Ethics*. Translated by David Ross. Oxford: Oxford University Press.

Ayer, A. J. (1936) 1971. *Language, Truth and Logic*. London: Penguin Books.

Bilgrami, A. 1992. *Belief and Meaning*. Oxford: Basil Blackwell.

———. 2006. *Self-Knowledge and Resentment*. Cambridge, Mass.: Harvard University Press.

Blackburn, S. 1993. *Essays in Quasi-Realism*. Oxford: Oxford University Press.

Boghossian, P. 2006a. *Fear of Knowledge: Against Relativism and Constructivism*. Oxford: Oxford University Press.

———. 2006b. "What Is Relativism?" In *Truth and Realism,* ed. P. Greenough and M. P. Lynch. Oxford: Oxford University Press.

Carnap, R. (1928) 2003. *The Logical Structure of the World*. Peru, Ill.: Open Court.

———. 1947. "Empiricism, Semantics and Ontology." In *Meaning and Necessity*. Chicago: University of Chicago Press.

Chang, R., ed. 1998. *Incommensurability, Incomparability and Practical Reason*. Cambridge, Mass.: Harvard University Press.

Chomsky, N. 2000. *New Horizons in the Study of Language*. Cambridge: Cambridge University Press.

———. 2009. "The Mysteries of Nature: How Deeply Hidden?" *Journal of Philosophy* 106 (4): 167–200.

Colodny, R. G., ed. 1965. *Beyond the Edge of Certainty: Essays in Contemporary Science and Philosophy.* Englewood Cliffs, N.J.: Prentice-Hall.

Davidson, D. 1973. "On the Very Idea of a Conceptual Scheme." *Proceedings and Addresses of the American Philosophical Association* 47: 5–20; reprinted in D. Davidson 1984.

———. 1980. *Essays on Actions and Events.* Oxford: Oxford University Press.

———. 1984. *Inquiries into Truth and Interpretation.* Oxford: Oxford University Press.

———. 2001. *Subjective, Intersubjective, Objective.* Oxford: Oxford University Press.

———. 2004. *Problems of Rationality.* Oxford: Oxford University Press.

Dupre, J. 1995. *The Disorder of Things: Metaphysical Foundations of the Disunity of Science.* Cambridge, Mass.: Harvard University Press.

Feyerabend, P. 1965. "Problems of Empiricism." In Colodny 1965.

Fodor, J., and E. LePore. 1992. *Holism: A Shopper's Guide.* Cambridge, Mass.: Basil Blackwell.

Frankfurt, H. 1971. "Freedom of the Will and the Concept of a Person." *Journal of Philosophy* 68 (1): 5–20.

Goodman, N. 1978. *Ways of Worldmaking.* Indianapolis: Hackett Press.

Griffin, J. 1977. "Are There Incommensurable Values?" *Philosophy and Public Affairs* 7 (1): 39–50.

Hales, S. D. 2011. *A Companion to Relativism.* Oxford: Basil Blackwell.

Hardy, H., ed. 2002. *Isaiah Berlin: Liberty.* Oxford: Oxford University Press.

Hare, R. 2003. *The Psychopathy Checklist.* Toronto: Multi-Health Systems.

Hare, R. M. 1952. *The Language of Morals.* Oxford: Clarendon Press.

Harman, G. 1975. "Moral Relativism Defended." *Philosophical Review* 84 (1): 3–22.

Hempel, C. 1950. "Problems and Changes in the Empiricist Criterion of Meaning." *Revue Internationale de Philosophie* 41 (11): 41–63.

Hobbes, T. (1660) 1996. *Leviathan.* Oxford: Oxford University Press.

Hume, D. (1740) 1978. *A Treatise of Human Nature.* Edited by L. A. Selby-Bigge. Oxford: Oxford University Press.

———. 1751. *An Enquiry concerning the Principles of Morals.* Oxford: Clarendon Press, 1999.

James, W. (1890) 1981. *The Principles of Psychology.* Cambridge, Mass.: Harvard University Press.

———. (1897) 1979. "The Will to Believe." In *The Will to Believe and Other Essays in Popular Philosophy.* Cambridge, Mass.: Harvard University Press.

Kagan, S. 1989. *The Limits of Morality.* Oxford: Oxford University Press.

Kant, I. (1781) 1998. *Critique of Pure Reason*. Translated by P. Guyer and A. Wood. Cambridge: Cambridge University Press.

———. (1785) 1997. *Groundwork of the Metaphysics of Morals*. Translated by M. Gregor. Cambridge: Cambridge University Press.

Kolbel, M. 2002. *Truth without Objectivity*. London: Routledge.

Kolodny, N. 2005. "Why Be Rational?" *Mind* 114 (455): 509–563.

Kuhn, T. S. 1962. *The Wright Structure of Scientific Revolutions*. Chicago: University of Chicago Press.

Levi, I. 1990. *Hard Choices: Decision-Making under Unresolved Conflict*. Cambridge: Cambridge University Press.

MacFarlane, J. 2005. "Making Sense of Relative Truth." *Proceedings of the Aristotelian Society* 105: 321–339.

———. 2007. "Relativism and Disagreement." *Philosophical Studies* 132: 17–31.

———. 2008. "Relativism about Truth Itself." In *Relative Truth*, edited by M. Garcia-Carpintero and M. Kolbe. Oxford: Oxford University Press.

———. 2009. "Nonindexical Contextualism." *Synthese* 166 (2): 231–250.

Mackie, J. L. 1977. *Ethics: Inventing Right and Wrong*. London: Penguin Books.

McDowell, J. 1986. "Critical Notice of Bernard Williams: *Ethics and the Limits of Philosophy*." *Mind* 95 (379): 377–386.

———. 1998. *Meaning, Knowledge, and Reality*. Cambridge, Mass.: Harvard University Press.

Moore, G. E. (1903) 1993. *Principia Ethica*. Revised edition. Cambridge: Cambridge University Press.

Nagel, T. 1974. "What Is It Like to Be a Bat?" *Philosophical Review* 83 (4): 435–450.

———. 1986. *The View from Nowhere*. Oxford: Oxford University Press.

Parfit, D. 1984. *Reasons and Persons*. Oxford: Clarendon Press.

———. 2011. *On What Matters*. Oxford: Clarendon Press.

Quine, W. V. (1953) 1980. "Two Dogmas of Empiricism." In *From a Logical Point of View*. Cambridge, Mass.: Harvard University Press.

———. 1960. *Word and Object*. Cambridge, Mass.: MIT Press.

Quine, W. V., and S. Ullian. 1978. *The Web of Belief*. New York: McGraw-Hill.

Raz, J. 1986. *The Morality of Freedom*. Oxford: Oxford University Press.

Recanati, F. 2007. *Perspectival Thought: A Plea for (Moderate) Relativism*. Oxford: Oxford University Press.

Rorty, R. 1972. "The World Well Lost." *Journal of Philosophy* 69 (19): 649–655.

———. 1982. *Consequences of Pragmatism*. Minneapolis: University of Minnesota Press.

———. 1989. *Contingency, Irony and Solidarity*. Cambridge: Cambridge University Press.

Rovane, C. 1998. *The Bounds of Agency: An Essay in Revisionary Metaphysics.* Princeton: Princeton University Press.

———. 2002. "Earning the Right to Realism and Relativism in Ethics." *Philosophical Issues* 12 (1): 264–285.

———. 2005. "On the Very Idea of an Ethical Scheme." *Iyyun: The Jerusalem Philosophical Quarterly* 54: 109–128.

———. 2008. "Did Williams Find the Truth in Relativism?" In *Reading Bernard Williams,* edited by D. Callcut. London: Routledge.

———. 2010. "Why Scientific Realism May Not Refute Relativism." In *Naturalism and Normativity,* edited by M. De Caro and D. MacArthur. New York: Columbia University Press.

———. 2011. "Relativism Requires Alternatives, Not Disagreement or Relative Truth." In Hales 2011.

———. 2012. "How to Formulate Relativism." In *Language, Meaning and Mind: Themes from the Philosophy of Crispin Wright,* edited by A. Coliva. Oxford: Oxford University Press.

Ryle, G. 1945. "Knowing How and Knowing That." *Proceedings of the Aristotelian Society* 46: 1–16.

Scheffler, I. 2000. "A Plea for Pluralism." *Erkenntnis* 52 (2): 161–173.

Sen, A. 1977. "Maximization and the Act of Choice." *Econometrica* 65 (4): 745–759.

Smart, J. J. C., and B. Williams 1973. *Utilitarianism For and Against.* Cambridge: Cambridge University Press.

Stevenson, C. L. 1944. *Ethics and Language.* New Haven: Yale University Press.

Strawson, P. F. 1959. *Individuals: An Essay in Descriptive Metaphysics.* London: Methuen.

———. 1962. "Freedom and Resentment." *Proceedings of the British Academy* 48: 1–25.

Stroud, B. 1968. "Transcendental Arguments." *Journal of Philosophy* 65 (9): 241–256.

Whorf, B. 1956. *Language, Thought and Reality: Selected Writings of Benjamin P. Whorf.* Edited by J. Carroll. Cambridge, Mass.: MIT Press.

Williams, B. 1981. "The Truth in Relativism." In *Moral Luck.* Oxford: Oxford University Press.

———. 1985. *Ethics and the Limits of Philosophy.* London: Fontana.

Wright, C. 1992. *Truth and Objectivity.* Cambridge, Mass.: Harvard University Press.

———. 2001. "On Being in a Quandary: Relativism, Vagueness and Indeterminacy." *Mind* 110 (437): 45–98.

———. 2006. "Intuitionism, Realism, Relativism and Rhubarb." In *Truth and Realism,* edited by P. Greenough and M. P. Lynch. Oxford: Oxford University Press.

———. 2007. "New Age Relativism." *Philosophical Issues* 17 (1): 262–283.

# Acknowledgments

I have been teaching, lecturing, and publishing on the topic of relativism for some years now, and received many stimulating comments from many people on many occasions—more than I can possibly acknowledge.

Among my students at Columbia University, I would especially like to thank Samuel Preston, who never took a course with me on the subject, but who read my book manuscript with as much responsive and acute philosophical attention as a fully mature colleague.

Among my colleagues, I would like to thank David Albert, John Collins, Haim Gaifman, Philip Kitcher, Achille Varzi, and Katja Vogt for patiently hearing me out at one time or another on my ideas about relativism, and in some cases reading one or another bit of my writings about them.

I would especially like to thank my oldest and closest philosophical friends for their sustaining companionship and help over the years, and constant willingness to read whatever I write: Donald Davidson and Peter Strawson, both of whom I miss very much; Michael Della

Rocca, Isaac Levi, and Stephen White, who have never failed to engage whenever I have had something on my mind; and, *as always,* Akeel Bilgrami.

Finally, I would like to thank the anonymous referees for this book, all of whom made helpful comments.

# Index

Agency, 209–210. *See also* Choice;
    Deliberation; Freedom; Rationality;
    Values: action-guiding character of
Agreement: normative significance of,
    20, 54; moral, 101–102, 220, 249–250,
    256–260, 269; and holism, 151–153,
    180–181; across scientific paradigms,
    160–165, 168, 176, 176n21. *See also*
    Contractualism; Conventions: moral;
    Principle of charity
Alienation, 98–99
All-things-considered judgments, 64–68,
    207–208, 210–212, 215, 218
Alternatives: defined, 58, 74, 77, 79, 97,
    100; intuitive conception of, 70;
    alternative conceptual schemes, 137;
    vs. Kuhnian incommensurability,
    160–166; unknowable, 180–181,
    186–193; and incommensurability of
    values, 220. *See also* Dilemma for

Alternativeness; Exclusion; Indiffer-
    ence; Multimundialism, defined;
    Multimundial stance; Normative
    insularity; Truth: true for
Analytic-synthetic distinction, 139, 141,
    148
Anscombe, G. E. M., 201n9
Antinomies of Pure Reason, 23
Antirealism, 12, 34, 44, 83, 88, 92–93,
    102–103, 228
Aristotle, 210n17
Assessment relativism, 59–70. *See also*
    MacFarlane, J.; Semantic relativism;
    Truth: relative
Atomism, 147
Ayer, A. J., 22n2

Berlin, I., 213n21
Bilgrami, A., 48n15, 151n16, 154n17,
    196n2, 209n16

Bivalence, 81. *See also* Truth-value gap

Blackburn, S., 201n8

Boghossian, P., 96n14

Burden of proof, 38, 40, 78, 112–118

Carnap, R., 73, 73n4, 126, 129–136, 141

Categorical imperative. *See* Kantian moral theory

Chang, R., 212n20

Choice, 196, 207, 217–218. *See also* Agency; Deliberation; Freedom: of the will; Options

Chomsky, N., 129, 150, 150n15, 171n19, 187–190, 187n27, 193

Cognitive abilities, 187–193. *See also* Chomsky, N.; Epistemic limitations; Language; Modularity of mind

Cognitive science, 187–188, 190–192. *See also* Facts: mental

Cognitivism, 205–206, 207n14, 241n35. *See also* Noncognitivism; Objectivity: in morals; Truth: moral

Coherence: logical, 19–20, 63, 81–82, 93–95, 98, 113–114, 268; philosophical, 39, 56, 64n19. *See also* Consistency; Incoherence

Collins, J., 95n13

Commensurability of values, 212–221, 232–237. *See also* Consistency: as transitive ordering; Incommensurability: of moral values; Rationality; Transitive ordering of values

Commitments: normative, 196n2; evaluative, 207, 207n14

Common sense: and relativism, 116; and philosophy, 117–118, 169; and science, 169–170

Comparative evaluation. *See* Commensurability of values; Deliberation; Rationality; Transitive ordering of values

Completeness, logical, 80–81

Concepts: as clusters of beliefs, 142; evaluative, 202–203. *See also* Consis-tency: of evaluative response; Moral values: thick; Moral values: thin

Conceptual schemes, 128, 178–179. *See also* Davidson, D.; Linguistic frameworks; Paradigms, scientific; Scheme-content distinction; Translation: translatability

Conflict, practical, 49–50, 203, 207. *See also* Contradiction; Disagreements: moral; Exclusion

Conjunction, 94, 129, 189. *See also* Consistency: and cotenability; Law of conjunction

Consistency: and cotenability, 77, 129, 172, 189, 219, 226; of evaluative response, 202–203, 253–254; as transitive ordering, 207, 211, 219. *See also* Conjunction; Dilemma for Alternativeness; Law of conjunction; Unimundial Ideal

Constructivism. *See* Conventions: moral; Language: constructivist account of

Context: context of use, 36, 37, 59–62, 69; context of assessment, 36, 59–63; moral, 44, 55, 61–62, 66–68, 103, 224, 242–246, 249–250, 255, 260–261, 266, 268; and interpretation, 151–154; and comparative evaluation, 213. *See also* Social conditions

Contractualism, 225, 233. *See also* Conventions: moral; Harman, G.; Hobbes, T.; Self-interest

Contradiction, 31, 32, 35, 37, 44–45, 49, 53, 64, 69–70, 72, 74, 104, 176. *See also* Conflict, practical; Disagreements; Exclusion; Law of noncontradiction

Conventions: moral, 11–12, 227–239; linguistic, 133, 136

Conversion, 107–110, 164

Davidson, D., 48, 73–74, 126, 128, 136–170, 150n15, 178–183, 196n2, 247, 249

Decisive experiments, 175–177. *See also* Feyerabend, P.

Deliberation, 65–66, 196, 207–208, 210–211, 217–219, 231

Dilemma for Alternativeness, 75–76, 78, 98, 117, 129, 146–148. *See also* Alternatives; Conjunction; Contradiction; Exclusion; Logical relations; Normative insularity

Direction of fit, 201n9. *See also* Anscombe, G. E. M.; Facts: fact-value distinction; Noncognitivism; Values: action-guiding character of

Disagreements: irresoluble, 15–16, 18, 22–27, 32, 89, 106–107, 110, 115, 156–157, 163–168; relativism-inducing, 16, 27, 30, 32, 46, 53, 57, 65, 69, 72, 75, 95, 104, 110; normative significance of, 18–20, 30–33, 51–53, 56, 58, 68, 106, 115; ordinary, 21, 25, 30, 32, 42–43, 69, 110, 115, 164; resolution of, 21–22, 25, 31, 43, 46, 57; Hegelian attitude toward, 25; intelligibility of, 143–145, 151; moral, 269–270. *See also* Conflict, practical; Contradiction; Dilemma for Alternativeness; Disputes of inclination; Exclusion; Epistemic relativism

Disengagement. *See* Alienation; Engagement; Indifference; Multimundial stance

Disputes of inclination, 16, 27, 74–75. *See also* Disagreements

Dogmatism, 108, 157, 174. *See also* Feyerabend, P.

Doubt, 23, 116. *See also* Mill, J. S.; Peirce, C. S.; Pragmatism; Skepticism

Dupre, J., 172n20

Egoism, 197, 199, 224, 227, 234–237. *See also* Conventions: moral; Harman, G.; Hobbes, T.; Moral theory; Rationality: as foundation of morality; Self-interest

Emotivism, 201–204. *See also* Ayer, A. J.; Hume, D.; Expressivism; Noncognitivism; Prescriptivism; Stevenson, C. L.

Empiricism: empiricist criterion of cognitive significance, 22, 132, 135; dogmas of, 126, 139–140, 147–148. *See also* Atomism; Feyerabend, P.; Objectivity: and empiricism; Observation, theory-ladenness of

Engagement, 98, 100, 153, 173, 209, 220–221, 234, 240, 264, 270. *See also* Alienation; Indifference; Inquiry; Multimundial stance; Unimundial stance

Epistemic limitations, 26–27, 26n5, 187–190, 193. *See also* Alternatives: unknowable; Cognitive abilities; Epistemic relativism; Skepticism

Epistemic relativism, 4, 18, 26, 32, 156

Error theory, 200–201. *See also* Mackie, J. L.

Eudaimonism, 222n26

Examples, use of in philosophy, 38–40, 46–47, 78, 102, 113, 149n12

Exclusion: due to logical conflict, 51, 75, 104; as basic to relativism, 52–56, 69, 74, 103–105; due to normative insularity, 78, 96–97. *See also* Alternatives; Conflict, practical; Contradiction

Explanations, 162, 168, 170–172, 177–178

Expressivism, 201. *See also* Emotivism; Noncognitivism; Prescriptivism

Facts: fact-value distinction, 112, 136, 195–196, 201, 203; natural, 125–126, 147, 191, 195–196; mental, 136; moral, 200, 214–215. *See also* Mind-world relation; Objectivity; Realism

Feyerabend, P., 73, 73n2, 108n18, 126, 128, 156–157, 173–178, 177n2, 248–250, 259, 261

First person point of view. *See* Point of view

Fodor, J., 149, 150n13

Frankfurt, H., 209, 209n15. *See also* Freedom: of the will; Wantons

Freedom: compatiblist account of, 161; of the will, 209. *See also* Agency; Choice; Frankfurt, H.; Hume, D.; Values: irreducibility of

Friedman, M., 98n15

Goodman, N., 73, 73n4, 136
Griffin, J., 213n22

Happiness, 223. *See also* Utilitarianism
Hare, R., 198n5
Hare, R. M., 202. *See also* Prescriptivism
Harman, G., 228–238, 229n30, 230n31, 237n33. *See also* Contractarianism; Conventions: moral; Egoism; Hobbes, T.; Self-interest; Truth: relative
Hempel, C., 132n4
Hobbes, T., 228, 228n29, 234
Holism: of meaning and belief, 48–49; of meaning, 104n17, 126, 141, 165; uncontained, 108, 147, 154, 160, 167, 176, 248–249, 261; of confirmation, 126, 140–141, 157–159, 166–167, 175; of belief, 142–145; objections to, 147–153; in the domain of morals, 258, 260–261. *See also* Concepts: as clusters of beliefs; Davidson, D.; Observation, theory-ladenness of; Principle of charity; Quine, W. V. O.; Web of belief
Hume, D., 147–149, 148n10, 161, 195, 196n1, 201–204, 204n11. *See also* Emotivism; Facts: fact-value distinction; Laws: causal; Laws: psychological
Hypocrisy, 265–266

Idealism, 173
Identity, 242–245
Ignorance, 214–215, 218–219. *See also* Alternatives: unknowable; Epistemic limitations; Skepticism
Incoherence, 28, 64, 79

Incommensurability: in science, 24n4, 104, 126–127, 155–166, 171–177, 259; within a point of view, 212–221; distinguished from pluralism, 213; of moral values, 235–236. *See also* Commensurability of values; Disagreements; Epistemic relativism; Holism: of confirmation; Kuhn, T.; Normative insularity; Science: revolutions in; Transitive ordering of values; Web of belief
Indexical relativism, 37, 44
Indexicals, 36, 44, 59–60
Indifference, 57, 89–90, 98–100, 116, 126, 146, 216–218. *See also* Alienation; Engagement; Multimundial stance
Induction. *See* Hume, D.; Inferential relations; Laws: causal; Laws: scientific; Logical relations
Inferential relations, 94–95. *See also* Concepts: as clusters of beliefs; Holism; Laws: logical; Logical relations
Inquiry: ideal limit of, 85–88; and Unimundialism, 86–90, 99; and Multimundialism, 99–100; scientific, 169, 194; moral, 214n24, 234, 245–247, 263, 267–268, 270. *See also* Levi, I.; Pragmatism; Science: normal
Interpretation, 47–48, 51–54, 151–153, 161, 165, 182, 252, 267, 268–269. *See also* Davidson, D.; Principle of charity; Psychological attribution; Quine, W. V. O.; Translation: radical translation
Intuitions: about relativism, 15–17, 38–39, 56, 72–76, 91–93, 105; linguistic, 47–48, 154n17. *See also* Common sense; Examples, use of in philosophy

James, W., 88, 108, 108n18, 150, 150n14

Kant, I., 23, 83, 97, 130–131, 183, 185. *See also* Kantian moral theory;

Transcendental argument; Transcendental idealism

Kantian moral theory, 221–222, 224–225

Knowledge: self-knowledge, 154n17, 183–186, 190; of other minds, 180, 183–186, 190, 192; knowledge that vs. knowledge how, 189–193. *See also* Cognitivism; Empiricism; Inquiry; Objectivity; Science

Kolbel, M., 28n7

Kolodny, N., 211, 211n19

Kripke, S., 113n21

Kuhn, T., 24n4, 72–73, 72n, 104, 126–128, 155–177, 155n, 248–250, 259, 261

Language: formal, 77, 80–81, 132–133; natural, 132, 189–190, 192; constructivist account of, 136. *See also* Chomsky, N.; Cognitive abilities; Conceptual schemes; Epistemic limitations; Interpretation; Intuitions: linguistic; Linguistic frameworks; Translation

Law of conjunction, 77, 94. *See also* Conjunction; Consistency; Laws: logical; Logical relations

Law of noncontradiction, 16, 19, 28, 32, 54, 57, 63, 69, 75, 77, 96, 105. *See also* Contradiction; Exclusion; Laws: logical; Logical relations

Laws: logical, 95; causal, 148–149, 161, 204n11; psychological, 150, 154, 196, 204n11; scientific, 161–162, 168. *See also* Facts: mental; Law of conjunction; Law of noncontradiction

Levi, I., 23n3, 196n2, 214n24

Life projects, 223

Linguistic frameworks, 73, 133–135, 140. *See also* Analytic-synthetic distinction; Carnap, R.; Conceptual schemes; Empiricism; Language: formal; Objectivity: and empiricism

Linguistics. *See* Intuition: linguistic

Logical positivism, 22–23, 132–133, 158, 202

Logical relations, 79, 89–90, 94–95, 97, 108, 133, 145, 148–149, 160, 175–176, 199, 202, 204n11, 209, 211, 231–235, 243, 248, 259. *See also* Commensurability of values; Dilemma for Alternativeness; Inferential relations; Laws: logical; Normative insularity; Transitive ordering of values

MacFarlane, J., 28n8, 38n13, 58n16

Mackie, J. L., 200–201, 200n1, 201n1, 241n34

McDowell, J., 210–211, 211n18, 242n36

Meaning. *See* Analytic-synthetic distinction; Holism; Interpretation; Language; Translation

Metaphysics, 79–80, 83–85, 88, 91–92, 98, 109, 135, 172, 263

Methodological pluralism. *See* Pluralism: methodological

Mill, J. S., 21, 31, 31n10, 115, 177n22

Mind-world relation, 109n20, 128, 137, 179, 182–185, 191. *See also* Davidson, D.; Rorty, R.; Scheme-content distinction; Triangulation

Modularity of mind, 188. *See also* Chomsky, N.; Cognitive abilities

Moore, G. E., 195–196, 196n1. *See also* Moore's paradox

Moore's paradox, 52, 86, 95–96

Moral platitudes, 249–250, 253–262, 266n39. *See also* Agreement: moral

Moral reflection, 197–199, 221, 226, 253, 255, 261, 264. *See also* Moral values: domain of; Socrates's question

Moral theory, 43, 197, 199, 221–226, 255, 264

Moral values: domain of, 195–199, 204, 228, 243–244, 255, 264; thin, 223–226, 255, 264; thick, 223–224, 226, 239–246, 251, 254–261. *See also* Commensurability of values; Moral platitudes; Moral reflection; Moral theory; Socrates's question; Values

Multimundialism, defined, 10, 91, 100, 132. *See also* Alternatives; Normative insularity; Worlds

Multimundial stance, 93, 99–101, 118, 126–127, 146, 179, 192, 209, 212, 220, 234–236, 238, 265–270. *See also* Incommensurability: of moral values; Indifference; Normative insularity; Worlds

Nagel, T., 84, 188, 188n28
Natural facts. *See* Facts: natural
Naturalism, about morals, 195–196. *See also* Hume, D.; Moore, G. E.; Values: irreducibility of
Natural kind, 152
Nihilism, 204, 241–242
Noncognitivism, 201–205, 241n35
Nonindexical contextualism, 38n13
Normative insularity: defined, 79, 92, 94, 96–97; of linguistic frameworks, 133–136; in the domain of natural facts, 146–148, 153–154, 156, 160, 165–166, 178, 187, 193, 260; in the domain of morals, 212, 219–220, 227–231, 234–236, 238, 250, 257, 262. *See also* Exclusion; Facts: fact-value distinction; Incommensurability: of moral values; Indifference; Logical relations; Multimundial stance; Worlds
Notional confrontations, 103–110

Objectivity: in science, 132, 156, 173–174, 193; and empiricism, 132–135, 157, 173–174; in morals, 213, 241, 263. *See also* Cognitivism; Mind-world relation; Realism; Truth; View from Nowhere
Observation, theory-ladenness of, 158–159, 165, 166–167, 174. *See also* Analytic-synthetic distinction; Empiricism; Holism; Web of belief

Omniscience, 64n20, 182, 186–189. *See also* View from Everywhere
Options, 207–208, 216–219, 238, 258. *See also* Choice; Possibilities: practical

Paradigms, scientific, 72, 104, 161–167, 259. *See also* Incommensurability: in science; Kuhn, T.; Science: normal
Paradox, 29n9, 81, 113n21. *See also* Moore's paradox
Parfit, D., 198n4, 226n28. *See also* Moral theory
Peirce, C. S., 85–87, 115–116. *See also* Inquiry: ideal limit of; Pragmatism
Persons, 264–266
Physics, 10, 172–173, 187
Pluralism: methodological, 175; with respect to moral values, 213, 214, 220, 222–223, 228. *See also* Incommensurability: of moral values; Moral values: thick
Point of view, 80, 84, 87, 160, 180, 191–192, 198–199, 212–215, 226, 246
Possibilities: metaphysical, 84–85, 128, 180; logical, 97, 128, 146–148; conceptual, 128, 135, 178–182, 231; practical, 233, 238, 245, 259–260. *See also* Options
Pragmatism, 23, 85–88, 115–116, 192. *See also* Peirce, C. S.; Rorty, R.
Prescriptivism, 202, 204. *See also* Expressivism; Hare, R. M.; Noncognitivism
Principle of charity, 128, 137–138, 141–145, 186, 247–248, 269. *See also* Davidson, D.; Holism; Interpretation; Quine, W. V. O.; Translation: radical translation
Progress, epistemic, 86–87, 108. *See also* Pragmatism; Realism: scientific; Science: progress of
Projectivism. *See* Error theory; Quasi realism
Propositional knowledge. *See* Knowledge: knowledge that vs. knowledge how

Psychological attribution, 49, 151–154. *See also* Context: and interpretation; Holism; Interpretation; Knowledge: of other minds; Laws: psychological

Psychology. *See* Cognitive science; Facts: mental; Laws: psychological; Psychological attribution

Psychopath, 197–198. *See also* Egoism; Hare, R.; Moral reflection

Quasi realism, 201n8. *See also* Blackburn, S.

Quine, W. V. O., 36, 48, 126, 132n4, 138–143, 139n7, 141n8, 142n9, 166–170, 174–175. *See also* Analytic-synthetic distinction; Empiricism: dogmas of; Holism; Principle of charity; Translation: radical translation; Web of belief

Rationalism. *See* Rationality: as foundation of morality

Rationality: internalist conception of, 23–25, 89–90, 115–116; failure of, 64n20, 66; as foundation of morality, 205, 236–238; ideal of, 207–212, 215, 218. *See also* All-things-considered judgments; Deliberation

Raz, J., 212–221, 215n25. *See also* Incommensurability: within a point of view; Incommensurability: of moral values

Reactive attitudes, 204. *See also* Strawson, P. F.

Realism: scientific, 35, 108, 152–153, 173, 178; Tractarian, 80, 83–84; and relativism, 83–84, 88, 92–93, 102, 108–109, 127–128, 173, 191–193, 241; modal, 92; moral, 103, 241; metaphysical, 192. *See also* Cognitivism; Mind-world relation; Naturalism, about morals; Objectivity; View from Nowhere

Reduction. *See* Science: special sciences; Science: unity of; Naturalism, about

morals; Truth: reduction of; Values: irreducibility of

Regulative ideal, 82, 85–86

Relativism: as a metaphysical doctrine, 15, 18; as a universal doctrine, 28–29, 39, 111, 113n21; as a domain-specific doctrine, 29, 39, 82, 111. *See also* Alternatives; Assessment relativism; Epistemic relativism; Indexical relativism; Multimundialism, defined; Normative insularity; Semantic relativism

Revision: of belief, 56–57, 82, 86–87, 89–90, 101, 106, 140–141, 145–146, 166–170; of common sense, 118–119; of logic, 120, 140; of meaning, 140–141. *See also* Engagement; Holism: of confirmation; Science: revolutions in; Unimundial stance; Web of belief

Rights, 223–225, 264–265

Rorty, R., 73, 73nn5,6, 100, 109–110, 136

Ryle, G., 190n29

Scheffler, I., 172n20

Scheme-content distinction, 128, 137, 179. *See also* Analytic-synthetic distinction; Conceptual schemes; Davidson, D.; Empiricism: dogmas of; Holism; Linguistic frameworks; Mind-world relation

Science: revolutions in, 156, 163–166; normal, 163–166; special sciences, 171–172; unity of, 171–172; progress of, 173–174. *See also* Cognitive science; Empiricism; Facts: natural; Laws; Objectivity: in science; Paradigms, scientific; Physics

Self-criticism, 66, 196, 198, 210

Self-interest, 224–228, 232–236. *See also* Contractualism; Egoism

Self-knowledge. *See* Knowledge: self-knowledge

Semantic relativism, 28, 35–38, 44–45, 58, 62–70, 96, 231. *See also* Assessment relativism; Indexical relativism; Truth: relative

Skepticism, 5, 88, 116, 128, 137, 174, 179, 182–186, 192. *See also* Doubt; Transcendental argument

Social conditions, 109, 235–239, 241–246, 251, 254, 257–260. *See also* Context: moral

Sociology, 54, 67, 245

Socrates's question, 197–199, 204, 209, 227–228, 234, 245, 253, 261, 264. *See also* Moral reflection; Moral values: domain of

Solipsism, 197. *See also* Egoism; Psychopath

Stance. *See* Multimundial stance; Unimundial stance

Strawson, P. F., 183, 183n25, 205. *See also* Reactive attitudes; Transcendental argument

Stevenson, C. L., 202n10

Stroud, B., 183, 183n25

Theory-observation distinction. *See* Analytic-synthetic distinction; Empiricism: dogmas of; Holism: of confirmation; Observation, theory-ladenness of; Scheme-content distinction; Web of belief

Tolerance, 240, 269

Transcendental argument, 183, 192–193. *See also* Epistemic limitations; Kant, I.; Realism; Strawson, P.F.; Stroud, B.; Transcendental idealism

Transcendental idealism, 83, 129–131, 185, 191. *See also* Kant, I.

Transitive ordering of values, 207, 213–214, 218–222, 226, 228, 243–246. *See also* All-things-considered judgments; Commensurability of values; Consistency: as transitive ordering; Rationality

Translation: translatability, 45–46, 73–74, 137, 159, 164–165, 180–181; radical translation, 141. *See also* Interpretation; Language

Triangulation, 183–186. *See also* Davidson, D.; Knowledge: of other minds; Knowledge: self-knowledge; Mind-world relation; Skepticism; Transcendental argument

Truth: relative, 16, 28–38, 44–45, 52, 62, 69, 96, 200, 231; universal, 29n9, 96–99, 113n21, 118, 245, 255, 263–264, 266; moral, 35, 42–44, 61, 67, 199, 200–206, 219, 231, 241–242, 255, 258, 263, 266; conceptual, 39–40; Peirce's definition of, 86; reduction of, 88, 192; true for, 96–100, 102, 138, 219; Tarski's definition of, 137; apparent, 200–201. *See also* Cognitivism; Knowledge: knowledge that vs. knowledge how; Mind-world relation; Quasi realism; Realism

Truth-value gap, 53, 81. *See also* Bivalence

Unimundial Ideal, 82–89, 267. *See also* Regulative ideal

Unimundialism, defined, 79, 82. *See also* Engagement; Logical relations; Truth: universal; Worlds

Unimundial stance, 82–83, 88–90, 99, 118, 127, 145, 153, 157, 171–177, 179, 181, 209, 220, 234, 240, 245, 250, 256, 266–270. *See also* Engagement; Inquiry; Truth: universal; Worlds

Utilitarianism, 212–213, 221–222, 224–226

Values: antirealist account of, 35–36; irreducibility of, 125, 136, 195–196; naturalist account of, 125, 195; action-guiding character of, 197, 201, 206, 219, 223–224, 244–245, 255, 260–261. *See also* Facts: fact-value distinction; Facts: moral; Moral values; Truth: moral

View from Everywhere, 84, 93, 119, 129, 131n, 180–182, 187–188, 190–191, 199, 242, 246. *See also* Unimundialism, defined; View from Nowhere

View from Nowhere, 84. *See also* Nagel, T.; Objectivity; View from Everywhere

Virtue, 42, 210

Voluntarism, 236–237

Wantons, 209, 218. *See also* Frankfurt, H.; Nihilism; Rationality

Web of belief, 142, 145, 166–170, 248. *See also* Concepts: as clusters of beliefs;

Holism: of confirmation; Logical relations; Observation, theory-ladenness of; Quine, W. V. O.; Revision: of belief

Whorf, B., 73, 73n4, 136

Williams, B., 74, 103–110, 103n16, 104n17, 153, 197, 199, 222–226, 242n36, 255

Wittgenstein, L., 79–80, 184n26

Worlds, 79–80, 85, 88, 92–94, 97–99, 101–102, 112, 129, 130, 134–136, 163, 166, 179, 186, 190–191, 219–220, 236, 238, 246, 256–258, 262, 266, 270

Wright, C., 27n6, 28n8, 29n9, 34n12, 38n13